URBAN

JOSEPH

URBAN

ARCHITECTURE · THEATRE · OPERA · FILM

RANDOLPH CARTER

ROBERT REED COLE

ABBEVILLE PRESS · PUBLISHERS

NEW YORK · LONDON · PARIS

Editor: Walton Rawls
Designer: Alex Castro
Copy Chief: Robin James
Production Manager: Dana Cole

Frontispiece: Joseph Urban in his Yonkers, New York, studio with one of his set models. 1927.

Library of Congress Cataloging-in-Publication Data
Carter, Randolph, 1910–
    Joseph Urban : architecture, theater, opera, film / Randolph
Carter, Robert Cole.
        p.   cm.
    Includes bibliographical references and index.
    ISBN 0-89659-912-4
    1. Urban, Joseph, 1872–1933—Criticism and interpretation.
2. Theater architecture—United States.   3. Architecture. Modern–20th
century—United States.   I. Cole, Robert, 1942–
II. Title.
NA737.U7C37   1992   92-15386
720′.92–dc20   CIP

CONTENTS

He had but one philosophy, called the Joy of Living. This was the essence of all he did, of all he said, and of all he believed. To create beauty and by so doing create happiness was his approach to life, and to spread happiness was his accomplishment, not only through his most sincere and lovable nature, but by an unflagging devotion to the creation of beautiful things. Believing that life to be joyous must be beautiful, and conversely that through beauty life could be made more joyous, to create beauty became his goal, and by virtue of that he lived and died a great artist. . . . The joyous spirit dwelt with him, grew with him, and went out from him into others' lives. . . .

Otto Teegen

PREFACE

More than thirty-five years ago, Joseph Urban's second wife, Mary Porter Beegle, with his daughter, Gretl Urban, presented to Columbia University's Brander Matthews Dramatic Museum his papers and his art files. The more than 27,000 papers, architectural plans and designs, drawings, paintings, photographs, and stage models document a career that began in turn-of-the-century Vienna and later included assignments at the St. Louis Exposition in 1904, stage designs for the Boston Opera Company, productions for the *Ziegfeld Follies* and the Metropolitan Opera in New York, and architectural plans for such New York landmarks as the Ziegfeld Theatre, the Hearst International Magazine Building, and the New School for Social Research. The sketches and plans for these that were built and many other proposals that were never built, such as the Reinhardt Theatre, illustrate the richness of his conceptions and the grandeur of his imagination.

In recent years studies have been published on Urban's work as a designer of the Ziegfeld Follies and the more than fifty Metropolitan Opera productions that he completed from 1917 until his death. Until now there has been no complete biography, so the present volume is especially welcome. The more than two hundred illustrations in both color and black and white present a graphic history of his achievements in all his artistic endeavors. All publications on Urban have drawn almost exclusively upon the resources of the Joseph Urban Collection now housed at Columbia University's Rare Book and Manuscript Library. The collection has, in addition, provided stage designs and models for exhibitions: at the Kennedy Center in Washington; on the occasion of the opening of Lincoln Center; for the hundredth anniversary of the Metropolitan Opera; and for a major retrospective at the Cooper-Hewitt Museum in New York.

The rediscovery of and growing appreciation for the contributions made by Joseph Urban are sure to continue as more aspects of the artist's genius unfold. Students and scholars, curators and librarians, writers and art critics are among those whose research and scholarship will benefit from the remarkable evidence of his work in the original documents at Columbia University and in the monuments that survive.

Kenneth A. Lohf
Librarian for Rare Books
and Manuscripts
Columbia University

Joseph Urban and his brother-in-law, Heinrich Lefler, jointly illustrated a number of children's books. Lefler, costume designer for the imperial theatres, drew the figures, and Urban provided the architectural features and the decorative borders. This set of illustrations is from an edition of Grimms' tales published in 1902.
Left. "Marienkind." (The Christ Child)
Center. "Hansel and Gretel."
Right. "Sleeping Beauty."
Gerhard Trumler.

decoration. In an article in the May 1934 *Architecture*, which was part of a memorial tribute, Deems Taylor observed:

> There were three Joseph Urbans working in the theatre. One was the poetic illustrator whose sensitive and whimsical imagination had invented the illustrations for Hans Andersen's fairy tales, the fairy-tale calendar, and the *Three Princesses.* Another was the ultra-modern decorative artist who conceived the color scheme for the Chicago Exposition and designed smart hotel bars and the Katharine Brush apartment. The third was the architect who designed the Tsar's Bridge and the Hutton House [Mar-a-Lago] and the Ziegfeld Theatre.... You could have what you wanted of his gifts—fantasy, realism, abstract decoration, architectural solidity. He could do superbly many things that his contemporaries could not do at all. And because he stood for more than a single phase of his art, he could not be trade-marked; and a man who cannot be trade-marked is at a disadvantage in an era of specialization.[1]

During his lifetime Urban's career was marked by good fortune and brilliant success. A man of great charm, extravagant and generous to a fault, he moved effortlessly among the rich and powerful—tycoons, crowned heads, famous artists—and, in true Renaissance style, never lacked for patrons. Fate decreed that Urban was usually in the right place at the right time. His good luck may be said to have begun with his birth in Vienna and his maturing in that fabled Habsburg capital during a period of its greatest intellectual ferment and artistic creativity.

In many respects Vienna was unique among European capitals. Poised precariously between the Orient and the Occident, it had served for centuries as a stormy outpost between Christendom and the Turks, withstanding sieges in 1529 and 1683. In 1687 the Hungarian diet had recognized the hereditary right of the Habsburg dynasty to the throne of Hungary, and this led to Vienna's establishment as the hub of a vast multiracial empire. The amalgam of Hungarians, Germans, Czechs, Poles, Croatians, Slavs, Slovaks, Russians, Italians, Magyars, and Jews lent a unique temper to Vienna, an exotic tone heightened by the sumptuous trappings of the Habsburg court.

At the Congress of Vienna, 1814–1815, convened to reshape Europe after the downfall of Napoleon I, Habsburg rule was further extended to the Tyrol, Dalmatia, Galacia, and Salzburg. When one of the participants was asked *"Comment marche le Congrès"* ("How goes the Congress?"), the diplomat is said to have replied, *"Le Congrès ne marche pas, il danse"* ("It doesn't march, it dances"). And dance the city did! Music was everywhere. Waltzing the evenings away, the Viennese were carefree and happy, if often a bit frenzied. A nineteen-year-old named Richard Wagner observed the man responsible for it all, Johann Strauss the Elder, conducting his lively compositions at the dance hall Sperl. Wagner's account could be applied even more strongly to the younger Johann Strauss, the immensely popular Waltz King of the reign of Franz Joseph:

> I shall never forget . . . the passions bordering on mad fury with which the wonderful Johann Strauss conducted. This Daemon of the ancient Viennese folk-spirit trembled at the beginning of a new waltz like a python preparing to spring, and it was more the ecstasy produced by the music than the drinks among the enchanted audience that stimulated that magical first violin to almost dangerous flight.[2]

These sensuous celebrations were, in reality, an escape from the restraints of daily life in Imperial Vienna, where political expression was harshly suppressed and insistence on the "correctness" of social contact and appearance was almost fanatical.

Within a remarkably short period of time, between 1850 and 1870, Vienna had developed from a walled medieval town into one of the most splendid capitals of Europe. In 1874 the British antiquarian Major Byng Hall noted:

> To one who returns after a lapse of years, the changes that have taken place are nothing short of astounding. The fortifications by which the ancient city was embraced have been torn down and replaced by a magnificent boulevard some four miles long, the Ringstrasse. Elegant apartments, public gardens, lakes, pleasant walks and a noble opera house to crown the whole has been conjured into being. The extensive suburbs are now, as it were, joined to the city; the ancient portion and that which heretofore was a small but lively town, has now been transformed into a superb metropolis.

The fortifications referred to by Major Hall had successfully defied the Turks but not Napoleon, and during the revolutionary year of 1848 they were suddenly appropriated by insurgents. Because they had outlived their usefulness, and to unite the old city with its new suburbs, Emperor Franz Joseph had ordered the encompassing fortifications demolished in 1857, creating the route for a magnificent thoroughfare. The resulting wide, empty space that surrounded the city on three sides (the fourth was bounded by the Danube Canal) became the Ringstrasse. Perfect for strollers, parades, and carriage rides, the new boulevard also had military advantages: its width discouraged barricades but could be used for troop formations, either defensive or ceremonial. Napoleon III was also redesigning Paris during this period with the same considerations.

More significant is the fact that a number of imposing new public buildings were erected on the Ringstrasse. They represented an extraordinary variety of architectural styles. The historicist epoch was at its height, and its cardinal rule was that a building be tied to a historical period associated with its intended function. Consequently the classical Parliament was designed to celebrate the glories of ancient Athens, the university reflected the Renaissance, the Rathaus (town hall) recalled medieval guild houses, the Burgtheater evoked Italian Baroque, and the opera house united design elements of the French Renaissance, Gothic, Florentine, and even Venetian styles. For such architects as Theophil Hansen, August Siccard von Siccardsburg, Eduard vander Nuell, and other leading representatives of historicism, the Ring represented the high point of modern architectural achievement; to later architects and designers like Urban, Otto Wagner, Otto Albrecht, and Adolf Loos, who came to maturity during the last decade of the nineteenth century, these imposing structures were to be viewed with scorn.

Hermann Bahr, a spokesman for the modern movement in Austria, would write in 1900, in his book *Secession*, of the "artistic deceit" of the Ringstrasse architecture: "If you walk across the Ring, you have the impression of being in the midst of a real carnival. Everything is masked, everything disguised. . . . To disguise . . . behind borrowed forms is both silly and ugly. Earlier, people used to demand that a building should look like something; we demand that it 'be something.' " [3] But during the latter half of the nineteenth century the middle classes were in the ascendant, and for them the splendor of the Ringstrasse, with its monuments, parks, squares, and tree-lined avenues (ideal for military parades and processions), was a viable link to the existing order under which they had achieved their success. They came to be some of the most ardent supporters of Emperor Franz Joseph and the system he represented.

At the time of Urban's birth, Franz Joseph had been on the throne almost a quarter century. He would remain another forty-four years, a potent symbol, backed by the black-and-yellow Imperial colors and the double-headed eagle. His portrait was everywhere, and so were those in his service:

> Everywhere the gendarmes wore the same cap with a feather or the same mud-coloured helmet with a golden knob and the gleaming double eagle of the Habsburgs, everywhere the doors of the Imperial tobacco monopoly's shops were painted with black and yellow diagonal stripes; in every part of the country the revenue officers carried the same green (almost flowering) pommels above their naked swords; in every garrison town one saw the same blue uniform blouses and black formal trousers of the infantry sauntering down the Corso, the same coffee-coloured jackets of the artillery, the same scarlet trousers of the cavalry.[4]

And in his autobiography, *The World of Yesterday*, Stefan Zweig evokes the epoch as "the golden age of security":

> Everyone knew how much he possessed or what he was entitled to, what was permitted and what was forbidden. Everything had its norm, its definite measure and weight. He who had a fortune could accurately compute his annual interest. An official or an officer, for example, could confidently look up in the calendar the year when he would be advanced in grade, or when he would be pensioned. . . . In this vast empire everything stood firmly and immovably in its appointed place, and at its head was the aged emperor; and were he to die, one knew (or believed) another would come to take his place, and nothing would change in the well-regulated order. No one thought of wars, of revolutions, or revolts. All that was radical, all violence, seemed impossible in an age of reason.[5]

Josef Karl Maria Georg Urban was born in Vienna on May 26, 1872, to a thoroughly respectable middle-class family of lawyers and teachers. His father, also named Josef, was an educator of some local renown, holding a position roughly equivalent to a high school principal and with at least two books on pedagogy to his credit. The family apartment was located on Neustiftgasse in the seventh district, a thoroughly respectable middle-class neighborhood. The household, tended by two efficient servants, a cook, and a housemaid, included an elder sister, Fanny; a younger sister, Carola; and their mother, a gentle matriarch who usually managed to keep her husband, himself a strict disciplinarian, under firm control. Music was the chief art the family enjoyed and participated in at the level of gifted amateurs. Urban senior played the piano acceptably, and Urban junior endured violin lessons. There was nothing special in his family background to give any clue to the source of Joseph Urban's remarkable artistic talents.

Education was understandably highly valued by the Urban family, and it was assumed that young Joseph would go to the university. With a few exceptions, the boy's early school years gave little indication of much interest in matters academic or artistic. Professor Dorner, who taught German composition to young Joseph, remembered:

> He was a lovable, smiling and good-natured child, but so full of zest for life, so turbulent, so incapable of submitting to any discipline, that we would never have kept him in school had his father not been a dear colleague and already sufficiently worried about the obstreperousness of his unnatural offspring. Yet the Urban Pepperl ["Pepi" is a Viennese nickname for Joseph] had an extremely retentive mind and managed to scrape through his examinations even though he considered it beneath his dignity ever to study his lessons.
>
> His powers of observation were extraordinary for a boy, and if the subject of a composition interested him, his descriptions of anything observable by the eyes were of such finesse, of such acuteness of perception that it startled, in spite of his almost illegible writing and inky smudges.[6]

A very young Joseph Urban, whose family enjoyed playing chamber music together. Gretl Urban collection.

The one subject that really interested the reluctant student was mathematics. From Professor Dorner's recollections of Urban's work in this field one can discern the beginnings of Urban's meticulous draftsmanship, which is so evident in his later professional work:

> This boy, whose very touch meant inkspots and grease, kept his algebra and geometry books most tidy and clean; his drawings were perfect, and he took to the propositions and their proofs like a duck to water. The logic of algebra he immediately understood. Rhomboids, triangles, circles and their tangents he never tired of drawing and shading with minute care.

Urban's father decided that his son would become a lawyer and earn the esteemed title of "Herr Doktor," assuring a future safe, respectable, and full of dignity. A law degree was the key to a successful career in government, with attendant prestige and security. Joseph was expected to find a niche in the imperial circles of Vienna from which he might rise to a high position, perhaps even a ministry, and retire finally with a suitable pension. The boy had reservations about the course his family had planned, but at his mother's urging he was finally persuaded to attend the university and study law. As might be expected, law did not long hold the attention of the restless young man. Architect Karl Stöger recalled his friend's mood as a law student:

> He was not sad or depressed, a man of his temperament, so sunny, could not be, but he was restless and talked for hours on end of geometry in furniture, of simplicity and purity in architectural expression, of mass being more important than detail. He took long solitary walks, spending hours gazing at the *Hofstallungen* [the imperial stables where the Lippizaner stallions are kept], whose simple Biedermeier lines enchanted him, while thinking wild, fantastic thoughts of what he would do were he an architect.

The ceramic double-headed eagle of the Austro-Hungarian Empire that Urban designed for Vienna's Rathauskeller, which was probably done first for a book cover of an imperial publication. Gerhard Trumler.

On Stöger's advice Urban enrolled in 1890 at the Polytechnicum for courses in architectural engineering. Soon he was also attending classes at the Imperial and Royal Academy in architectural design and aesthetics under the famous, if conservative, architect Baron Karl von Hasenauer, who had designed the two imposing state museums, the Burgtheatre, and the new wing of the Hofburg, the imperial residence in Vienna. For the first time Urban's heart was truly in his studies. No longer bound by the rigid discipline and fixed schedules of the university, he quickly gravitated into the Bohemian life of his fellow art students who worked hard for a week or so and then celebrated at one of the city's dance halls, usually the Sperl. The proprietor was delighted to have the students as patrons and even extended them credit, since a great many customers were drawn to the Sperl to observe the revels of the aspiring artists.

Pepi was frequently the center of attention. Not only were people drawn to him for his charm and good humor, but they also came to hear him sing. He had a powerful baritone voice, good enough to cause him briefly to consider a singing career. The idea was abandoned when the great tenor Leo Slezak told him that smoking and drinking champagne were forbidden if he truly wished to become a successful singer. Urban's specialty was a song called *"Der schönste Mann von Wien."* Though a traditional song, new words were provided, and for Urban it became a musical emblem.

Urban's antics were the source of considerable amusement among his friends. One memorable night he even climbed to the top of the monument to Empress Maria Theresa, where from his perch on the empress's shoulders he delivered a speech on the merits of champagne. A policeman arrived and ordered the orator to descend, but Urban pretended dizziness and demanded that fire engines be summoned to effect his rescue. Finally, according to one of his friends, "his lasciviously comic gestures to our poor and morally so severe Empress during his downward climb had us and the policemen weeping with laughter."

These escapades were abruptly terminated by Urban's father, who was less than pleased to learn from an acquaintance, a professor at the university, that no student by the name of Joseph Urban was enrolled therein. The discovery that money designated for tuition and legal texts was actually being squandered on classes at not one but two art schools precipitated a crisis of such magnitude that family ties, though not broken, were severely strained.

The young khedive of Egypt, who before ascending his throne had lived in Vienna, decided to add a European wing to the Abdin Palace in Cairo. It was Urban's good fortune that Baron von Hasenauer recommended his nineteen-year-old student for the job. In October of 1891 Urban left for Egypt, where he labored strenuously for eight months on the project, at the same time luxuriating in the opulence of the royal court. Urban returned to Vienna with a taste for strong Turkish cigarettes and an ample supply of exotic stories about harem life, stories that became more elaborate with each retelling. The most important result of the trip, however, was unquestionably his sharpened awareness and appreciation of color:

> My arrival in the Harbor of Alexandria was really my first impression of color. The strange deep blue of the Mediterranean, the white city, the flaming sails of the boats, the riot of color in the costumes, and over all a purple sky—this enormous impression followed me my whole life and dominated for years my color schemes. I think the indescribable blue of the Egyptian sky created my life-long love of blue.[7]

After completing his studies at the academy in 1893, Urban worked under Ludwig Baumann, the emperor's official architect, a situation that offered few opportunities for personal expression. At the age of eighty-three, Baumann recalled his association with young Urban:

> He worked for me more or less regularly: he helped on the designs for the new Ministry of War, the new concert house, and several other government buildings. Continuously I had to suppress his simplifications, as the city of Vienna at that time and for that type of building demanded the conventional richness of Hasenauer's tradition.
>
> He was a difficult young man and too utterly independent for my requirements, yet he was such a magnificent draftsman, I could completely count on him when any difficult architectural designing was demanded at short notice, that I put up with his fantasies, always realizing that I was harboring a great talent that would develop into a true genius with the right kind of opportunity.
>
> I think he considered me an awful old fossil at that time, and had it not been for his veneration of my beautiful wife, he probably would not have deigned to remain in my office at all.

Urban always regretted that, unlike his classmate Josef Maria Olbrich, he never had the opportunity of working directly under Otto Wagner, the dean of modern Austrian architects. In a tribute on his seventieth birthday, Wagner was hailed as "the antithesis of the Ringstrasse," "the father of modern Viennese architecture," and "educator of an entire generation." [8] As Hermann Bahr stated, "Without Wagner's blazing audacity, no one would have had the courage to believe once again in Austria's artistic future." [9] And Urban later wrote: "His radical departure from all period work, his fantastic and interesting plans for monumental and domestic building, museums and churches inspired me to try and get on my own feet to work independently in my own style." [10]

"The time was on the move," wrote Robert Musil of the Austrian fin de siècle. "People who were not born then will find it difficult to believe, but the fact is that even then time was moving as fast as a cavalry-camel. . . . But in those days, no one knew what it was moving towards. Nor could anyone quite distinguish between what was above and what below, between what was moving forwards and what backwards." [11] In any event, during the last decades of the nineteenth century, figuratively at least, fissures were beginning to develop across the monumental façades of the Ringstrasse. The fragmented Austro-Hungarian Empire was held together by an inflexible bureaucracy, the most efficient censorship in Europe, and a formidable military machine; the cumbersome structure, embellished by parades and endless rounds of official festivities, manifested an order at least outwardly intact.

Society was, however, occasionally shaken by such untoward events as the murder-suicide of Crown Prince Rudolph and his lover Baroness Marie Vetsera at Mayerling in 1889 and by the assassination of his mother, Empress Elisabeth, in 1898 by the anarchist Luigi Luccheni. Luccheni's goal had been to kill someone of royal blood. The empress had been fatally stabbed as she boarded a Lake Geneva steamer because the pretender to the French throne had not arrived in Geneva as announced. Luccheni lacked the money for a trip to Italy to kill King Umberto, so Elisabeth became his victim. Urban was chosen to design a memorial to her that was erected in Baden.

Though no sense of approaching disaster was shared by the complacent middle class of Vienna, there were unmistakable signs of intellectual ferment

Urban's sketch for Empress Elisabeth's memorial in Baden. 1904. Columbia University.

in artistic and literary circles, ever the most sensitive seismographs of internal and external events. Vienna has been described as a city where psychoanalysis *needed* to be invented, and it was, of course; but Freud himself was both ignored and denounced there. As Otto Friedlander wrote despairingly:

> Vienna, between 1900 and 1910, was one of the intellectual centers of the world, and Vienna had no idea of it. Vienna is no sounding board. Two or three thousand human beings speak words here and think thoughts here which will overturn the world of the next generation. Vienna does not know it.
>
> What an extraordinary gap!
>
> Only a small group of human beings: writers, politicians, educators, journalists, artists, civil servants, attorneys, and doctors live here who are alarmed by all the problems of this time and who are thinking and forming the future.

16

They are an island; no bridge leads from them to the Viennese. Only a few disciples stand behind these far-seeing men. No crowds.

Indolent and gay vegetates the slumbering city, never dreaming what great things are being thought and created there.[12]

A good part of this undetected renaissance was initially generated in the coffeehouses of Vienna. Given the city's chronically poor housing conditions, they assumed great social, intellectual, and artistic significance as gathering places. Bruno Walter recalls that the coffeehouses were "the scenes of decisions and events of historical and cultural importance, of weighty political and scientific discussions, and were naturally also a hotbed of intrigue and endless gossip." [13] Typical of these avant-garde enclaves was the Siebener Club. In 1895 seven young men began meeting every Thursday at the restaurant Zum Blauen Freihaus and later at the Café Sperl. The original seven were the architects Joseph Urban, Josef Hoffmann, Josef Maria Olbrich, and Karl Stöger, and the artists Kolomon Moser, Ludwig Koch, and Karl Schuster. The club's debates and discussions on matters of artistic import soon attracted additional members and led directly to the creation of the two most important artistic organizations in Vienna at the end of the century, the Secession and the Hagenbund.

The *Gesellschaft für vervielfältingende Kunst* (Society for the Reproduction of Art) was one of the most important artistic agencies of the government in the 1890s. It operated under the Ministry of Culture, had considerable money at its disposal, and commissioned many original works of art, especially graphics and book illustrations. The society's president frequently attended the Siebener Club's meetings and was sufficiently impressed to suggest that some of the members prepare a series of historical illustrations for the society's publication, *Für Schule und Haus*. Urban's first submission, an illustration depicting a medieval town, was immediately accepted and exhibited in the fall of 1895 at the Künstlerhaus, the headquarters of the Viennese artists' union. There it attracted the attention of noted illustrator Heinrich Lefler, a professor at the academy.

In addition to designing costumes for the imperial theatres, Lefler also taught costume design at the Vienna Academy. These knights are sketches he made in the early 1890s. Author's collection.

Urban continued doing illustrations, but those for which he is best known today were done in collaboration with Heinrich Lefler, already a distinguished artist. Lefler and his family had long been in the service of the emperor, starting with his great-grandfather and grandfather, who had been in charge of the imperial stables and the famous Spanish Riding School with its Lippizaner stallions. Lefler's father was a respected and admired court-appointed mural painter in the accepted nineteenth-century style, and his work adorned many government buildings. Young Heinrich wanted to become an artist also, but his interests lay in the fields of costume design and illustration. His father saw to it that the boy studied with the best teachers in Munich and Vienna and also tutored him himself while he attended the academy. Earning a doctorate for a historical study on costume, Lefler was appointed a professor at the academy in that subject area and held the position for the rest of his life. In addition, Lefler's own costume designs were so beautifully and authentically executed that theatres throughout Europe sought his services. In 1900 the emperor appointed him lifelong art director of the imperial theatres, a position of great influence and prestige.

Shortly after Joseph Urban returned from Egypt in 1892, he was introduced to Lefler by Leo Slezak, a mutual friend. Lefler was so impressed

with the enthusiastic younger man that he invited him to his studio the next evening. Urban took an immediate liking to his fellow artist and admired the works he displayed in his studio. Without much prompting, Urban talked about the splendors of ancient Egypt and illustrated them with a few deft pencil strokes. He also, in Gretl Urban's words, "painted a few samples of the glorious blues of the Mediterranean and in particular of the sensuous, velvety blue of the tropical sky, a color he always loved and later successfully used on his famous cycloramas." [14] This blue came to be called "Urban blue."

Except for the artistic talent that both possessed and recognized in each other, the two men were direct opposites who nevertheless became so closely identified that they were known as the Twins, the Castor and Pollux of Viennese art circles. Lefler, ten years older and a bookish introvert, was thin, even frail, in striking contrast to Urban, who was robust and had a carefree, impulsive nature. In spite of temperamental differences, they became fast friends, and their artistic collaboration resulted in works that neither would have achieved alone. Prior to his association with Urban, Lefler's work was light, even delicate, employing a very fine line and soft pastel colors. Once they began to collaborate, Lefler's figures became more substantial, his color bolder; as Urban developed his modernistic ideas, restrained occasionally by Lefler, his work became more refined and mature.

The work of Urban and Lefler, like that of most of the artists connected with the modern movement, was strongly influenced by Art Nouveau, or *Jugendstil* as it was designated in Germany. During the nineties this style,

18

whose evocative power rested on its linear rhythm, was heralded all over Europe as a new international art form free of the traditional imitation of the historical past. While not strictly true, since its roots were grounded in the Gothic with Celtic, Byzantine, Indian, and Japanese branches, it served as an important bridge between the prevalent naturalism and later trends in twentieth-century art and decoration. The fluid, undulating linearity of the book illuminations and temperas of William Blake were a major influence in the development of the new style, as were the works of Whistler, the Pre-Raphaelites, and William Morris. In Vienna the style achieved special elegance, not only in the designs of Urban and Lefler, but also in those of their illustrious contemporaries Josef Hoffmann, Josef Maria Olbrich, Alfred Roller, Kolomon Moser, and Carl Otto Czeschka, a brilliant graphic artist whose illustrations for Keim's *Niebelungen* rank among the finest examples of *Jugendstil*.

The first joint project of Urban and Lefler was a commission by Baron Karl von Wiener, the minister of culture, to illustrate in black and white the story *Roland's Squires* by J. K. Musaeus. Urban was then enjoying a rather strenuous affair with a countess, and both the baron and Lefler felt that a sojourn in the country, away from temptation and distraction, was indicated. It took considerable persuasion to induce Urban to go with Lefler to his parents' villa near Brunn, but the rewards were substantial. With Lefler drawing the figures and Urban providing the architectural backgrounds, the illustrations proved so successful that the artistic collaboration of the two became permanently sealed.

Another bond was also forged. In the wake of Urban's intensely physical affair with the countess, the purity and innocence of Lefler's younger sister, Mizzi, proved irresistible. They were married later that same year, 1896. A daughter, Margarete (Gretl), was born in 1898; Helene (Elly) in 1900. Gretl remembers a marriage that was not always serene:

> There is no question about their being very much in love when they married. Father used to tell me he was immediately charmed. Mother was demure

Portrait of Mizzi Urban by her brother, Heinrich Lefler. Gretl Urban collection.

Portrait of Gretl Urban by her Uncle Heinrich. Gretl Urban collection.

and elegant. Because of Heinrich she was well acquainted with the art world and understood what the moderns were striving for and was enthusiastic about this new movement in all the arts that was pervading the very air of Vienna. She was well read, much more than Father, intelligent, quite a good painter, and utterly spoiled.

Mother said Father courted her enchantingly: flowers every day and rides, always chaperoned by her haughty mother, who disapproved of Buschi's [Gretl's pet name for her father] rather ardent ways and frivolous life. She had chosen a rich young lawyer, a baron, as her daughter's husband, but Mizzi and Buschi were in love and her father and Heinrich were on their side, so they were married in style and went to Semmering in the Austrian Alps for their honeymoon.

Mother knew nothing of physical love before she married, her mother having only told her that as a dutiful wife she had to submit to her husband's desires, no matter how distasteful. That was the unholy custom of those days, which preordained a fear of sex with an attitude that there was something not very nice about it. This attitude Mother never changed throughout her long life; any free discussion of sex always embarrassed her and made her feel uneasy.

After I was born, Father began looking for his pleasures elsewhere. From what Mother told me, after Elly was born, though she still adored Father, she refused any further physical contact, not only because she disliked it but also because she wanted no more children. Father always treated Mother with great tenderness, but inevitably they drifted apart.

The tremendous difference in temperament, unnoticed when they were first in love, became dangerously apparent. There was also Mother's habit of indulging in hysterics whenever things went wrong. I still remember her wandering around at night weeping bitterly because Buschi had not yet come home. She would rush to the window at every hoofbeat in the street and fall weeping into Father's arms when he arrived in the early morning hours. This performance alarmed us, particularly my little sister, Elly, until we finally got used to it and paid no attention anymore.

There were, of course, still many happy times Mother and Father shared. The great balls and galas, the parties at our apartments with music and dancing, the marvelous Christmas Eve festivities for which we children were permitted to stay up, with lavish gifts for one and all under the huge Christmas tree hung with candies and decorations and lit by real candles. Elly and I always had to perform. You should have seen plump Gretl, happily dancing in from the atelier as a snowflake, while poor Elly, almost in tears and nervous, was the Christmas tree, waiting for snow.

Lefler-Urban designed the 1898 jubilee calendar celebrating Emperor Franz Joseph's fiftieth year on the throne. This spread was for the month of July. Gerhard Trumler.

There were also times when we, Heinrich, and Minna, Uncle's lovely wife, moved to the country in the summer where there were no temptations, and Heinrich and Buschi worked hard and with much joy in their collaboration. We girls, Mother, Minna, and the governess would go for walks in the woods and, if the water was warm enough, have a swim in the small river that bordered our garden. It was the only exercise that Buschi and Heinrich joined us in, although occasionally Buschi would go to a nearby wood to pick his beloved bluebells and wild saffron. When we had to return to Vienna, Mother always wept bitterly. She said she just dreaded what she knew would happen during the winter season.

Mother knew nothing about money, and Father's idea of money was to spend it. Mother would complain that hardly had she gotten used to one salon or dining room than Father designed and furnished a new one. He said he was experimenting, which I suppose was true but also very costly. Many a time Heinrich had to help out until Father was able to pay his debts. Heinrich always laughed about his insistence that Father pay him back every cent with interest so he would learn about finance. Father never did.

The first work in color completed by the Twins was a watercolor triptych panel illustrating Poe's *Mask of the Red Death.* Exhibited in 1897, the painting captured all the color and horror of the tale and won the highest award for artistic achievement, the Emperor's Prize, a purse of one thousand ducats. Lefler was ill at the time, and Urban went alone to shake the emperor's hand, a rare honor, and collect the green silk bag from the emperor's paymaster. Urban took the purse to Lefler's bedside, and while dividing the gold coins they decided to put aside equal amounts for a celebration with their friends. The festivities lasted a week.

Exquisite illustrations for Andersen's and Grimms' fairy tales, decorative calendars, and a children's songbook, now a classic, entitled *Kling Klang Gloria,* followed. There were also numerous government commissions for stamps, bonds, and banknotes. This official patronage caused the minister of culture to be severely criticized for favoritism shown the Twins; he was, in fact, one of their greatest patrons. The minister's wife, Baroness von Wiener, recalled the courteous reply her husband always used: " 'Is not

21

Many choice government commissions went to Lefler-Urban, partly as a result of their undeniable talent and partly due to Urban's friendships with members of the nobility and imperial ministries. Stamps and a thousand kronen bank note by Lefler-Urban. Gerhard Trumler.

Urban's work better than anyone else's; is not the Lefler-Urban combination perfect? Can you suggest anybody else better qualified?' As there was not, there was no answer, and the fault-finders had to suffer in silence.'' The minister himself said that some thirty years after their appearance he still considered the colored fairy tales ''masterpieces of illustration, which will live forever.'' Today the Lefler-Urban illustrated books and calendars are highly prized among antiquarian book collectors; the very first color illustration in the Museum of Modern Art's 1986 exhibition catalog for the ''Vienna 1900'' show was a page from one of their calendars.

In 1898 a great celebration was planned to mark the emperor's fiftieth anniversary on the throne. The Künstlerhaus arranged a massive exhibition that proved too large to house in its own building and required the use of additional space in the Musikverein, Vienna's famed concert hall, across the street. In a competition to build a span linking the two buildings, Joseph Urban's design was selected from more than one hundred entries. This was the first structure he designed and built according to his own ideas. Instead of designing a bridge that looked as though it had always joined the two buildings, as the other entrants had done, Urban proposed a modern wooden structure that was obviously both of a festival and temporary character. It included the exuberant flowing curves of the *Jugendstil*, representations of the imperial double eagle, and the use of bright colors rather than plaster painted to look like stone. A window was cut that afforded a splendid view of the Baroque Karls Kirche, and traffic was rerouted so that a sculpture garden could be built. The bridge aroused great passions; those who liked it called it ''The Emperor's Bridge,'' and those who did not named it ''The Urbanaeum.'' One of the major objections, and a frequent criticism of Urban's work in Vienna, was its cost.

Urban was also in charge of arranging displays within the two halls. In the concert hall he placed models of about fifty buildings that had been erected during the emperor's reign and separated them by floral arrangements and bay trees. Precious tapestries from the emperor's personal collection that had never before been publicly exhibited were hung from the boxes and over the orchestra seats. The Künstlerhaus was so pleased with Urban's preparations that he was given the privilege of greeting the emperor on the bridge and escorting him to the Musikverein, where Urban had stationed in the gallery about three hundred singers and members of the Vienna Philharmonic who, when the emperor entered the hall, broke into Haydn's ''Hymn to Austria.'' The old gentleman was so moved by the display and the music that he forgot the strict etiquette of the court, turned, and shook the young architect's hand. This was the second of the three handshakes Urban was to receive from the emperor. To Urban the gesture was especially significant since he felt that the emperor's expression of satisfaction boded well for the success of the new artistic movement.

The Lefler-Urban contribution to the exhibition was a series of illustrations for another tale by Musaeus bearing the ungainly title of *The Book of the Chronicle of the Three Sisters*. This was the most beautiful work the two men did together. The drawings brought the Twins the Austrian gold medal for fine arts and a purchase by the German government, which published the illustrated tale in a limited deluxe edition. The book was exhibited as part of Germany's contribution to the 1900 World's Fair in Paris, where it was awarded a grand prize. The tale gave both artists the opportunity to use their

individual and combined talents to the fullest extent. Lefler contributed knights in elaborate costumes riding horses fitted out with their own ornate trappings, ladies in elegant gowns, and rustically clad villagers. An illustration entirely of his own work presents a fair maiden in a pink-and-gold gown sitting with her knight. The couple is on a pale-colored lawn accented by a single striking white birch tree with gray tree trunks filling the top of the illustration. Urban exercised his architectural fantasies by designing a medieval village, a castle in green accented with red roofing tiles, and a black-and-white neo-Gothic dream palace. The last major illustration in the text is a glorious piece of *Jugendstil* design, complete with a gold-and-lavender peacock.

Lefler and Urban were not immune to the influence of other artists. Their black-and-white illustrations draw inevitable comparison to Aubrey Beardsley, who worked in the same medium and employed the sinuous lines of the Art Nouveau style. In the use of both color and line, the pure *Jugendstil* piece from the *Three Sisters* bears quite obvious resemblance to Gustav Klimt's work.

Ludwig Hevesi, the art critic who supported the new art movement and the work of its practitioners, detected the influence of Eugène Grasset in the Twins' drawings. Grasset was born in 1841 in Switzerland, but he became a French citizen in 1891. The very range of his efforts invites comparison to the Twins: paintings, stained glass, tapestries, calendars, covers for magazines and popular songs, illuminated projections, playing cards, and postage stamps. He was a master of decorative art perhaps best known today for his

A huge exhibition was held jointly in the Musikverein and the Künstlerhaus in 1898 as part of the celebration marking the Emperor's fiftieth anniversary. Urban's entry won the competition to build a bridge joining the two buildings. The "Kaiser's Bridge" marked the real beginning of Urban's architectural career.
Left. An 1898 photo of the bridge.
Gerhard Trumler.
Right. Urban's original color drawing. 1898.
Columbia University.

contribution, along with Lautrec, to the development of the French Art Nouveau poster style.

After the success of the Emperor's Bridge, Urban's career as an architect was assured, and he received many important commissions from noble Austrian families as well as from the Crown. At an exhibition of modern interiors in the Museum of Art and Industry in 1898, Lefler and Urban designed their first modern interior: a lady's boudoir. Twenty years later Urban would laugh at this "crazy" room, which, nevertheless, was brimming with novel ideas. The room attracted the attention of Count Karl Esterhazy and his wife, of the ancient Hungarian noble family that was once Haydn's patron. So impressed were they with Urban's work that they gave him several commissions.

The Esterhazys first asked Urban to build them a pleasure palace, or *Lusthaus,* on their estate in St. Abrahams, in Hungary. He seized this opportunity to let his fantasies run free by designing a series of rooms in a *Jugendstil* extravaganza. These included a central hall, a hunting room, a ladies' salon, and a garden room, which were attached to the original building by a glass gallery. The façade was of white marble with golden rose-shaped medallions, and a light green was discreetly added as a third color. Only the very best materials were used in this luxury pavilion, for cost was no object. Urban designed all the interior appointments and decorations as well.

This initial project so pleased the Esterhazys that they gave Urban two more important commissions: a hunting lodge and another château, this one featuring an elaborate fountain of green marble studded with amethysts.

The plans for the new City Hall in Vienna had included space for an enormous restaurant, the Rathauskeller, and although the building was completed in 1883 the city fathers did not decide what to do with the space until the fall of 1898. The coveted commission to decorate this immense

Count Karl Esterhazy and his wife were so attracted to a woman's salon Urban had exhibited that they gave him three major architectural commissions.
Top. Fireplace in the Esterhazy Castle in St. Abraham, Hungary. 1899. Columbia University.
Bottom. Exterior drawing of the St. Abraham castle. 1899. Gerhard Trumler.

Original color drawings for rooms in the St. Abraham castle. 1899.
Top left. Salon with daybed.
Top right. Dining room.
Bottom. Bedroom.
All from Columbia University.

restaurant was awarded to the Twins, who were given six months to complete the daunting task. The work was finished by February 1899 and featured huge murals painted by Lefler and Alexander Goltz. Urban provided an overall architectural and decorative scheme that accommodated the massive interior with its huge arches, and he designed the furniture used in the various rooms of the hall.

The Middle Ages, that recurring source of inspiration to the *Jugendstil* artists, provided a great deal of the decorative material for the Twins. There were, however, several murals that established the Rathauskeller's uniquely Viennese character: representations of important scenes in the city's history, four of its suburbs, three of its current officials including Mayor Karl Lueger, and even some Viennese slang expressions were depicted. A very suitable motif of green and red grapes was applied to the ceiling arches. Hevesi was very pleased with the results, which showed that the Twins had "achieved such a collaboration, such a power to supplement each other that they work as one." [15] The Rathauskeller, he concluded, "is the first great test of this new movement of the day and is its perfect vindication." [16]

One year later the smaller Volkskeller opened, also decorated by the Lefler-Urban team. Urban installed red-colored wooden arches in the low-

Rathskeller-Stiege.

The choicest plum that Vienna could award an architect as the turn of the century neared was for the restaurants beneath City Hall. The commissions went to Urban. Original drawing for the entrance to the Rathauskeller. 1899. Columbia University.

Named after two of Vienna's waltz kings, the Strauss-Lanner Room in the Rathauskeller was for small private parties.
Top left. Urban's original color drawing for the Strauss-Lanner Room. 1899. Columbia University.
Top right. Photo of the finished room. Gerhard Trumler.
Bottom. More than ninety years after it opened, it is still possible to enjoy fine Viennese cuisine under the Rathauskeller's arches with their grape motif. Gerhard Trumler.

Top. Photo of the Volkskeller showing the ceiling decorations, the light-red wooden arches, and some of the room's nine bays. 1900. Columbia University.
Center. Larger than the Volkskeller, the Rathauskeller in Vienna's city hall opened in 1899. Lefler's murals depicting events from Vienna's past were in the style of the Lefler-Urban book illustrations. 1900. Columbia University.
Bottom. The Lefler-Urban decorations for the Rathauskeller received both critical and public acclaim. 1900. Columbia University.

ceilinged room that culminated in rosettes used to conceal lighting elements; cups and grapes made of copper were applied to natural wooden panels, and there were nine bays or loges along the sides of the room that Urban decorated in Viennese themes. Hevesi again praised the Twins' effort by noting that "for the inauguration of modern art and its appreciation amongst the lower stratas, such a Volkskeller does more than any up-to-date gallery." [17]

The year 1900 was extraordinarily busy for Urban. Baron von Wiener, representing Austria as minister of culture, attended the Paris World's Fair, and Urban accompanied him as delegate architect for the artists' union, the Künstlerhaus. Urban was responsible for the final selection and arrangement of works to be displayed, but to his bitter disappointment, Gustav Klimt's three panels for the new university (*Justice*, *Medicine*, and *Astronomy*) were rejected by the French critics. The trip, however, was obviously successful on other fronts, as attested by the baron's recollections of this visit to fin de siècle Paris:

> Champagne was cheap then and money plentiful, so champagne we had at lunch, at dinner and at supper. There was not a restaurant or cabaret we neglected. After the day's labor we did not go to bed, but stayed up all night to see the sights. La Rue and Carton were our favorite rendez-vous for dinner; the sculptors Rodin and Bartolomé, the painter Puvis de Chavannes usually joined us there. We met Monet and Renoir. There was no feeling of patriotism or antagonism to mar our pleasure in each other; we felt as one in the fellowship of art and ambition.
>
> Those truly were the good old days! Before the evening was very old, we went to either the Bal Tabarin or the Moulin Rouge where Paris's most beautiful and brilliant women were to be found. With some of these lovely ladies we adjourned to more intimate locale where Pepi inevitably sang *"Der schönste Mann."* Sometimes at dawn we went to *les Halles* where Pepi brought huge bunches of flowers for the ladies, while he enthused over the gorgeous display of fresh meats and vegetables piled in boxes higher than a man. He was particularly pleased with the neat display of brilliantly red radishes and vivid orange carrots—and how he loved onion soup; never did he tire of it.
>
> Cléo de Mérode we met and Sarah Bernhardt; Jean de Reszke and Emma Calvé. From February until late April we enjoyed the gaiety and splendid beauty of this gracious city.

The Künstlerhaus possessed the only viable exhibition space in Vienna, but younger artists had become increasingly dissatisfied with the artists' union, which either refused to exhibit their modernistic works or else would include but a few pieces in exhibitions dominated by conservative or mediocre talents. In 1897 a group of artists led by Gustav Klimt, Josef Olbrich, and Josef Hoffmann (the latter two original members of the Siebener Club) formed a new organization, the Secession, and by April 1898 had laid the foundation stone for their startling exhibition hall designed by Olbrich. The Viennese watched, mostly in horror, as the building took shape. Dubbed the "Assyrian convenience," it was described as a cross between a glass house and a blast furnace, and after the addition of Olbrich's golden cupola, an openwork sphere of laurel leaves and berries, it became known as the "Golden Cabbage." A phrase borrowed of Hevesi, defiantly stating the Secessionist creed, appeared over the entrance: "To the time its art, to art its freedom." Though he had no part in its conception, Urban greatly admired this handsome pavilion, the first building in the Decorative Arts style.

The emergence of the Secession severely strained the Siebener Club; conflicts and jealousies inevitably resulted. In 1900 twenty-one artists led by Urban and Lefler formed their own group, which they called the Hagenbund, borrowing the name *Haagen* from the proprietor of their beloved Blauen Freihaus. Prominent members included Franz Barwig, Ludwig Graf, Wilhelm Hejda, Josef Heu, Rudolph Junk, and August Roth. Lefler was the new organization's president and Urban the vice president. While each organization had a lively appreciation of the other's talents, definite rivalry, occasionally bitter, developed. As Josef Hoffmann remembered:

> The Hagenbund could not give a special feast or exhibit without the Secession doing the same thing and vice versa; if we decorated a cabaret, the Hagenbundlers did the same thing, and if our group had an exhibit in Germany, you could be sure they would be there soon also with a show of their own. There was much rivalry and heated fighting and we took it all most seriously. Children as we were, of course, but this competitive spirit and jealousy helped tremendously in our development and modern artistic achievements.

The members of the Hagenbund remained within the Künstlerhaus until November 1900, while the Secession, as their name implies, withdrew from the association. For the Hagenbund's first two exhibitions, the Künstlerhaus provided rooms for display, and both exhibitions were extremely successful. In fact, they were so successful that animosities were aroused among other members of the Künstlerhaus, forcing the union to deny the Hagenbund space for a third exhibition. After the success of a third exhibition, held in a private gallery, the Hagenbund began to look for a permanent home. Sponsors in government and among the aristocracy encouraged them, and Mayor

Urban's original drawing for the Golden Cross Sanitarium in Baden. 1903. Gerhard Trumler.

Sketch of the Secessionists' exhibition hall in Vienna designed by Josef Maria Olbrich, which opened in 1898.

The Hagenbund, a rival artists' union to the Secession, was founded by Urban, Lefler, and some of their friends. Their exhibition hall was an old market pavilion remodeled by Urban. 1901. Gerhard Trumler.

Lueger, one of Urban's ardent supporters, finally offered the group the old city market hall on Zedlitzgasse. A wealthy builder furnished materials needed for renovation, and additional money was provided by other patrons. Despite Urban's best efforts to minimize expenses, money ran out and thirty thousand kronen had to be raised through an auction of members' artworks.

One of Urban's first moves was to allow artists from all the various ethnic and national groups within the empire to participate in the Hagenbund exhibits, provided, of course, they had the requisite talent. The Hagenbund was first to tap this pool of talent that was previously excluded from Viennese art associations, and an unexpected benefit was the approval and support of the emperor.

Although his personal tastes were notoriously conservative, Franz Joseph frequently visited the Hagenbund. Whichever artist was on duty had the honor of escorting the emperor on his brief and usually silent inspections. If Urban was there, however, Franz Joseph would linger, listening to his guide's jokes and occasionally even chuckling. Another royal visitor was Archduke Franz Ferdinand, heir to the throne, whose assassination at Sarajevo would trigger the First World War. The archduke hated modern art, but since the Hagenbund exhibitions were always a topic of conversation, curiosity forced him to see what the talk was all about. One day he arrived at the hall unannounced. As he was leaving, according to Karl Stemolak (then president of the Hagenbund), he asked Urban if they were quite alone, and when Urban replied that they were, the archduke whispered, "Then I count on you not to tell anyone that I have been to see such a disgusting mess. Art: pooh!"

For the four or five shows the Hagenbund mounted each year, Urban skillfully arranged the exhibition rooms with a view toward providing intimate spaces to best display the individual works of art. He also designed the furniture, fixtures, floor and wall coverings, posters, and catalogs. Professor Stemolak recalled the work Urban did on the Hagenbund interiors:

> Walls were changed about completely and new coverings were made for them; new pedestals were designed for sculpture; new lighting there was, new furniture and rugs; often platforms were built and stairs; whole rooms

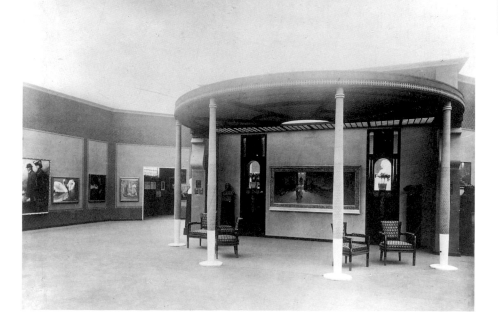

Urban, both a founder and president of the Hagenbund, installed most of the exhibits and designed catalogs and posters.
Left and center. Undated photos of Hagenbund exhibits.
Columbia University.
Above. Hagenbund posters.
Gerhard Trumler.

In the image: "I.R. SCHOOL FOR ARTS AND CRAFTS OF THE AUSTRIAN MUSEUM VIENNA"

In 1904 Urban first came to America to install the artworks in the Austrian pavilion at the St. Louis world's fair. His initial project in America earned him a gold medal. Photo of an exhibition room in the pavilion. Columbia University.

were raised or lowered as the works of art demanded. Costly silks were used for the walls and the bands that held them were ever new and enchanting: silver or gold, white or black metal or wood, and every bit of it came out of Pepi's fertile brain.

Photographs of the exhibitions show bright, airy, and uncluttered rooms with strikingly modern decorative details. Some of the installations were so modern that they could easily be confused with exhibitions Urban arranged in New York thirty years later. In 1902 the group presented a show called "Art in the Life of the Child," which Urban later reproduced for his own apartments, for many of his clients, and even for a motion picture, *The Wild Goose*, that he designed for Hearst in 1920. Other important exhibitions mounted by the Hagenbund included Arnold Boecklin in 1903, Max Lieberman in 1904, Constantin Meunier in 1906, and Oskar Kokoschka in 1911. The Hagenbund also exhibited in Munich, London, Rome, and, most importantly for Urban, in St. Louis in 1904.

The Austrian Pavilion at the St. Louis World's Fair was one of the most popular displays at the celebration marking the hundredth anniversary of the Louisiana Purchase. Ludwig Baumann, Urban's former employer, designed a building in the Secessionist style, then totally new to America, and Urban was responsible for the rooms allotted to the Hagenbund. His rooms received a grand prize and a special gold medal for the best-arranged art exhibit at the fair. Urban's trip to St. Louis in 1904 was his first to America. He sensed that the country offered great opportunities for an architect, but rejecting several tempting offers he returned to Austria and the city he loved.

By 1905 Urban had become successful enough to move his family into a splendid new apartment near the Ringstrasse, 8 Nibelungengasse. Abandoning the *Jugendstil*, he decorated the rooms in the modern style, uncluttered and serene. There were none of the usual ornate tile stoves, and the floors were covered with plain gray carpet accented by small brightly colored rugs of Urban's design. Ideas that Urban had explored in the 1902 Hagenbund

exhibition were put to practical use in the strikingly innovative room for his children. Urban hated disorder and untidiness, two sins of which children were likely to be guilty. In his design he eliminated all opportunity for clutter and disarray. The walls were painted in white enamel so that finger marks and smudges could be wiped away easily. Drawers that might be left half-open or filled to overflowing were done away with. Toys could be hung on specially designed knobs on the walls or stored on a bench beneath them. The only purely decorative elements in the room were his Andersen and Grimm fairy-tale illustrations that lined the walls.

The Urbans entertained lavishly. Frequent guests included Leo Slezak, Gustav Mahler, and Felix Weingartner from the Hofoper; Paul Schlenther of the Burgtheater; Hagenbund artists Josef Heu, August Roth, and Ludwig Graf; actors, singers, and composers Mélanie Palffy, Selma Kurz, Josef Kaniz, and Léo Fall; and government officials Count Kielmannsegg and Baron von Wiener. Dinner served with fine wines was followed by musical entertainment in the salon. Lefler's wife, Minna, of the Volksoper, sang, accompanied by Mizzi Urban and Urban himself on the violin. Depending on visiting artists, the music extended from Mozart to Wagner to Franz Léhar. The end of the evening was signaled by a rendering of "*Der schönste Mann*," though special friends frequently lingered until the early hours.

The new apartment contained a studio where Urban and Lefler worked together. Gretl remembers life with her family at 8 Nibelungengasse:

Disorder of any kind was abhorrent to Urban. In designing a room for his two young daughters he created an environment that would prevent mess or clutter. The walls were painted in enamel so smudges could be easily removed, wall pegs were provided for clothes, and there were chests along the wall for toys.
Top left and right. Children's room in Vienna apartment. 1905.
Gretl Urban collection.
Bottom left and right. Urban's studio in his apartment. 1905.
Gretl Urban collection.

Drawing for the dining room
in Urban's apartment. 1905.
Author's collection.

In my childish memory the studio looms a huge white room with two towering windows; between the windows was a large table on which artists' supplies were neatly arranged. There were art books also and ceramic heads. Once in a while I was allowed to visit, provided I sat still. Father sat at his worktable and Heinrich at his easel, clouds of smoke above their heads. Father was the talker, Heinrich the listener. Father was a big man, exuberant, brimming with energy. He smoked incessantly, but somehow there never seemed to be a speck of ash anywhere. Uncle Heinrich was a small man, quiet, introspective, with lovely big eyes, but otherwise quite homely. Their concentration on whatever they were doing was intense, and though I loved them both I soon became bored.

I also vividly remember Grandfather Urban. I can see him quite clearly, standing in our ultramodern salon and frowning at an Impressionist portrait of two little girls that had been painted by one of Buschi's friends. The unfamiliar background bewildered him, and the extravagance of our life worried him profoundly.

On Sunday afternoons while Father and Heinrich were working in the studio, Mother would preside over afternoon coffee. Grandmother Lefler and Minna were regular visitors. Grandfather Urban would have his coffee and talk to the ladies or watch them at a game of tarok. He then would wander into the toy room and play with us for a while, finally retreating to the studio where Buschi kept special cigars for him. After some small talk (Buschi humoring him with a tolerant smile), Grandfather would drift off home.

In later years, reminiscing about his father, Buschi felt that they had lost touch from the minute he had embarked on his artist's career. They had nothing more in common, yet pathetically his father kept looking for the boy who used to play in his quartet.

Urban's architectural projects from 1900 to 1911 were mainly done for friends and patrons who asked him to design homes or to decorate apartments for them. For Baron von Wiener and his wife, Urban designed a home that used gas for lighting, heating, cooking, and washing in order to spare them

The influential British art journal *The Studio* published a special issue in 1906 dedicated to "The Art Revival in Austria." The black-and-white photographs of interiors designed by Urban are from this issue. The color photographs by Gerhard Trumler show the same interiors as they appeared in 1990.
Top left and right. Dining room, with mahogany doors inlaid in mother-of-pearl.
Bottom left and right. Winter garden.

Entrance to a Vienna apartment designed by Urban. Ca. 1905. Gerhard Trumler.

the mess of coal dust. The use of gas and the built-in furniture were but two of the innovations Urban provided his client, patron, and friend. The von Wieners later sold their home, but the baroness continued to walk by to look at it with fond memories even though the new owners had drastically altered the original design. Her account of the home reveals many of Urban's stylistic and ornamental trademarks:

> The exterior of the house was very simple: whitish stone, window boxes with forget-me-nots and a round balcony. The only ornament was a painted frieze of pine cones, done in bluish gray, about two meters wide, around the entire lower part. The furniture too was extremely simple in line and the walls painted in neutral colors. The dining room had ornaments of brilliant blue grapes; the salon walls were decorated with intertwining stems, leaves and blossoms of morning glories; however, one year later Pepi, who was a frequent visitor in our home, got tired of this latter and forced us to cover it with plain gray material.

Evidence of Urban the illustrator is found in his covering surface areas with floral decorations, stenciling, wallpaper he designed, and medallions, as well as the patterned rugs and carpets he also designed. He managed to combine both the curving motifs of the *Jugendstil* and the strictly geometric patterns that Josef Hoffmann had adopted. One notices also a return to much more simple lines in the furniture, away both from the excesses of the Ringstrasse Historical Style and the early *Jugendstil.* Urban, among others, was borrowing from the homey and simple Biedermeier style popular in Austria around the 1840s.

Whatever he built or designed was carried out with only the finest craftsmanship and materials, creating a feeling of great elegance and luxury without heaviness or oppressive solemnity. Captions taken from illustrations of Urban interiors that appeared in a special 1906 edition of *The Studio,* entitled "The Art-Revival in Austria," give an indication of the elegant materials employed and the effects created: "Dining room in mahogany inlaid with mother-of-pearl"; "Library in mahogany inlaid with ivory and mother-of-pearl [with old silver fittings]"; "Boudoir with walls of purple silk and mahogany inlaid with mother-of-pearl"; "Sitting room in Hungarian natural oak with gilded fittings and wall hangings of emerald green and red silk." [18]

In 1906 Paul Schlenter, director of the Burgtheater, commissioned the Twins to design parts I and II of Goethe's *Faust.* Urban had made his debut as a scenic artist in 1905, with a play by Arthur Schnitzler also directed by Schlenter. Fellow Hagenbund artist Alexander Goltz, who assisted Lefler with the costumes for *Faust,* recalled that "there was such a vital glamour about the Urban scenes that spontaneous applause arose as the curtain revealed one of them.... This *Faust* was for its beauty and acting one of the most perfect that had ever been seen... It was through the medium of this performance that Urban's great gift and unparalleled imagination as stage-decorator was discovered."

Vienna was seething with plans for a *Festzug* in honor of the emperor's sixty-year reign in 1908. All were frustrated by the specter of the tremendous costs involved, but Urban viewed it as an enormous opportunity for himself and his fellow artists in the Hagenbund and was not deterred. The Twins had garnered a considerable following among the wealthy and influential elite of Vienna, and Urban arranged an elaborate banquet at the Hagenbund in order to enlist their support. Karl Stemolak described the scene in the exhibition hall:

> Never have I seen such splendor; on a slightly raised dais stood the huge table, decorated by Urban with gorgeous silver and a profusion of flowers; the walls were newly covered and hung with paintings all expressing the joy over the Kaiser's long reign. There were three huge sculptures: one, an enormous bust of the Emperor cut in wood by [Franz] Barwig and two groups of life-size soldiers done by myself. At the very end of the hall was a glass mosaic by Ludwig Graf, subtly illuminated.
>
> Our rooms were rather frigid, and as Pepi decided that warmth was an essential for the good fellowship we wished to create, he heated the entire place with cleverly concealed electric stoves, a thing never heard of before and causing much gaping amongst our guests.

Apparently proper warmth was generated, for by midnight, awash with music and champagne, sponsorship of the *Festzug,* with Urban at its helm, was assured.

The event that took place on June 12, 1908, might best be described as the final extravaganza of the Habsburg dynasty and, indeed, of the Austro-Hungarian Empire itself. The Ringstrasse was ablaze with flags, banners, and flower-bedecked street lamps. Conceived on a mammoth scale, the program of pageants and floats (each designed by a different artist) consisted of eighteen tableaux of events in the Habsburg reign, ranging from the marriage of Maximilian I in 1500 through the Thirty Years' War, the siege of Vienna by the Turks, and, most elaborate of all, the representation of the reign of Maria Theresa, as designed by Heinrich Lefler. The parade that followed these spectacles included ten thousand marchers in folk costumes that reflected the diverse nationalities of the empire, soldiers, marching bands, pages, heralds and banner bearers, cavalry, court musicians, and eighteen imperial coaches gilded and decorated with flowers. The whole was climaxed by a gigantic float drawn by six pairs of horses and populated by actors and actresses from the Imperial Theatre.

Head of a bronze statue of Mark Antony by Artur Strasser, for which Urban was the model. Ironically the statue is next to the building of the Secessionists, friendly rivals to Urban's Hagenbund. Gerhard Trumler.

Ludwig Hevesi praised the day's events extravagantly:

A *Festzug* like this one has never been equalled and never will be equalled again. Only those who never saw it can belittle its importance and splendor. . . . Taking everything into account, it was a festival for the eyes that is not often experienced and has once again proved that Vienna, thanks to its temperament and artistic and quasi-artistic tendencies, is, indeed, the capital for this kind of spectacular festivities. It is now most appropriate to name it "The City of Festival Pageantry." [19]

Ten-year-old Gretl, though not seated with her father in the imperial pavilion, with its crownlike top, was enchanted by the pageantry and impressed by the magnificent assemblage. It was a day of triumph for Joseph Urban.

Bottom. An elaborate parade and pageant in Vienna celebrated Franz Joseph's sixtieth anniversary on the throne. The elderly emperor remained standing in his *Kaiserpavillon*, designed by Urban, throughout the lengthy festivities. 1908. Columbia University.

40

This drawing of the Emperor's pavilion with a representation of his crown forming the top appeared on the jubilee's commemorative program. 1908. Columbia University.

The weather was perfect; the city was jammed with visitors; there was general jubilation. The complicated pageantry of the parade and the various historic episodes meshed to perfection. Urban was personally congratulated by the emperor, who, heroically and despite his seventy-seven years, remained standing throughout the entire presentation. And since the emperor stood, the other guests in the splendid *Kaiserpavillon,* especially designed by Urban, were also obliged to stand. On this occasion Urban received his third and final handshake from Franz Joseph.

Thoroughly exhausted, having worked day and night to perfect every facet of the vast undertaking, Urban and family departed for a vacation in Grado, a resort on the Adriatic. It was not long before ugly rumors reached them of venomous gossip emanating from Vienna about what was being called the "Urbanfest." As Arthur Schnitzler observed of his fellow Austrians in the novel *The Road to the Open*: "Our indignation is as little genuine as our enthusiasm. The only things genuine with us are our malice and our hatred of talent." [20] So it was inevitable that Urban and Lefler—like Mozart and Mahler and many others—would encounter this peculiarly Viennese form of jealousy. When the storm broke, the first attacks came from the Künstlerhaus in a spate of newspaper articles accusing Urban of having awarded most of the important assignments to personal friends. This was vehemently denied by Urban, who contended that he had chosen only artists whom he considered best qualified and, in any event, everyone, himself included, had donated their time and talent out of respect for the emperor. Urban was also accused of reckless extravagance.

Rudolph Junk later reflected on the matter of the *Festzug*'s cost: "Vienna at the time was one of the richest capitals of Europe. Had it not been for professional jealousy, there would have been no outcry." The issue of cost was really unimportant given the fact that the emperor had paid for all or most of the celebration out of his private funds, with only minimal, if any, drain on the public treasury.

Urban had been responsible for assigning numerous contracts for construction and supplies, and one recipient of a large contract for lumber had expressed his gratitude by giving Urban a diamond ring. Unfortunately, the presentation had been made in public, and rumor spread around town that Urban had taken commissions while the other artists had worked for nothing. Against the advice of Lefler, Urban sued the perpetrator of the rumor for libel. Because of insufficient grounds on both sides, the court threw the case out, which did nothing to temper the scandal.

The Künstlerhaus, of course, had never forgiven Urban for luring Lefler and other important artists from its fold, but when members of his own Hagenbund started attacking him, he was shocked and bewildered. Attendance at the 1908 autumn Hagenbund exhibit was noticeably smaller than before. Complaints from within grew louder as sales of the members' works diminished, and Urban found himself no longer the Hagenbund's popular president. To save the organization he helped found, he offered his resignation, which was accepted. Lefler and other supporters also resigned. Stemolak, who did not resign, later viewed the outcome with obvious regret: "Alas, we let him go. He could have saved us by staying. . . . He was our guiding spirit."

Fortunately the worlds of music and theatre were completely removed from the dispute, and Urban was kept busy with theatrical productions. Lefler, never physically strong, had suffered a heart attack, which undoubtedly was brought on by tensions generated by the *Festzug* and its aftermath. Deprived of his twin, Urban was obliged to work alone, designing scenery not only in Vienna but in other cities within the empire and Germany. Between 1909 and 1911 Urban saw twenty-five of his stage designs realized: an incredible output even for one so active. Lefler joined him for their final collaborations on two productions in 1911, one of which was *Pelléas et Mélisande*. It had unexpected and far-reaching consequences for Urban's life and career.

Urban went to Paris to discuss with Debussy the *Pelléas* that he and Lefler were preparing for Vienna, but also present was Henry Russell, the impresario of the Boston Opera Company. So taken was Russell with Urban that he offered the designer the post of artistic director with his company. Gretl Urban recalls the events that followed:

> In spite of Heinrich's urging, Father was reluctant to accept the offer. One day in a state of indecision he wandered into St. Stephan's Cathedral and found himself face to face with the famous Madonna. On the spur of the moment he asked: "Should I go to the United States?" It may have been wishful thinking or perhaps the play of light from the candles or the stained glass, but Father always swore the Madonna nodded.
>
> Buschi, too cowardly to face Mother's hysteria, left, ostensibly for a new production in Germany, but actually to sail from Bremen. Poor Heinrich was left to tell Mother, who carried on as expected. We girls were very excited about our Buschi venturing into a strange land. Within a couple of weeks he sent us a cable stating that he had signed a five-year contract with

Russell. Mother at first refused to leave Vienna, but on the urging of Heinrich and the pleading of us children, we finally left for America.

One evening in 1915, seated in the pretty garden of Mother's rented house in Swampscott, Father recalled: "It was such a flawless day for me: little did I know then that the *Fest* marked the end of a very important chapter in my life. If it were not for the *Fest* we would probably be suffering in Vienna and I undoubtedly in the army instead of enjoying life here in peace and security."

The person who sacrificed most when the Urbans left for America was, of course, Heinrich Lefler. Fully cognizant that he was not well enough to make such a drastic change, Lefler said he was content to fulfill contractual obligations to the imperial theatres. Not only did he lose thereby his closest friend and collaborator, whom he affectionately called *"Dickes,"* but also his beloved sister, Urban's wife, and his two little nieces whom he adored. There was one happy reunion in Venice, but once the First World War broke out, Lefler never saw any of the Urban family again. In a sense, however, Lefler did go with Urban to America, since the production of *Pelléas* that he and Urban mounted in Vienna in 1911 was reproduced in Boston in 1912.

B O S T O N
1 9 1 1 - 1 9 1 4

On his return from Europe in the late summer of 1912, H. T. Parker, the perceptive critic of the *Boston Evening Transcript*, lamented the current state of American stage design in an article entitled "The New Stagecraft." After analyzing advanced trends in Germany, Austria, and Russia, he concluded: "And the wonder of it all is that we in America have sat these many years blind to all the changes in the scenic arts of the theatre, content with the old outworn ways—the most conservative of countries instead of the most advanced, as we fondly and foolishly consider ourselves." [1] The article added, however, the hopeful note that "There is to be a German stage director at the Boston Opera House next season." The "German" was, of course, Joseph Urban.

Actually, Urban had joined the Boston Opera the previous fall, but his presence had not been acknowledged until the announcement of his engagement as general stage director in the spring of 1912. He had arrived with Rudolf Adler, his business manager, Adler's wife, and the painters Karl Koeck, Otto Weber, Max Kamerzell, and their wives—all cloaked under the name of a Viennese scenic design company. He brought with him three complete opera productions for Boston and since his arrival had been adding his own touches to some of the company's existing productions.

Urban's major achievement in Boston would be the introduction of "the new stagecraft" to America. Today these innovations in lighting, direction, and design are so much a part of the theatrical experience that it is difficult to understand the fervor and controversy with which they were initially received.

Essentially, the aim of the new stagecraft was to fuse all the various elements of a theatrical piece—settings, costumes, lighting, stage movement, and, in some cases, music—into a unified artistic whole that would have maximum aesthetic and emotional effect upon the audience. Richard Wagner, an early exponent of this concept, gave it the name *Gesamstkunstwerk*.

Detail of Urban's design for the Boston Opera production of *Louise*. 1913. Columbia University.

45

With regard to scenery, this meant that no longer would a painted piece of canvas, essentially a greatly expanded, often wrinkled, easel painting, appear on stage with a white light thrown on it. Scenery was now crafted to be viewed only in a theatre under specially conceived theatrical lighting.

John Corbin, theatre critic of the *New York Times* when Urban's work first appeared on the New York stage, has left us an account that simply and most effectively describes just what Urban achieved, how he obtained the desired effects, and how they contrasted with the old stagecraft. In his review of *The Riviera Girl* for the daily *Times*, Corbin commented on the setting: "The scenes which are all keyed to the velvet, impenetrable blue of a Mediterranean sky, are of monumental stateliness and rich simplicity of color. The costumes give the note of variety and rapid change, but discreetly blend throughout with the dominant tone of music and scene." [2]

Corbin followed up with more extensive comments in the Sunday theatre section:

> A scenic artist of the elder and realistic school would no doubt have shown the azure coast of the Mediterranean in all its detail of creamy marble villa and cyprus shade, its vanishing perspective of rocky promontory and rocky ledge. At the rise of the curtain the backdrop, if adequately painted and lighted, would call forth many an oh! and ah! from the audience. Painters of the new school know that such delight is childish and transitory, irrelevant to the purpose of true illusion. The scene that elicits it begins by distracting attention from the true source of dramatic effect, which is the art of composer, librettist, and actor; and it ends in the paradox of a background of still life—of trees unmoved by any breeze, of waves that are forever breaking and never break—set against a world the very essence of which is variety, change, progress. What at best has been a distraction becomes a tedious monotony. When it is not at its best it is simply appalling. In "Rambler Rose," to cite the latest example, the backdrop shows a hill up which winds a road—a road which is marked with a distinctness of line all out of drawing, and which puzzles and baffles throughout the act. At the curtain the reason becomes manifest. The motor car of the rambling heroine buck-jumps along the road, pulled by a string from off stage. That is scenic realism with a vengeance. [3]

To this Corbin contrasts, almost in awe, Urban's work, especially the blue sky effect, one of his trademarks:

> In the three pictures of Joseph Urban, the Mediterranean is not seen, nor any detail of villa or foliage, of ledge or shore. Only the sky is visible, and it is without cloud or star. But the coloring, the lighting, of this sky has exhausted the resources of the modern theatre. It is a deep and magic blue; velvety in texture, yet suggesting limitless regions of heaven. It is a symbol, if you wish, of the Mediterranean—the very breath and spirit of the Côte d'Azur. And it dominates the successive scenes with a sense of imaginative unity only less persuasive and compelling, than that of the music. The architectural features of the foreground are similarly broad and harmonious—monumental in line and spacing, richly simple in color. Avoiding every detail that may distract the eye, or weary it, they strike a note of beauty, stimulate the imagination in full accord with the mood of the composer. [4]

Here, simply stated, are the keys to all of Urban's scenic designs: color, light, simplicity, and fidelity to the intentions of the composer and/or author.

In its brief life of five seasons—from a November 8, 1909, opening to a splendid 1914 finale in Paris—the Boston Opera Company frequently matched

New York's Metropolitan in overall numbers of performances, variety of repertory, production values, and its roster of famous international singers and conductors. In the company's first season, there were ninety-three performances in Boston and on tour, and twenty operas were presented, including such spectacles as *Aïda, Les Huguenots, Mefistofele, Faust, Lohengrin,* and *Il Trovatore.* That all this, including the construction of a superb theatre, was achieved between the fall of 1908, when the cornerstone was laid, and the spring of 1910, a period of only eighteen months, can only be described as truly staggering.

If the Boston Opera was not entirely Henry Russell's creation, its genesis and success were certainly due to his exertions as impresario, or managing director, as he preferred to be designated. He was a small man with little capacity for self-effacement, and his character was hardly sufficient to mask his overriding vanity and self-destruction. On the other hand, these qualities may have been the very ones that, linked with a fluency in languages, innate taste, flair, and sound musical knowledge, enabled him to move relatively unscathed in the world of grand opera, a realm convulsed by artistic temperament, caprice, critical confrontation, and financial embarrassment.

As a vocal coach in London, with a studio in fashionable Curzon Street, Russell was noted as having attracted such famous singers as Lillian Nordica and Nellie Melba. His teaching method, based on "the study of the art of breathing and the physiology of the throat," cured Eleanora Duse of a "taut and fatigued throat" [5] and led to close association with Duse and Gabriele D'Annunzio in the production of several of D'Annunzio's plays. Russell could make the piano thunder like an orchestra, and he delighted D'Annunzio by playing his own reductions of Wagnerian scores. Russell also became a close friend and associate of Maurice Maeterlinck and a frequent guest in the poet's beautiful old abbey of Saint Wandrille in Normandy. In dread of returning to the "comparatively dull life of a singing master," [6] Russell turned his multiple talents to that most intricate of arts, grand opera, as manager of the San Carlo Opera Company. In his memoir, *The Passing Show,* he observes: "It has been my strange destiny to spend at least half my life with very rich people, opera being one of those expensive luxuries that demand the support of millionaires." [7] One such tycoon was Eben Jordan, Jr., heir to the Jordan Marsh Company, Boston's finest department store.

During America's copper panic of 1907, Russell, on a transcontinental tour with the San Carlo Opera, found himself in New York with twenty-six artists and a chorus, but with no cash to meet the payroll. Recalling Jordan's publicly expressed enthusiasm for the San Carlo Opera's Boston performance the previous season, Russell put in a call to Jordan's residence:

> . . . to my bitter disappointment, the telephone was answered by the butler, who said Jordan was in Hot Springs, Virginia. I made up my mind, however, that he was my only hope, and, collecting the few remaining dollars I possessed, I took the train that night to Hot Springs. . . .
>
> He was a distinguished looking man, a little blunt in manner, but his eyes had the kindest expression I have ever seen. His voice was deep and gruff, and by the way he spoke I gathered my visit considerably surprised him.
>
> "What the devil have you followed me to Hot Springs for?" was his greeting. This made me so nervous I was rendered speechless. . . . But within half an hour of the time that I had entered the room, Jordan handed me a certified check for $20,000. [8]

And Russell concludes: "Little did I realize that the ultimate outcome of my visit to Hot Springs that terrible day would be the building of one of the finest opera houses in America, and my appointment as managing director." [9]

The period of 1906 to 1911 was one of widespread operatic expansion. Otto Kahn, patron-financier of the Metropolitan Opera, had conceived the ambitious scheme of spreading grand opera throughout the country with interlocking companies including Philadelphia and Chicago. Oscar Hammerstein was not only challenging the Metropolitan with his highly successful Manhattan Opera House on West Thirty-fourth Street but was building an opera house in Philadelphia and further extending his influence to Baltimore, Chicago, and Washington. With typical optimism Russell wrote to Otto Kahn in 1913: "I cannot help feeling that, if the operatic situation in North America is properly handled and concentrated, the day will come when we can control the operatic destinies of the world." [10] In such a climate it seemed entirely suitable that Boston, which considered itself the cultural center of the nation, should have an opera house of its own, or so it appeared to Eben Jordan and a shivering crowd of two hundred "lovers of music, song-birds of the stage and patrons of the art" [11] gathered on upper Huntington Avenue on a chilly November 30, 1908, for the ceremony attendant to the laying of the cornerstone for the new opera house. Telegrams of congratulations from Otto Kahn and the entire Metropolitan board of directors and from Emma Eames, Geraldine Farrar, Alice Nielson, and other artists were read by Henry Russell.

The opera house was designed by the noted architect Parker B. Haven. Lawrence Gilman of *Harper's Weekly* magazine pronounced the exterior of red brick, gray limestone, and terra-cotta "in admirable taste and reticent beauty, rather than prodigal sumptuousness." [12] The interior, also understated, was decorated in tones of ivory and antique gold under a sky-blue ceiling with white clouds and a huge chandelier. Seating twenty-seven hundred, with fifty-four boxes, and including a splendidly equipped stage 48 feet wide and 39 feet high at the opening, with 130 feet of vertical fly space, it was certainly an opera house worthy of Boston. Philip Hale wrote of the new house in the *Boston Herald*:

> [At last] a building artistic in design, structure, ornamentation, equipment, in which the spectacle is not through necessity only on the other side of the footlights; for there is at last the opportunity for the display of fair women in gala costumes which in an opera house adds so much to the brilliance of the scene and ... performances; which gives to the opera certain—if the word is sadly abused—aristocratic distinction. [13]

Of more immediate concern to the audience was the ambience of the new house. Everyone from President Lowell of Harvard to Mrs. John L. Gardner expressed delight in the ample lobby space, the promenade, and the Palm Room, a "dignified but cheerful chamber on the second-tier box floor fitted out with 'graceful chairs and round tables' ... was adopted ... as a smoking room, 'men taking the hint from a cigar case in one corner and match safes on the tables.' " [14] There was also an "elaborate soda water and ice cream fountain, 'expected to be used by the women.' " [15]

The three productions Urban brought with him from Vienna and presented within roughly a month of each other were *Pelléas et Mélisande, Hänsel und Gretel,* and *Tristan und Isolde.* While it is, of course, impossible to fully appreciate Urban's artistry from photographs or even his own meticulous drawings, we do have the benefit of commentaries by two

perceptive and eloquent critics concerning Urban's work and how audiences reacted to it. Philip Hale wrote for the *Boston Herald* and Henry Taylor Parker served the *Evening Transcript. Pelléas* was the first of the three Urban productions staged, January 10, 1912.

Henry Russell realized that *Pelléas* in and of itself would not fill his large opera house. The work had already appeared in Boston under Oscar Hammerstein's aegis and thus no longer could be deemed a novelty. Publicity was therefore focused on the authenticity of the production and its faithfulness to the intentions of its creators. Conductor André Caplet was a protégé of the composer, Claude Debussy, and both he and Russell had conferred with him in Paris during the summer of 1911. In addition, Russell had long been an intimate of the poet Maurice Maeterlinck, whose play Debussy had set to music. Georgette Leblanc, known as Mme. Maeterlinck,[16] was the Mélisande for the early performances, to be followed by Mary Garden, who sang the part when the opera had its Paris premiere.

To spur ticket sales, Russell arranged an elaborate hoax that he justified as follows: "Apart from my dread of giving a new opera to a half-empty house, the cost of the production was so great that I feared the prospect of a heavy financial loss."[17] With Georgette's approval, or so he claimed, Russell informed the press that Maeterlinck would be in Boston for the premiere and had bet him a thousand dollars that he could land in New York without being recognized. There was not a word of truth in any of this, as Russell later admitted, for Maeterlinck had no intention of leaving his walled estate in France.

The *New York Herald* picked up the story and asked: "Will he enter New York disguised as a nobleman or in the steerage? M. Maeterlinck is confident that only the heaven born genius of Arsene Lupin [a detective created by Georgette Leblanc's brother, Maurice] will be able to detect him. He is determined to reach Boston without being interviewed."[18]

Debussy told Urban that he did not like the spindly trees most designers provided for the forest scenes in *Pelléas et Mélisande.* Accordingly, Urban created the dense grove shown in this model from the 1912 Boston Opera Company production. Columbia University.

The ruse worked. Russell dressed up a member of the chorus to look like a European artist, and had him register at the Hotel Westminster—whose owner cooperatively announced to the anxious press that a mysterious "Monsieur M." had indeed checked in. The opera house was filled with patrons hoping to catch a glimpse of the elusive poet; members of the press stayed in the hotel lobby with the same intentions—and with the same degree of success. Russell was elated.

The production itself was praised by both Parker and Hale. Parker went so far as to write an editorial stating that "nothing like them [the settings] has ever been seen in any opera on the American stage."[19] The lights coming up on each scene gave the audience, Parker wrote, "the sensation of the sudden opening of an illuminated mediaeval manuscript."[20] The dimming of the lights at the close of each scene produced an effect, according to Hale, of "a series of dissolving pictures that came suddenly from the darkness and at the end of each scene gradually faded."[21]

To make the opera more intimate on the enormous stage, Urban used one of his favorite devices, a stage within a stage. However, with its raised platforms the set seemed boxlike and cramped to some, particularly to Mary

Garden, who assumed the role of Mélisande on March 30. She threatened not to sing because the sets were so small: "I can hardly turn around." [22]

Debussy had told Urban he never liked the spindly trees that always seemed to be used in the forest scene, for he could not imagine Golaud's getting lost in such a woods. Urban developed this as the key to his design and set the opera in a very real medieval Normandy rather than in some vague dreamlike fantasy kingdom. Arkel's castle appeared as if made of rough-hewn stone and was furnished with rudely carved furniture. The stark interiors were relieved by unexpected bright patches of color such as the red, black, and gold canopy over Mélisande's bed and the open missal in Arkel's gallery.

For *Hänsel und Gretel* Urban again used a reduced stage to make the children's opera more intimate. A golden border similar to what he and Lefler had used to frame their fairy-tale illustrations encompassed the sets, creating the effect of a giant children's picture book. *Tristan,* like *Hänsel,* was better received by the public than *Pelléas* had been, but its debut was marred by difficulties with the lighting. Urban wanted lighting effects to underline the lovers' emotions in the second-act love duet, but the stage technicians were incapable of meeting his complex demands. Problems with lighting dogged Urban's Boston productions and provided his critics with one of the few real sources of ammunition against his designs.

At season's end, Russell boasted of the company's achievements: "Without making the music itself secondary to the dramatic action, we have endeavored, I may say even succeeded, in making music and action a harmonious whole, and we have carried the illusion into scenic surroundings." [23]

Shortly before the start of the opera season, either late October or early November 1912, Urban's family joined him. He had rented two separate apartments in a building on Huntington Avenue, which was near the opera house and home to other members of the company. When Mrs. Urban first inspected the rooms, before her husband's late arrival on the scene, her reaction was, according to Gretl, "This looks like a convent school." Urban had been able to decorate only the living room using his own designs. The other rooms were either sparsely furnished or filled with store-bought furniture, which until then had never been seen in an Urban apartment. Because of his work at the opera, he had been unable to design more furniture, and after paying Lefler every penny he owed him, he could afford little else.

The family soon felt rather at home in Boston since they had a Viennese cook, the company of Viennese artists who worked with Urban, and even old friends from Vienna such as Leo Slezak and the Felix Weingartners. Urban and Gretl were also to meet several great artists they would later reencounter at the Met, among them Caruso, Bori, Matzenauer, Garden, and the de Reszkes.

Gretl described her introduction to Boston:

> At first we were a little snobbish about Boston, which contained not one decent pastry shop and, after Vienna, seemed rather bland, but we all loved the beautiful opera house, especially the interior. Buschi had learned an amazing lot of English, and Elly and I were pretty good at it too, as we had had an English governess for the previous two years. Mother was laughed at by a saleslady at Filene's department store when she attempted to make a purchase, and when Mr. Jordan was informed, he said it never could have happened at Jordan Marsh, a model department store that had invented the slogan "The customer is always right."

Urban's studio in the Boston Opera House. The designer had complete responsibility for everything not related to music that took place onstage, including sets, costumes, props, and lighting.
Gretl Urban collection.

We were taken up by Boston society, and even Mrs. Jack Gardner, a rather homely but very gracious woman, entertained us at her amazing house, Fenway Court, which was Venetian in style, with a formal garden under a skylight. Her portrait by Sargent featuring her back, her best feature, was displayed surrounded by small clipped bushes and occasional tables with plates containing semiprecious stones.

It was evident that Buschi was an important figure; as the opening of the opera season approached, his name appeared almost daily in the press. For the opening, *The Tales of Hoffmann,* on November 25 we were guests in Henry Russell's box in the second tier center. We had been to several rehearsals and had heard so much from Father about the problems with electricians and the light cues that we were quite nervous. We need not have been. Everything worked perfectly; Buschi and the artists enjoyed a real triumph.

The elaborate prospectus for the upcoming 1912–1913 season (probably designed by Urban) focused, in part, on Urban's role with the company:

The Boston Opera House will be the first in America to avail itself of these [the new stagecraft's] improved methods. Mr. Josef Urban, who is thoroughly familiar with these methods and is the originator of many of them, has been engaged as general stage director for the coming season. The designs for not only the scenic settings, but for the costumes, for the stage properties and accessories, and for the lighting effects will be supplied by him.[24]

In short, Urban was responsible for everything that took place onstage, including the directing of the cast. All musical aspects of the operas were under the control of conductor André Caplet.

A writer for the *Transcript* with the improbable name of Adalbert Albrecht described the new facilities Eben Jordan provided the opera company in an article entitled "The Opera's Factory of Illusions." The first of the two facilities was an annex to the opera house itself, which contained rehearsal rooms for the chorus and ballet and offices for Caplet and Urban. Albrecht also left us an invaluable firsthand account of Urban's working methods as he pictured him in his new office designing *The Tales of Hoffmann*:

> Here is the place where Mr. Urban sits bent over his drawing-board and carries out sketches to the finest detail in line and color. Here, on paper, he already tries to catch and hold fast the spirit of each separate act. Already he plans a wide-open door with a view of a fresh, early-morning rose garden gay with blossoms, tries to suggest the muffled conviviality of a cellar restaurant, makes the moon peep through latticed windows, groups the actors in their costumes round heavy tables with tankards, places the prima donna on a couch of his own designing, deposes the lovers in cosy corners.[25]

Costumed figures were grouped around the central drawing of the set, with each figure painted in color and in great detail:

> We even see the faces of these people; in a few strokes the character of the role is indicated: the roué with his scanty hair combed carefully over his bald head, the jeune première with a blue ribbon twisting about her locks, the venerable old servant with a beard that flows down onto his breast and bushy, yellowish eyebrows. And then every table and every chair, every lamp and candlestick must be drawn and painted so that not even the slightest trifle fails to agree with the setting and disturbs the artistic illusion.[26]

When the sketches were completed, Urban conferred with his staff on the practical details of actually constructing the sets to best effect, but at the least possible cost. The next step was for Urban's Viennese artists to prepare models of each set on the scale of 1:25. Albrecht was enchanted with the models and compared them to the cut-out cardboard Christmas mangers so popular when he was a child:

> These models are the most fascinating little works of art, made of cardboard, and one of their main uses is to show whether all parts of the scene are visible from the auditorium, whether all the proportions of the different parts produce the desired effect and whether the whole impression conforms, on the one side, to the requirements of the design in line and picturesqueness and, on the other, to those of the stage management. . . . In these models . . . colored tissue paper is pasted over the windows. . . . On the walls of these models hang in miniature the gobelins and pictures that are used in performance; the light fixtures, the furniture is there, in short, we see the stage as it will be when the curtain rises the first night.[27]

Fortunately, some models prepared for Broadway and Metropolitan productions have been preserved in good condition in the Urban archives at Columbia University. When photographed, they are difficult to distinguish from the actual stage sets.

The Urban family outside their Boston apartment. Urban was so busy with the opera company that he did not have time to design his own furniture. This was Gretl's first contact with a store-bought bed. Gretl Urban collection.

GUESTS: GENTLEMEN·

·NICKLAUSSE·   ·HOFFMANN·

COPPELIUS·

·1912·
·BOSTON·
·URBAN·

Costume sketches that Urban prepared for the 1912 production of Offenbach's *The Tales of Hoffmann*. In Europe Urban had only designed scenery since Lefler made the costumes for productions they jointly created.
Columbia University.

Once the models were pronounced perfect, preparation of the actual scenery began. This work was carried out in the other new facility the company acquired in 1912:

> Quite close to the railway station in Swampscott, hidden from the street by a few apple trees and workingmen's houses, lies the scenic studio of the Boston Opera Company—from outside nothing but a vast, low, whitewashed shed. No passerby suspects that here is the greatest factory of illusions of our country, that here men are at work carrying out with sure purpose a part of the intentions of the greatest musical geniuses of all ages. No one guesses that here reforms are in process which may be of exceeding importance not only to the American stage but to our whole young culture.[28]

Since the cyclorama of the Boston Opera House was 64 feet high and 170 feet wide, or 10,880 square feet, enormous pieces of canvas were needed to make the sets. To paint them, they were laid out flat on the studio floor, which was 75 by 150 feet. First the artists drew in the scenery's outlines with pieces of charcoal on the ends of long poles, then came the all-important mixing and application of the colors. Albrecht continues his account:

> It is hard to believe how much study and practice is necessary in choosing the colors for the decorations so that the intended effect is obtained. Above all, the colors must be "light-proof," for they are often subjected to the most varying and intense electric light for hours at a time. And the art of the painter, who works by daylight, consists in so mixing the colors that they produce the proper effect by artificial light.[29]

One of the principles of the new stagecraft was that scenery was intended to be viewed only in the theater under proper lighting conditions. The "pointillist" technique Urban used to achieve some of his greatest effects is described by Albrecht:

> Incredible effects can be obtained with the electric "four-colored lights," presupposing, of course, that they are used under the direction of an artist who understands how to make light and painting go hand in hand. Thus, for instance, in a background, the clear, sunny atmosphere can be produced, the wonderful shimmer of golden sunshine can be obtained, by stippling with different colors the blue canvas that represents the air. Then, when the proper shade of electric light is thrown on it, the effect is most deceptive.[30]

BACCHANAL· GUESTS·BY·GIULIETTA·   ·II· GIULIETTA ·

Finally, Albrecht pays homage to the artistry of Urban's workers and explains how they actually painted the huge canvases:

> These dimensions [of the stage] demand not only an artistic comprehension of the whole effect and the highest technical skill, but also truly athletic strength. To handle the enormous brushes heavy with paint, the tremendous rulers, the gigantic palettes mounted on four wheels, all day and all week long requires great physical endurance. But what makes such work most wearing is that it has to be done with all speed. The colors must not be allowed to dry; hence the painters work with a haste that reminds one of a game of polo. They run from one end of the studio to the other, work with outstretched arms, kneel to rub certain spots of color, etc.[31]

The studio contained numerous other departments: a carpenter shop, areas devoted to upholstering and draperies, and spaces for the manufacture of papier-mâché objects such as vases, shields, and armor. The wives of the Viennese artists presided over a sewing room and, among other effects, mounted leaves on gauze that was invisible under stage lighting. Shoe, wig, and costume departments also hummed. In total, almost one hundred people worked at the opera's "factory of illusions."

H. T. Parker also visited conductor Caplet and stage director Urban in their new offices. From his account of the visit, one might have anticipated nationalistic conflict, but Parker assured his readers that "there is a Franco-German pact of eager ambition and tireless work over the opera":

> For Mr. Caplet the music is French music that has never yet spoken with its true and characteristic voice to American audiences. He will try to set that voice free. For Mr. Urban the tales are German tales written by a German for Germans that have never yet received their due setting and atmosphere in America. He will try to achieve it.[32]

Urban's methods for designing a production have been covered in some detail to show how carefully he considered his work; just as much attention was given to his role as stage director. (Today the tasks he took upon himself—settings, costumes, lighting, and direction—might be distributed among as many as four different people.) He first studied the libretto, referring to original sources whenever possible, in this case E.T.A. Hoffmann's classic tales, and then he would research the historical period of the story. Finally, he would prepare a fully detailed analysis of each scene that described the movements of the cast, as well as their motivations. Interspaced throughout these analyses were jewellike colored renderings of the scene that showed the disposition of the characters on the set at a particular moment. Fortunately the "script" Urban prepared for *Hoffmann* survives, and part of it is reproduced here.

Urban's stage pictures underlined both events in the plot and the personalities of characters. In the Olympia act, for example, flowers and floral images predominated:

> The guests . . . form as it were a bouquet of flowers in the foreground, that is, a dark bouquet formed by the bright colored costumes of the ladies, in which the men in their green, blue and brown costumes figure as the stems and leaves. The ladies wear flowers in their hair, which are so placed that when they turn their backs to the audience, they form a wreath around Olympia. These flowers must not be of the same color as the costumes of the principals.[33]

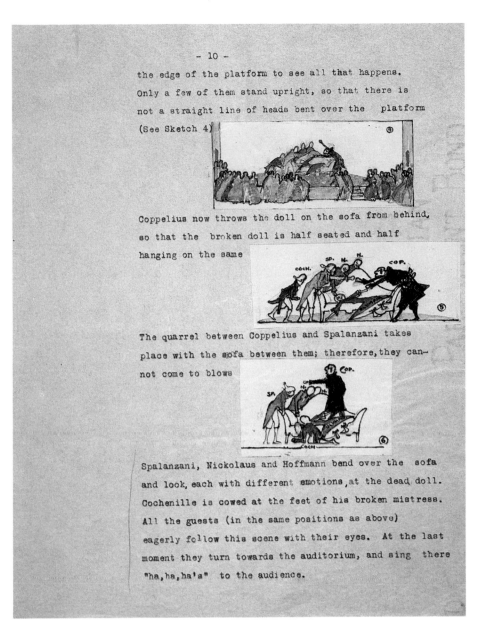

the edge of the platform to see all that happens.
Only a few of them stand upright, so that there is
not a straight line of heads bent over the platform
(See Sketch 4)

Coppelius now throws the doll on the sofa from behind,
so that the broken doll is half seated and half
hanging on the same

The quarrel between Coppelius and Spalanzani takes
place with the sofa between them; therefore, they cannot come to blows

Spalanzani, Nickolaus and Hoffmann bend over the sofa
and look, each with different emotions, at the dead doll.
Cochenille is cowed at the feet of his broken mistress.
All the guests (in the same positions as above)
eagerly follow this scene with their eyes. At the last
moment they turn towards the auditorium, and sing there
"ha,ha,ha'a" to the audience.

Urban tied each act to the others by the costumes and positions of the villain, the heroine, and the servant. At the curtain of each act, the servant was dressed to provide a red accent, while Hoffmann was always in blue:

> Regisseur should try as a standard motive to have the servant at the feet of his mistress at the end of every tale (the red spot) as in the Olympia Act, kneeling and crying, bent over the broken doll. In the Giuletta Act, at the feet of his mistress departing in the gondola. In the Antonia Act, kneeling at the arm-chair of his dead mistress. Also in all three tales the black appearance of the bad element must always be seen at the end (dominant position).[34]

Parker's review in the *Transcript* on the twenty-sixth ran to three columns with the headline "THE OPERA OUTDOES ITSELF . . . 'Tales of Hoffmann' Produced as Never Before in America."

> Last evening, the fourth season began at the Opera House with a more finely-tempered and revealing performance of "The Tales of Hoffmann" than has hitherto been accomplished in America. . . . The performance was

In addition to his duties as designer for the Boston Opera, Urban was also the stage director. He prepared a detailed analysis of blocking and stage directions, complete with jewellike colored illustrations, for each scene of an opera. This is a page from his "script" for *Hoffmann*. 1912. Columbia University.

Models for three scenes from
The Tales of Hoffmann. 1912.
Top. The prologue and
epilogue at the tavern.
Center. The Olympia act.
Bottom. The Giulietta act.
Columbia University.

clothed in scenery, costumes, and light that seemed unmatched on the American stage in illusion of time, place and atmosphere, in imaginative suggestion and in intrinsic pictorial beauty.

Mr. Urban discarded the footlights and other outworn means of illumination and resorted to newer devices that brought soft and suffused glows and natural play of them over the faces that they caught. . . . He even set the three tales that Hoffmann tells on a raised platform that they might seem as things of the imaginations apart, whereas Prologue and Epilogue passed on the ordinary stage level. . . . He used color in masses or in telling spots; he cultivated plane surfaces; he eschewed finicky details; he sought the effect of a fluid and atmospheric picture. . . .

Sketch of the costumes and set for the Antonia scene in *Hoffmann*. 1912. Gretl Urban collection.

Working side by side with Mr. Caplet, he [Urban] it was who had freed the singing-players from the outworn conventions of operatic acting, persuaded them to sink themselves into their parts and to adjust their parts to the play; who had given the performance its shifting variety in essential unity. . . . Music, drama, and setting were wholly fused into the compassing of perfect atmosphere and illusion.[35]

Parker concluded his review with this prophetic statement:

Some day, the records may say that a revolution in the setting and lighting of the American stage dates from these innovations at the Boston Opera House—with "Pelléas," with "Hansel and Gretel" and now with "The Tales of Hoffmann." Then how proud we Bostonians shall be of ourselves—even though we did not half suspect it while it was actually going forward.[36]

Louise Edvina, as Antonia, was praised for her exquisite rendering of Offenbach's passionate, lyric music. Philip Hale went so far as to describe her portrayal of the fragile heroine as "ideal." Canadian by birth, Edvina had studied in Paris with Jean de Reszke and had created the title role in *Louise* at Covent Garden as well as Maliela in *The Jewels of the Madonna*. Her pure lyric voice had great sensuous charm and her acting was unmannered and spontaneous. When she married Cecil Edwardes, the son of a British peer, she changed her name from Martin to the Latin version of her husband's surname.

Urban was enchanted. From the first, their professional relationship was ideal. *Louise* followed *The Tales of Hoffmann* on December 18, 1912. By the premiere of *The Jewels of the Madonna*, a month later, a romantic alliance, though discreetly conducted, was definitely established. His daughter Gretl also was enchanted:

> Louise Edvina was a tall, slim actress with a liquid, lyric soprano voice that she knew how to use with seemingly effortless mastery. As I had a real crush on her and treasured the photographs she had given me, I could readily understand Father's admiration for a great artist and his passionate love for a famous prima donna. He wrote her long letters in English, and I had to help him with the spelling or a word he didn't know. I never read any of the letters, but they were exquisitely done in his characteristic handwriting. I thought it was all most romantic and their separation tragic.
>
> Edvina, his "divine diva," he enjoyed saying in English because it made music the way she did. My romantic Buschi!
>
> He became interested in her at the very first rehearsal of *The Tales of Hoffmann*. She was the only one who immediately understood what he was after in raising the fantasy parts of the opera above stage level while leaving its reality on stage level. She was also good at following his direction to use the solidly built setting to lean against, et cetera, and make it part of her acting, which, she assured him, helped her tremendously in the portrayal of the frail heroine.

An Impressionistic Montmartre was rendered by Urban for Charpentier's *Louise*. 1913. Columbia University.

Louise Edvina in the costume Urban designed for her role in Wolf-Ferrari's *Jewels of the Madonna*. 1913. As a token of their offstage affair, Urban gave the soprano a specially made set of sketches of the costumes he had designed for her.
Columbia University.

Buschi took infinite pains in the designing of her costumes and was in his element when he sketched the bejeweled habit for *The Jewels of the Madonna*. He made copies of some of his sketches for her as a memento of a unique collaboration and also of their affair, which, as she had told him frankly from the start, would have to be ephemeral and casual, not only because Buschi was married, but also because she loved her husband and would never do anything to hurt him or jeopardize her position in London society and at Covent Garden. Because of this frank understanding, in privacy and in work, their love affair lasted until the war.

For his other work in the 1912–1913 season, Urban received generally favorable notices from the critics, but the public's reaction was often less supportive. When Charpentier's *Louise* was presented for the first time, with Edvina in the title role, operagoers had expected to see realistic representations of Paris; instead, Urban provided impressionistic sets in soft tones of blue, green, and lavender. He was attempting "suggestion and atmosphere rather than literal truth," as Philip Hale had appreciated.[37] Cries of protest arose when *Hänsel und Gretel* was revived, for some felt that a new designer had desecrated one of the company's best-loved productions. The golden stairway used by the angels in the forest dream sequence was gone, and the forest had become so dark that the audience was unable to see what the children were doing. There was little recognition that Urban had been the original designer and was now rethinking one of his own works.

A lengthy article defending Urban and his art appeared in the *Transcript* on January 11, 1913. The writer, not H. T. Parker in this case, tells us how little the Boston audiences understood Urban's work:

61

MADAME·BUTTERFLY·BY·PUCCINI···II·ACT·   ·1912·-·BOSTON··URBAN·

A very *Jugendstil* design for Puccini's *Madama Butterfly*. 1913. Columbia University.

No one seems able to judge the results as unique art products, creating and demanding new standards. No one observes that for the first time in America the setting and lighting of music-drama are as artistic and integral a part of the total effect as the music. Naturally nobody remarks that this has been the way in all the German houses for the last ten years. No, we all have the fidgets over something new. For after all, revolution is revolution.

. . . If Mr. Urban were parading himself as a notably eccentric personality, instead of quietly doing his work, or if he had come to us as a much-heralded [Max] Reinhardt, the eyes that now mistrust his settings and his lights would have been quickly opened, and the grumbling or the sarcastic comments upon them quickly stilled. As it is his revolution may turn into nothing more than a rebellion unless the audience at the opera house free their minds from preconceptions and try to understand this new world of the theatre of which Mr. Urban is the prophet.[38]

These timely words must have comforted the beleaguered artist during a difficult and intense phase of his career, for he not only had to struggle in a new language but also had to settle his wife and children in their new home while maintaining a rigorous schedule at the opera house. During the 1912–1913 season Urban was responsible for six new productions and all that they entailed within the four-month season. In addition he had to oversee revivals of operas from previous years.

One of the new productions was Wolf-Ferrari's *Jewels of the Madonna*. Philip Hale's review is cited here because it makes an ironic link between Urban and Broadway: "Certain episodes in the first and third act will please many who dislike 'Pelleas and Melisande' and they will think for the time that they are attending a glorified performance of 'The Follies of 1912.' "[39]

This was not intended as a compliment, since the *Follies* was then known as a rather gaudy and vulgar entertainment. The irony is that only two years later Urban would be transforming the *Follies* into the elegant and sophisticated revues that became the very symbol of the 1920s.

The culmination of Urban's work in Boston came with Bizet's one-act opera *Djamileh* on February 24, 1913. Parker labeled the work itself a "trivial curiosity," but was most appreciative of Urban's lavish use of color in both the costumes and the single setting, which was within a sultan's palace.

> Haroun's chamber stood between curtains of deep, dull, dead reds over which gold arabesques, similarly stifled in hue, wandered. Between the curtains was the panelling of the walls now of blue and silver wrought in close oriental tracery and again of conventionalized and bosky shrubs that flowered luxuriantly in their greens; while here and there the dull red and gold subdued this brightness. Between the panels in the centre was the great circle of the window. Thick clusters of white flowers clung to the surrounding silver lattice. Beyond a tall rose tree flung up deep red patches of its flower. Above was a sky of velvet that moonlight slowly silvered. Within, light fell, soft and golden, from hanging braziers, and the naked gold of a great screen returned this soft radiance.[40]

Parker concluded his review with some remarks that show what this triumph meant for Urban personally:

> Hitherto America has known no such imagination in design and color in the theatre, and no such artistry of scenic accomplishment. The new, by its clear virtue at Mr. Urban's hands, has once more beaten down the old ways of the "tradition." There were no murmurings over the settings of "Djamileh." Rather they were its saving grace. Mr. Urban's victory had come slowly and in the face of many odds; but last night it came completely.[41]

Unfortunately, since the opera received only one performance, very few people were able to see it.

Urban drew on his experience in Egypt for the setting of Bizet's one-act opera, *Djamileh*. One critic saw this production as the vindication of Urban's controversial efforts as an exponent of the "new stagecraft." Only one performance of the opera was given. 1913. Columbia University.

In January of 1913, Russell announced that Urban was going to be retained for the following 1913–1914 season. Parker's article reporting Urban's reappointment shows how precarious the artist's position actually was and just how much opposition he faced. The critic praised Russell for having "steadfastly supported . . . [Urban] in the face of the opposition and even derision that some of his scenic innovations have excited."[42] Having witnessed Urban's hectic year, Parker described him as a "quiet and simple man; but he knows what it is to work and fight for an ideal."[43]

The 1913–1914 season, which was to be the company's last, began much the same way as the previous one. The major new production was *Die Meistersinger,* and once again there were illustrated stories in the Boston papers about what had been necessary to bring this work to the stage. Urban was said to be striving for authenticity in every detail: from the stools of the singers to the banners of the guilds. For this he drew on his youthful travels though Germany, just as he drew on his experiences in Egypt for *Djamileh.*

Another new production for the 1913–1914 season was Henri Fevrier's *Monna Vanna.* George Tyler, a Broadway producer of such spectacles as *The Garden of Allah* and *The Daughter of Heaven,* caught a performance and asked Urban to design the sets for *The Garden of Paradise,* a play based on Hans Christian Andersen's fairy tale "The Little Mermaid," which he intended to produce on Broadway in the fall of 1914. The challenge of myriad fantastic costumes and settings ranging from the mermaid's underwater kingdom to the prince's royal palace was irresistible to Urban. Under the watchful eye of his business manager, Mr. Adler, a contract was signed by the producers of the play and the Boston Opera Company that enabled Urban to work on his first Broadway production.

In the meantime, Russell was negotiating an enormously complex international deal involving Baron Frederic d'Erlanger, the millionaire composer; Lord Grimthorpe, Russell's onetime patron in London; Sir Ernest Cassell, the London banker; Clarence Mackay and Otto Kahn of the Metropolitan; Lord Rothschild; and, of course, Eben D. Jordan—a deal that would ensure a season of the Boston Opera in Paris. Quaintance Eaton offers two motivations for this Herculean endeavor: the deep-seated desire of a European-born American to show off his new accomplishments to the Old World and the desire of wealthy backers of opera to form an international cartel.[44] Russell not only pulled it off but turned it into the crowning success of his career.

The opera's final performance in Boston took place on March 28, 1914, and the company departed on May 29 on board the *Lapland*, the largest ship ever to enter Boston harbor. Rerouted from New York, it arrived two hours late to find a crowd of five thousand shivering on the windy docks. As crowds converged on the narrow pier, passengers became entangled with well-wishers, and the next day the *New York Times* detailed the casualties, from feminine faintings to manager McDonald's "injury around the stomach" to Mme. Lafitte's loss of handbag and tickets.[45] Russell and Urban, along with the technical crews, scenery, and props, had departed earlier on the *Olympic*, so Gretl, Elly, Mizzi, and Tommy, their German schnauzer, were escorted to their cabins by Mr. Adler. As the *Lapland* pulled away with its ruffled operatic complement, the cheering fans did not know and never would have believed they were witnessing the final performance of the Boston Opera Company.

It took all of Russell's skills, with no help from local opera managements and their press satellites, to make the company's April 25 opening of Montemezzi's *L'Amore dei Tre Re* at the Théâtre des Champs-Elysées a smashing social and critical success. High diplomacy was represented by President Poincaré and Ambassador and Mrs. Herrick, British Ambassador

Costume sketches for Wagner's *Die Meistersinger*. 1913. When the company presented this production in Paris in the spring of 1914, it was the first time in more than forty years that a complete German opera had been performed there in German.
Columbia University.

A scene from Mozart's *Don Giovanni* showing the lush dark blue for which Urban was famous. 1913. Columbia University.

and Lady Bertie, Italian Ambassador and Signora Tittoni; titled splendor was exhibited by Principessa di Stigliano Colonna, Comtesse de Gallifet, and Lady Lawther. The dress rehearsal attracted the artistic elite: Claude Debussy, Gabriel Pierné, Rejane and Maurice Bernhardt, Jean de Reszke, and composer Italo Montemezzi himself. Bostonians in the audience were led by Jordan, his wife, and daughter, and included Mrs. Gardner, Bayard Thayer, and Henry Dana. Urban's settings fitted neatly onto the stage of the Champs-Elysées, but ironically *Le Monde Musical* "found the architecture of the décors strictly American." [46] Edvina's Flora was described as a performance with "interior flame, and with pretty attitudes knowingly voluptuous." [47] Her costume for the second act, a daringly cut gown under a flowing mantle, caused gasps even in sophisticated Paris. King George and Queen Mary of England, who were in town on a state visit, sent emissaries to Edvina summoning her to a command performance at Covent Garden.

In the spring of 1914, no one, especially in Paris, could have credited the guns of August that in a few short weeks would totally fragment Europe's glittering façade. It was Gretl's first visit to Paris, and it proved a thrilling introduction to the City of Light. The family was royally established in a suite

66

at the Plaza Athénée, next door to the theatre where the company was performing. There were dinners at Maxim's, stylish receptions, shopping excursions, trips to museums, and, of course, an ascent to the top of the Eiffel Tower. Articles in newspapers and journals brimmed with praise for Urban's sets and costumes, declaring them to be superior to both those of the Opéra and the Opéra Comique.

The season ended in a sold-out gala on June 19 with an unlikely trio of scenes from *Tristan*, *Pagliacci*, and *The Barber of Seville*. Most of the company sailed for home June 21 on the *Cincinnati*, "conscious only of a job well done." [48] The Paris Opéra ruefully confessed that the Boston competition had cost their company more than six hundred thousand dollars in lost revenue.[49] Russell, full of plans for the coming fall season, retired with his entourage to a villa on the Riviera, where he enjoyed himself with Danna Shinn, a young American singer who had supplanted both his wife, Nina, and singer Alice Nielsen in his affections and whom he would eventually marry. Russell and Danna were in Monte Carlo when the blow fell in September: a cable from Jordan announcing the permanent closing of the Boston Opera.

Still hurt by the *Festzug*'s aftermath, Urban did not yet want to return to Vienna; however, a family reunion arranged for Venice delighted all, for Heinrich Lefler, unable to attend the Paris season because of festival performances at the Hofoper, was able to break away with his wife long enough to spend a couple of days with the Urban family in the city of the Doges. Gretl recalls the last meeting of the Twins as being curiously undramatic:

> I can see us quite clearly, sitting at table in the Piazza di San Marco— Heinrich, Minna, Buschi, Mother, Elly, and myself. We were having a bite to eat and making the usual desultory remarks one makes as the time of departure approaches. Then we put Minna and Heinrich on the train to Vienna. Buschi looked after the train for a long time and said, "He looked so tired and frail, I have never found it so hard to say *Servus*."

The family proceeded to Florence, where they heard the news from Sarajevo of the assassination on June 28 of Austrian Archduke Franz Ferdinand, heir to the Habsburg throne, and his wife. Rumors of war were rife, but Urban dismissed them as ridiculous, pointing out that though such incidents were not to be condoned, this was a civilized age and war was unthinkable. So, while ultimatums were delivered between the powers great and small, and flags were being unfurled all over Europe, the Urbans reveled in the glories of Florence.

On Saturday, August 1, a German ultimatum to Russia expired without a reply, and the German ambassador to St. Petersburg was instructed to declare war at five o'clock that afternoon. On August 2, Belgium rejected a German ultimatum demanding the right to send its armies through that country, and at twenty minutes past eleven on August 3, British Prime Minister Lloyd George dispatched the War Telegram: "WAR, GERMANY, ACT." The following day, with the German assault on Liège, Belgium, the first battle of World War I began.

Florence was thronged with American tourists, and virtual panic set in with the false rumor that Italy might honor the Triple Alliance and join with Germany and Austria. The situation for the Urbans was alarming. Although he had taken his first citizenship papers, Urban was indisputably an alien, possibly an enemy alien. Fortunately the American consul was a Bostonian and an opera buff and by some legerdemain declared Urban an instant, but

The palace setting from Verdi's *Otello*. 1914. Columbia University.

as it proved temporary, citizen. The family's problems, however, were by no means over.

The German and British fleets were moving ominously about the Mediterranean, and by the time the family arrived in Naples, passage home, even by freighter, was out of the question. Due to problems of exchange, they were running out of funds. Urban wired George Tyler, the producer of the show he was to design in New York, that he was stuck in Italy and would be unable to fulfill his obligations. Then, philosophically, he took his family on an extended tour of Pompeii. Tyler, in New York, frantic at the prospect of a delay or cancellation of his production of *The Garden of Paradise*, confided his problems to a man he identifies in his autobiography as "my strange and mysterious Italian friend from the East Side," who assured him that there was absolutely no cause for alarm—the matter would be attended to . . . pronto![50]

A couple of days later a dashing young Italian speaking broken but emphatic English appeared at the Urbans' hotel. Presenting a bouquet of roses to Frau Urban and identifying himself only as "a friend," he said that he had been informed of their plight, that passage had been arranged on a ship sailing the following day, and that all expenses had been met. He promised to meet them on the ship and departed, leaving the Urbans bewildered but delighted. Frau Urban even dried her tears, which had been flowing with increasing frequency. True to his word, the young man saw them comfortably settled in adjoining cabins in which flowers had been lavishly arranged, gave Urban two hundred dollars in gold, and, after depositing a basket of assorted wines and special rations for Urban's miniature schnauzer, bade them an enthusiastic bon voyage. Not until their arrival in New York did they realize that it was the notorious Black Hand, as the Mafia was then known, which had graciously stretched across the sea to bring them safely back to America.

THE URBANITY OF
ZIEGFELD'S FOLLIES

In his cable to Henry Russell about closing the Boston Opera, Eben Jordan had alluded to "financial difficulties," but the truth probably lay closer to the words of Richard Henry Dana: "He had had enough." Gretl Urban recalls the family's return to Boston:

> The Opera, which had really been a world apart, had vanished without a trace. At first we were very sad, but Father explained that it was "show business," and I think that he was really relieved, especially when Mr. Jordan, who was very apologetic, assured him that the Swampscott studio would be at his disposal. [The settings for Urban's next venture, *The Garden of Paradise,* and also those of the *Ziegfeld Follies* of 1915, 1916, and 1917, were prepared at Swampscott.]
>
> Buschi had found a lovely apartment for us with a large entrance hall. There was a big back porch that he had made into an outdoor living room with wicker furniture, awnings, and flowers. The neighbors were much amazed by this European custom, which had not yet penetrated the ambience of old Boston, and pretty soon some started imitating us. Both Elly and I were in school and we missed *The Garden of Paradise*—which didn't run very long.

The Garden of Paradise opened at New York's Park Theatre on November 28, 1914, to disastrous notices. Part of the problem, aside from a leaden script by the usually successful Edward Sheldon, was the extraordinary number of intermissions. A critic for the *New York Times* noted that the eight intermissions totaled fifty-one minutes, "interruptions so unfamiliarly frequent and so prolonged as dangerously to strain the interest in the dramatic story." [1] Unfortunately, it was Urban's massive and complex scenery that caused the delays between scenes, but once again Urban had found himself working with a fairy tale that gave his imagination great latitude for fantasy. Exquisite as Urban's settings were, they alone could not save the play, which closed quickly, leaving the production company bankrupt.

Detail from Urban's design for the musical *The Rose of China.* 1919. Columbia University.

When Florenz Ziegfeld saw the settings in Urban's first Broadway production, *The Garden of Paradise* by Edward "Ned" Sheldon, the producer immediately hired him to design the sets for his *Follies.* Undersea setting for *The Garden of Paradise.* 1914. Columbia University.

Louis DeFoe, in a *Greenbook Magazine* article entitled "A New Experiment with the Fairy Play," remarked on Urban's work:

> It is, indeed, Mr. Urban rather than the actors, or, even Mr. Sheldon, who is the most important factor in the story. I have no doubt that the play's whole meaning might have been as well transmitted to the audience without use of a spoken word. . . .
>
> *The Garden of Paradise* is likely to be revolutionary and artistically important . . . principally for the imaginative and interpretive quality of its nine superb settings. Lovelier visions than he has created of an imagined world which stretches above and below the sea have not . . . before been seen in our theatre. . . .
>
> A stately interior of a regal palace, a misty expanse of storm-swept sea, the dream-like loveliness of a fairy bower, the vague mystery of the ocean's translucent depths—mind pictures of these he invokes out of the imagination by splotches of broad color on simple surfaces and by ingenious methods of illumination. They create a sense of reality out of palpable unreality. . . . A glance at the flat, dark blue of an Urban seascape brings with it a sense of limitless distance. And all the mechanical contrivances and details of the *mise-en-scène* are so coordinated that they contribute to the unity of each effect. So in Mr. Urban's method of adorning the stage the old, unsightly and unillusory "borders," wrinkled and unstable "back cloths," and obvious, clumsy "cut-outs" of conventional theatrical scenery have entirely disappeared. Illusion through suggestion takes the place of pictured actuality.[2]

Gene Buck, librettist and songwriter, founder of ASCAP, and the man responsible for discovering many talents (among them Ed Wynn, W. C. Fields, Eddie Cantor, and Will Rogers), persuaded impresario Florenz Ziegfeld to see *The Garden of Paradise*. As they passed by the Park Theatre one evening, Buck suggested to Ziegfeld that they take in the play; he had heard that it was dreadful, but the settings were said to be quite unusual. Ziegfeld left us this account of his evening at *The Garden of Paradise*:

> There were about thirty people in the audience, but by the end of the first act I knew I wanted the artist who painted the scenes. We went outside and asked about him and someone said he was in Pabst's next door. We found Urban in the cafe drinking a glass of beer, and after introducing ourselves, I asked him if he had any work on hand. He said he had some orders ahead and I asked him how much he would make between then—it was January— and June. "About $10,000," he answered. "Here is a check for $10,000," I told him. "Consider yourself engaged by me to do the 'Follies.' " [3]

Urban may not have had $10,000 worth of pending business, but he probably owed at least that much, for the producers of *The Garden of Paradise* were to go bankrupt without paying him for the work he had contracted. Although the welfare of his family and the Viennese workers back in Boston was a prime concern, Urban immediately expressed his reservations to the well-known producer about working for what he considered a "girlie show." Ziegfeld assured Urban that it was the incomparable quality of his work he was after and made (and kept) a promise that he would never ask the designer to compromise or lower his standards.

A year earlier, when Florenz Ziegfeld, Jr., was forty-six, his fortunes might have been said to have reached an impasse. Had he looked back over his career, an unlikely prospect considering his propensity to plunge headlong into the future, it would have seemed to anyone a succession of extravaganzas, most successful, some distinguished by imagination and daring, but all flared by a genius for publicity. However, with his divorce from the fading, embittered Anna Held, his private life had fallen into chaos. An unruly passion for the dazzling Lillian Lorraine was nearing its end, but more distressing by far was the dimming of his professional standing as Broadway's most flamboyant showman. His famous yearly *Follies*, though widely acclaimed, were conspicuously lacking in artistic distinction, an intolerable situation for a man of Ziegfeld's innate good taste and extravagant vanity. Nevertheless, in 1914 two new stars were to cross his erratic orbit and profoundly change his life and career: Billie Burke and Joseph Urban.

In 1883 the president of the Chicago Musical College, Dr. Florenz Ziegfeld, was surprised to learn that his son, Florenz, Jr., had run off to join Buffalo Bill's *Wild West Show* as a sharpshooter at Cody's personal invitation after he bested Annie Oakley in a shooting match. However, the enforcement of child labor laws and a father's wrath soon ended that engagement. The elder Ziegfeld was to be no happier with Flo's next exploit, an ensemble called "The Dancing Ducks of Denmark." This act was eventually closed by the ASPCA, which found that the Danish ducks danced only because Ziegfeld literally gave them a hotfoot.

Flo's career as a showman finally took off in 1893 at the Chicago World's Columbian Exposition, when he presented The Great Sandow, a twenty-three-year-old German hailed as "The Perfect Man." Sandow's act included the lifting of a grand piano and concluded when three horses crossed a plank resting on his chest. After the Exposition closed, Sandow made a couple of highly profitable tours under Ziegfeld's aegis and became something of a national celebrity.

In 1896, at the Palace Theatre in London, Ziegfeld discovered a worthy successor to The Great Sandow: Anna Held. There was general agreement that her talent was fragile, but Anna's intimate style, studied artifice, and exquisite body—an hourglass figure that flaunted an eighteen-inch waist— fascinated audiences, especially when she sang with her captivating French accent:

> Won't you come play wiz me,
> As I have such a nice little way wiz me.

In Anna, Flo also found a mistress whose extravagance and flair for publicity were a match for his own. One of their most successful publicity stunts was the revelation that Anna took "milk" baths, which were said to be the secret of her beautiful skin. Rumors had circulated that forty gallons of milk were being delivered daily to Anna's suite at The Netherland, and Ziegfeld was more than happy to escort a delegation of reporters to view Miss Held in her bath. The resulting story rocked two continents. The newspapers also were led to believe that the two had been married in Chicago, and not until some years later, during divorce proceedings in which Anna was declared Ziegfeld's common-law wife, was it revealed that no marriage had ever taken place.

The Ziegfeld-Held extravaganzas were phenomenally successful: *Papa's Wife*, *The French Maid*, *The Parisian Model*, *The Little Duchess*, and, most gaudy of all, *Miss Innocence*, for which Ziegfeld erected the largest electric sign ever for a show in America. Lavish dance numbers, a sketchy plot, and plenty of girls were the major characteristics of all these shows. The beauteous Anna was described in detail by one appreciative critic when she made her first New York appearance in 1896 in *A Parlor Maid*: "Her eyes are long, narrow, and heavily circled; her nose is straight; her mouth is perfect, and, as for her chin people might go some ways to see it without regretting the experience." [4] About her talents, however, there were reservations: "She would not be a 'sensation' at all if the idea had not been ingeniously forced upon the public that she is inherently and delightfully naughty." [5]

The first *Follies* opened in 1907 at the *Jardin de Paris*, the roof garden of the New York Theatre. The original idea for the show may have come from Held, who is said to have told Ziegfeld: "Your American girls are the most beautiful in the world; if you could only dress them up chic and charmant you could do a much better revue than the *Folies Bergère*." [6] Indeed, the *Follies* was a "revue," a form of entertainment that reached its greatest development in the 1920s. A major precursor of the modern American musical, the revue helped nourish such composers as George Gershwin, Jerome Kern, and Irving Berlin, who were to be instrumental in developing the book musical. While Ziegfeld's *Follies* are today the best remembered, there were several popular and successful rivals or imitators. The Shuberts presented *The Passing Show*; John Murray Anderson was responsible for the *Greenwich Village Follies*; George White had his *Scandals*; Irving Berlin mounted his *Music Box Revues*; and Earl Carroll staged his *Vanities*.

In contrast to a musical, a revue had neither a book nor a plot, nor were its musical numbers intended to further the action of a story. Unlike a nightclub performance, a revue was presented on a proscenium stage, and unlike vaudeville, it was for "mature" audiences. Abel Green defines this form of theatre succinctly in his introduction to Robert Baral's book *Revue*: "Revue was an especially indigenous form of live legit entertainment which had its roots in the political 'cellars' or *koemische-kabaret* of the *mittel Europa* school but soon evolved into less-pointed and more-broadened extravaganzas featuring tall girls and low comedy." [7]

The *Follies of 1907* had "tall girls" aplenty: fifty beauties were billed as the "Anna Held Girls," but Anna herself was not in the show—Ziegfeld had fallen quite madly in love with the dazzling showgirl Lillian Lorraine, whom he dubbed "The Most Beautiful Woman in the World." Flo's ardor was so strong that he installed Lillian in a suite at the Hotel Ansonia, the same place he and Anna shared apartments.

So profitable was the seventy-performance summer run of the first *Follies* that Ziegfeld decided to do it again in 1908, and he won even greater popular acclaim. By 1909 the *Follies* had become an annual event, but it was not until the 1911 edition that it was called *The Ziegfeld Follies*. In 1913 the show moved into Abe Erlanger's New Amsterdam Theatre. Unfortunately, the artistic elements so successfully blended in the New Amsterdam auditorium—which the *New York Times* characterized as "without question the most beautiful color scheme to be found in any theatre of the city"—were hardly evident on its stage.[8]

Ziegfeld was still a year away from discovering the designer who would invest his lavish productions with elegance and individual style. Before they met, there is no evidence that Ziegfeld, who was uninterested in opera, knew anything of Urban's achievements in Boston, or that Urban, who had never attended a "girlie show," was more than vaguely aware of the *Follies*.

Urban brought a new level of sophistication and elegance to the *Follies*. This set with its traces of Art Nouveau appeared in the 1915 edition, Urban's first. Columbia University.

75

Nevertheless, the stage was set for an alliance that was to prove immensely profitable for both. It was the Broadway production of *The Garden of Paradise* that brought them together.

Gretl Urban comments on the relationship between these two unique men of the theatre:

> Although they worked beautifully together for so many years, understood and liked one another, they never became intimate friends. Except for the Ziegfeld shows, the *Follies*, and later the musicals *Sally, Rio Rita,* and *Show Boat,* they had very little in common. Ziegfeld had no interest in architecture, opera, or drama, all the fields that were Father's life. Nevertheless, Buschi never forgot how much he owed to Flo. After all, it was Flo and his *Follies* that first made his name known in New York. It was through the *Follies* that his introduction of modern stagecraft became known to audiences and critics. And Father was always deeply moved by Flo's implicit faith in him as his "good luck star."

The great *Follies* date from 1915, and Urban did much more than merely create a framework for the stunning performers. To be sure, his architectural stage decor was new, the opulence astonishing, the entire physical production polished to a brilliance, but in a very real sense even the crude, naive patterns of the former *Follies* began distinctly to reflect Urban's sophistication and artistry. In an article entitled "The Urbanity of the Follies," one commentator described the effect of Urban's work on audiences:

> He made it possible for intelligent and fastidious people to go to a "musical show" without receiving a gratuitous insult to the eye and taste. How successful this effort has been is evident from the fact that the character of the "Follies" entertainment has changed radically since his advent. Gazing at those glowing blues, the jade greens, those solidly constructed "sets" the other night, one realized that the audience which had come for frivolous entertainment was quite unconsciously absorbing the beauties of color and light, line and mass. . . .
>
> Today [1919] it is as impossible to imagine the Ziegfeld show without its Urban settings as without its girls. The young ladies may come and go, but Urban is fundamental.[9]

Ziegfeld now had his scenic designer. It remained for Billie Burke, who would become his second wife, to lead him to the costume designer he still needed.

In her memoir, *With a Feather on My Nose,* Billie Burke describes her first glimpse of Ziegfeld. On New Year's Day in 1914, Somerset Maugham, in whose play, *The Land of Promise,* she was starring at the Lyceum, escorted her to a ball given by the Sixty Club at the Hotel Astor. Billie tells of her arrival at two in the morning:

> Possibly I can permit myself to say I "made an entrance," for no actress in her right mind would attempt less in descending a great staircase on the arm of Somerset Maugham. . . . At the foot of the staircase stood this man. . . . He had a Mephisthophelean look, his eyelids lifting, curved upward, in the middle. Slim and tall and immaculate in full evening dress, he was in black and white contrast to the rest of the costumed party, and so—and for who knows what other reasons—I noticed him at once. Willie Maugham and I swept on and began to dance.[10]

Before Billie's arrival, Ziegfeld had had a tiff with Lillian Lorraine, who left the ball in anger. He had attempted to reach her by phone, but Lillian quickly got relegated to the past, at least temporarily, by the vision of Billie

Burke descending the staircase. She did not dance for long with Maugham. The orchestra started a John Paul Jones, and every time the whistle blew, Billie and Flo found themselves dancing together. Billie remembered that a woman made up as the Empress Josephine followed them with her eyes: "She was utterly beautiful, this Empress, strange and dark, with enormous jealous eyes. . . . She was Anna Held." [11]

Billie knew she was in love and also in trouble:

> Of course I knew that Ziegfeld was a dangerous man before I met him, and I felt the impact of his threat and his charm at once. But even if I had known then precisely what tortures and frustrations were in store for me during the next eighteen years because of this man, I should have kept right on falling in love. [12]

Ziegfeld laid siege to Burkely Crest, Billie's estate at Hastings-on-Hudson, turning up frequently, even unexpectedly, and he paid diligent court to Blanche Burke, Billie's enchanted mother. Ziegfeld even installed a private line to his office in the New Amsterdam so that Billie could call him directly. He flooded her dressing room with roses and even ordered a cow delivered to Burkely Crest.

On April 11, 1914, Flo and Billie were married between matinee and evening performances. Together with Billie's mother, they crossed over the Hudson River to a church in Hoboken, New Jersey. Billie described the back room of the parsonage where they were married as "crammed and disorderly with baby carriages and cribs, old paint buckets and step ladders." Because

This setting for the 1915 play *Behold Thy Wife* provides an example of Urban's interior design. The room is bright with colorful accents and elegant but uncluttered. The fire screen is Art Nouveau. Variations of the chairs in front of the fireplace appeared in Hagenbund exhibitions and in the New York branch of the Wiener Werkstätte of 1922. Columbia University.

Overleaf. The "Zeppelin over London" scene from the 1915 *Follies.* Ed Wynn, W. C. Fields, and George White were members of the cast. Columbia University.

77

the names on the marriage license were Ethelbert Burke and Florenz Ziegfeld, Billie goes on to say, the minister was very confused:

> "And now, Flo," he would say to me, "you stand here."
>
> "He's Flo, I'm Billie," I would say.
>
> "Oh, all right then, you stand here, Bill," he would say to Flo. And Flo would correct him.
>
> "I'm Flo, and she's Bill. I mean Billie."
>
> But he married us and I'm quite sure it was legal.[13]

Convulsed with laughter, they headed joyfully back to town in time for Billie's evening performance. Later there was a wedding party at the Brevoort, and the newlyweds finally retired to Ziegfeld's apartments on the eleventh floor at the Ansonia.

Before she met Ziegfeld, Billie had been buying clothes designed by Lady Duff Gordon through her West Fifty-seventh Street salon called Lucile's, Ltd. In 1915 Lady Duff Gordon, or Lucile, as she was known in the trade, staged a display of her creations as a wartime British benefit, and Billie persuaded her husband to join her. When Ziegfeld saw the presentation, he was determined that Lady Duff Gordon's beautiful silks and chiffons would flutter through future *Follies* and set the tone of elegance, chic, and high fashion that would become the show's hallmark. The designer had established herself as supreme arbiter of women's fashion in 1897 when she opened the elegant salon Lucile's on Hanover Square in London. Among other innovations, she was responsible for the evolution of the living mannequin. Rounding up beautiful girls from all over, Lucile instructed them in proper deportment, gowned them in her latest gorgeous creations, and allowed them to beautifully descend the steps of her Adam room while tea was served. The fashion-show dress parade was born.

Ziegfeld may have been impressed by Lucile's fashions, but he was positively stunned by one of her models, Dolores (Lucile's models were all identified by a single name), whose perfect body enveloped in an Eastern gown gleamed like an opal with every stately movement. Probably the most sensational beauty ever to appear in the *Follies*, Dolores was handed to Ziegfeld by Lady Duff Gordon ready-made. Flo celebrated the event in a stunning *Follies* number designed by Lucile and entitled "Ladies of Fashion, An Episode in Chiffon." Nine other Ziegfeld beauties appeared as models, but it was Dolores as Empress of Fashion, Discourager of Hesitancy, who took the town by storm, setting an all-time high for aloof, detached poise.

Interior decorator and society matron Elsie de Wolfe had earlier suggested that Lucile open a branch salon in New York, and other American friends had concurred: "Everyone will flock to you at first just for the sake of being dressed by a woman with an English title. Afterwards, of course, you will stand on your own merits and people will come to see you because they like your clothes."[14]

In April of 1910, in an article entitled "A High Priestess of Clothes," *Vogue* noted Lucile's arrival with marked asperity:

> An invasion of the avenues of trade by a woman of the aristocracy in England can only be explained by a superabundant artistic taste requiring scope, or by the pressing need for money—perhaps both. . . . [I]t is sufficient to know that she has "arrived," and that, too, in no vague remote sense, but in a distinctly literal way—with many trunks—for she has set up her trade in New York and invited the smart set to inspect what she has brought.

Lady Duff Gordon's claim to be "the greatest living creator of fashions" may be allowed to pass unchallenged as evidence of international courtesy.... [I]n the choice and blending of colors, it must be acknowledged that she is a supreme artist. Nevertheless, a survey of her creations ... leads one to question whether they are acceptable to our American taste.[15]

Vogue's doubts proved unfounded; from the very first Lucile was a smashing success. She arrived in New York with a collection of 150 designs and four of her choice mannequins: Gamela, Corisande, Florence, and Phyllis. Collectively, the girls were described as "Crusaders of the 'Dream Dresses'" and given the "great mission of spreading among New York's Four Hundred the cult of the dream dress, that wondrous product of the genius of Lady Duff Gordon."[16]

Lucile directed her talents toward the stage as well, both in New York and in London. In 1914 she set down for *Harper's Bazaar* her principles of stage design, which coincide exactly with those of the new stagecraft. Stage costumes and couture clothes were not interchangeable, she insisted; costumes were made specifically to appear their best only in the special environment the stage imposed:

> It is really much more interesting (though not so profitable) to design dresses for stageland than for private wear, and far easier, as "effect" is all that is aimed at and attention to detail is unnecessary.
>
> Stagedressing demands accentuation! The actress moves under conditions that exist no where else, and under auditory conditions also. She has even to change the whole look of her face by rouge and grease paints to produce any effect at all under those unnatural lights. For this reason her dresses have to be of broader effect and more vivid colouring. All subtle harmonies and gradations of tints are completely lost in this world of glare and show.[17]

Ziegfeld had long been willing to spend exorbitant sums on costumes, and Lady Duff Gordon was equally extravagant: "When I start out to evolve a gown, I do not consider what it will cost. The money question I set aside and work as if it were done without price."[18]

The Bath Scene was one of the most spectacular in the 1915 *Follies*. It featured Ziegfeld's lucky charms, elephants, spouting real water.
Columbia University.

81

Her superb costume designs were not the only contribution Lucile made to Ziegfeld glamour. It was she who introduced the concept of the Showgirl, who was simply there to look beautiful and wear beautiful clothes, in contrast to the chorus girl, who was required to sing and dance. Besides Dolores, a number of Lucile's top models went into the *Follies*, among them Gamela, Denagarde, Mauricette, Anangara, Isoult, and Phyllis. The regal manner and astonishing hauteur they brought with them became the image of Ziegfeld's Glorified Girls. Dolores, of course, never smiled, but the others granted an occasional glimmer.

In her memoirs, *Discretions & Indiscretions*, Lady Duff Gordon describes Ziegfeld as in all respects "exemplary" but designates Joseph Urban as merely his "aide-de-camp." To her mind Urban had an "unaccountable partiality for yellow lights." [19] She demanded blue lights as a background and a white flood on each dress as it appeared, and she frequently got what she wanted. For his part, Urban saw Lucile as something of a thorn in his side. "Keep that woman out of my way!" he warned Gretl when she was acting as his assistant, and he refused ever to enter her salon.

Whatever the personal relationship between these gifted people, their collaboration on five editions of the *Follies* was an artistic success. So important were the contributions of Urban and Lucile that one critic said of the 1917 edition: "The new 'Follies' is the best show that Joseph Urban and Lady Duff-Gordon ever wrote." [20]

There remained only two more ingredients to the ultimate formula for the *Follies*, the first of which was the famous staircase that became a trademark for both Ziegfeld and Urban. When properly designed, a staircase is the ideal way to display a maximum number of beauties in a minimal space, especially if they are all dressed in gowns with elaborate trains. In Paris the *Folies Bergères* has long used stairs out of necessity because its shallow stage cannot otherwise present a large cast. The Ziegfeld staircase originated with a production at the Century Theatre that Ziegfeld and Charles Dillingham, another top Broadway producer, presented in November 1916. Called *The Century Girl,* the lavish revue had a score by both Irving Berlin and Victor Herbert.

Produced every year from 1907 to 1915, when both Urban and Lucile joined, the *Follies* were continued annually until 1927, when there was a hiatus until Ziegfeld himself produced the final edition in 1931. The series between 1915 and 1922 has been called "The Great Follies," [21] with the 1919 edition generally regarded as the greatest of them all. Irving Berlin wrote a song for that show that John Steel sang as the Ziegfeld Girls, in Lucile's costumes, paraded across the stage in the unique, halting "Ziegfeld walk." The song was "A Pretty Girl Is Like a Melody," and it became the theme song of all subsequent *Follies.* However, following the 1922 show, many of the greatest stars began leaving the cast, and both Ziegfeld and Urban admitted to losing interest in the format.[22]

The usual schedule for an edition of the *Follies* called for tryouts in Atlantic City, New Jersey, followed by an opening in New York around the middle of June. After a run on Broadway of about 120 performances, the show would then go on tour. Once Urban had agreed to work for him, Ziegfeld took his new designer to see the 1914 version then playing on the road.

> We went to Indianapolis to see the show on tour, and he caught the idea of the entertainment quickly. The failure of "The Garden of Paradise" was largely due to the long waits between scenes necessitated by the heavy scenery. There can be no waits in the "Follies"; something must be happening every minute, and to do this there must be an alternation of "scenes in one" and heavier scenes. He adapted his art to the new requirements, and I can't imagine an edition of the "Follies" without him now.[23]

The staircase that later became a *Follies* tradition first appeared in *The Century Girl.* Producers Charles Dillingham and Florenz Ziegfeld collaborated to present this lavish revue. Irving Berlin and Victor Herbert composed the score. 1916. Columbia University

A song and dance number by Irving Berlin titled "They've Got Me Doing It Too" was staged in this setting representing the stage door of the Frivolity Theatre. *Century Girl.* 1916. Columbia University.

Fortunately, Urban's reaction to his first encounter with the *Follies* was recorded by Oliver Saylor, who was with him at the time: "Advertising posters! The best of their kind in America today, perhaps. But how much more can be done!"[24] The next day he set down his intentions: "I see great possibilities in the 'Follies.' I hope most of all to unify the impression of all these short scenes to give the entire evening a kind of keynote."[25]

Friends in Boston were against Urban's taking a job they felt was beneath him:

Most of my friends in Boston think I should remain with the serious and poetic drama and opera. But I do not see why it isn't worth while to do anything well. I believe you can make your fun and pleasure and your diversions artistic as well as your more serious plays. In America you have seemed to feel that you must do serious things seriously, but that you can do things meant for pastime very carelessly. That ought not to be so. You ought to take just as much care in providing your fun as you do your education. I think Mr. Ziegfeld believes in doing things thoroughly, no matter what the cost, and that is why I believe that I shall get along with him splendidly.[26]

Urban worked for ten weeks on his first *Follies*, which opened on June 21, 1915, at the New Amsterdam Theatre. The cast of the show included Ed Wynn, Ina Claire, Ann Pennington, Bert Williams, Leon Erroll, Mae Murray, George White, Olive Thomas, Kay Laurell, Justine Johnson, and W. C. Fields, who, previously known only as a juggler, spoke his first lines onstage. The real star, however, was Joseph Urban, as the *New York Times* affirmed: "It is the notably beautiful investiture which marks the 1915 'Follies' as something apart from the common or garden variety of revue or musical comedy. . . . It is not merely that he has used taste and a sense of color. He has used imagination."[27]

Opposite. Urban created a village decked out for a festival for *Miss Springtime*, a show in which P. G. Wodehouse made his Broadway debut as a lyricist. 1916. Columbia University. *Bottom.* This elegant interior of a Fifth Avenue apartment was seen in *Apple Blossoms.* The dancing team of Fred and Adele Astaire made their debut in the musical and drew raves from the critics. 1919. Columbia University.

85

The newsstand in Grand Central Station was the setting for Irving Berlin's "It Takes an Irishman to Make Love." *Century Girl*. 1916. Columbia University.

After seeing his settings safely to the stage of the New Amsterdam, Urban had joined his family, who still lived in Boston, at their rented summer home near Swampscott, Massachusetts. Every prior summer the family had gone back to Europe, but in 1915 the war made this impossible. Mizzi Urban had wanted a house with a garden, while Urban wanted a place near enough to his Swampscott studio to enable him to supervise the work of his artists. The person who was able to find a house suitable to both was young Benjamin Netwig, the son of operatic soprano Alice Nielsen. His father had died when the boy was ten, so little masculine attention had been paid to Benny until Urban used him as a sort of errand boy at the Boston Opera. Benny adored Urban, who soon discovered that his protégé was quite good at making foundations for the all-important set models.

During this quiet time, Urban and his two daughters formed, in Gretl's words, a "close tie of love and understanding that lasted all our lives." Elly, like her mother, was a skilled maker of lace, while Gretl concentrated on drawing. Her pleased father coached Gretl in the principles of perspective and the vanishing point and decided to enroll her in the Boston School of Fine Arts in the fall of 1916.

86

Urban, ever generous, bought his daughters a pair of saddle horses, which they boarded at the cottage where Benny Netwig lived. Benny himself was a great rider, and it was he who helped select the Urban horses. Two years later, in 1917, Urban presented his family with a new Marmon automobile, complete with chauffeur, so from then on the girls spent summer mornings on horseback and afternoons in the car.

The revue format, as noted above by Ziegfeld himself, required types of scenery and staging radically different from what Urban had dealt with in classical theatre and opera. Whereas opera settings usually could be shifted leisurely during intermissions, a revue was fast-paced and subject to split-second timing, with no long pauses possible between as many as twenty different numbers. A lavish production piece making use of the full stage would alternate with smaller scenes, or a star such as Will Rogers would appear in front of a drop or curtain while scenery on the full stage was quickly and noiselessly changed. However massive and solid a full set might appear, it had to be designed and constructed so that it could be quickly set up and just as easily struck and stored backstage.

At least in the early days of his association with Ziegfeld, Urban worked harder on the *Follies* than on anything else he did. Eight to ten weeks before each opening, the designer met with Ziegfeld, the writers, and the composers to discuss their plans.[28] He would learn, for example, that the show needed a full stage set with an Oriental theme for twenty Ziegfeld Girls or that a certain kind of drop was called for while a star sang the latest creation of Irving Berlin out front. Naturally, during these initial discussions and early rehearsals, numbers would be added, dropped, or changed.

Ziegfeld and Urban gave the 1916 *Follies* a Shakespearean theme. This drop depicts Broadway on the left and Stratford-on-Avon on the right.
Columbia University.

In response to America's entering World War I, the 1917 *Follies* featured two patriotic numbers. In one, a cast member appeared as President Wilson inspecting the chorus line in their red, white, and blue costumes. As the orchestra played "The Star Spangled Banner," a huge American flag unfolded. This setting was more likely for Victor Herbert's "Can You Hear the Country Calling?" which was the revue's finale. Columbia University.

The swan curtain was from the 1919 edition of the *Follies*, which was considered to be one of the very best of the series. Irving Berlin's "A Pretty Girl Is Like a Melody" was heard for the first time, and Eddie Cantor was hilarious in his routine "The Osteopath's Office." Columbia University.

Usually there were about a dozen full stage sets. For these, Urban followed much the same procedures he used in Boston. When sketches and final drawings were completed, a fully detailed ground plan was prepared to show exactly where each piece of scenery was to be positioned. Plans and drawings then went to the studio in Swampscott, or later to Yonkers, where artists prepared scale models for Urban's approval. The completed scenery was then shipped by rail to Atlantic City, where the tryouts were held. A *New York Times* account tells of the great attention Urban gave his designs even after they actually reached the stage:

> Most stage artists turn out the prescribed settings and let it go at that. Mr. Urban is never content to stop there. He must follow his designs onto the stage, and managers are more than glad to number him one of their technical staff clear up to the night of performance.
>
> When Mr. Urban's scenery has once reached New York, he is working through till sunrise every morning superintending the construction and prescribing the lighting. With the nineteen scenes of the *Follies* this means ten days of such increasing activity as not even the grandest of opera can necessitate.[29]

Of course, Ziegfeld was also an active participant in the shows he produced. Although Gretl Urban did not get to see a production of the *Follies* until 1920 (because her father did not think the environment suitable for a young lady), she then commented, as her father's assistant, on the work habits of the famous producer:

> Of course, at that time [1920] I was unaware of the sheer horror that went into the creation of a Ziegfeld show. Ziegfeld was a task master, impatient, mercurial, a maddening perfectionist, but there were no union regulations in those days and he was able to drive everyone to the point of exhaustion.
>
> Flo's rehearsals—especially when guests were present—were alarming affairs that could go on for days and nights. Sometimes Flo charged about like Simon Legree among his slaves, and sometimes he huffed and puffed over a train, a headdress, or even a petticoat. These operations frequently tried Buschi's patience, but he realized that Flo wasn't just showing off, he was seeing a costume for the first time and, with his uncanny genius for enhancing beauty, was composing and correcting until he knew it was completely right.
>
> Flo and Buschi paid as much attention to props and simple backdrops as they did to the spectacular settings and special effects. Gene Buck used to say it was a unique and exciting experience to watch Flo and Joe, two such entirely different men, working together as one to bring so much beauty and excitement to an audience.

Two of the greatest *Follies* were those of 1917 and 1918. For the first of these, Urban devised a number using ladders that showed he could achieve great effects with the simplest of means, not at all the typical concept of the *Follies* setting. Some of Urban's beautiful color drawings for settings of various *Follies* survive, but they give little idea of the subtle and all-important lighting effects the designer achieved or how the set appeared with the Ziegfeld Girls on display. Similarly, photographs that show the girls are inadequate since they fail to convey the color or lighting transformations. Fortunately, as for the Boston Opera, we have eloquent word pictures left us by appreciative contemporary critics. A writer for the *Times* describes not only the settings

Opposite top. A delicate setting, with gauze panels, from *The Rose of China*. The musical was a failure on Broadway but a smash hit on the road. P. G. Wodehouse was one of the collaborators on the book. 1919. Columbia University. *Bottom.* Urban's exquisite color sense is readily apparent in this lavish and complex set for *The Rose of China*. 1919. Columbia University.

for the 1917 edition but how one number flowed smoothly, almost cinematically, into the next:

> A setting of Chinese lacquer that came toward the end, when the eye was all but numb to the nuances of color, was unbelievably lovely. A glimpse of a city roof, a panorama of lower Manhattan in the background and a fruit-festooned parapet bathed in moonlight on either side of the middle ground, was another striking scene. When the former scene dissolved three sets of crossed ladders of red and gold against a black background with half a hundred girls in Chinese costumes climbing up and down in unison while the rung ends became incandescent. Another novel effect followed a flower song in which girls dressed to represent various flowers sprang up through a trap. When the opalescent backdrop of beads that formed the background was lifted the figures of two young Venuses were seen in what seemed to be huge iridescent soap bubbles.[30]

A scene in the 1918 *Follies* that caught the eye of Louis Sherwin, critic of the now-forgotten *New York Globe and Advertiser*, was the first appearance of Urban's staircase:

> The starlight scene is quite ravishing, a staircase of superb proportions— Urban was primarily an architect; hence the massive quality and sweeping lines which no other scenic artist achieves. This staircase is in the centre of the stage, leading up to a background of exquisite blue. At the top of the staircase, on either side, are two figures like gigantic Djinns, straight out of the pages of the Arabian Nights. These figures are suffused with a greenish light, whereas the stairs are luminous with a shade of mauve.[31]

The *Telegraph* reviewer recalled Lady Duff Gordon's "Episode of Chiffon," which he said was "nothing more than vast draperies of chiffon through which came in parade a dozen or more girls, each of whom was gowned in

one of Lucile's most exquisite creations. This number revealed, more than any other, the reckless extravagance which marked the entire production." [32]

Unfortunately there is no original colored drawing of this scene for the 1921 *Follies*, which was used for the number set in a Persian court. Columbia University.

In the June 27, 1918, issue of *Musical America*, there was a small note that Urban had been detained in Atlantic City, with "the charge being an alien enemy and spy, and [he] suffered much discomfort for several days until he could prove that he had taken out citizenship papers." [33] P. G. Wodehouse and Guy Bolton, both members of the *Follies* writing team, provide an explanation of Urban's arrest in their amusing history of Broadway, *Bring on the Girls!*

Urban was in Atlantic City for the tryouts of the 1918 *Follies*. America had finally entered the Great War, and the fear of German submarines off the coast was very real. The resort was filled with what Wodehouse and Bolton described as "volunteer spy-chasers," [34] some of whom were also publicity seekers. One of these "dollar a year men" noticed Urban's very pronounced accent and heard him speaking in German to his Viennese artists. In addition, the sleuth saw what he thought was Urban giving signals every morning from his hotel window; in fact, his arm waving was only sitting-up exercises performed daily in front of his open window. Based on this accumulation of evidence, the volunteer guardian alerted the Federal authorities.

Meanwhile, Urban had persuaded the beautiful Lillian Lamont of the *Follies* to join him in his hotel suite to see his drawings and sip champagne. According to the two writers, Urban's apparent amorous success was not all that difficult since Lillian "had a heart which, like the U.S. Navy, was 'open to all men from eighteen to eighty.'" [35]

No sooner had Urban escorted Lillian to his door and inserted the key than he was told he was under arrest. Ziegfeld was able to convince the official of Urban's importance to the show, so the designer was allowed a week, under constant surveillance, to complete his work. He subsequently

93

appeared in court in Philadelphia, was cleared, and returned to New York in time for the *Follies* opening. The final scene of his affair with Lillian, as told by Wodehouse and Bolton, took place in New York on opening night. When asked if it all ended happily,

> "Not so much happily," answered Joe. "I ask Lillian to have supper with me opening night, but she say she cannot. And then when I walk to Rector's after the show, what do I see? Lillian sitting handholding with the *verdampte* spy-chaser!" [36]

Ziegfeld produced many other shows on Broadway with designs by Urban. Some of these will be considered in a later chapter; what remains to be covered here is an adjunct to the *Follies* called the *Midnight Frolic*. Following a performance of the *Follies*, it was possible to take a special elevator ten floors up to the roof of the New Amsterdam to see a more intimate, cabaret-style revue, which featured established Ziegfeld stars or new talent working their way to the big time. Patrons, who paid a five-dollar admission fee, could have dinner or sip champagne at tables as they watched a show staged by Ned Wayburn with sets by Urban and costumes by Lucile. The *Frolic*, which started in 1915, was suspended upon the arrival of Prohibition and briefly revived between 1928 and 1929.

The show was presented on a stage that slid out over the dance floor and was surrounded by tables on three sides. At the rear, Urban provided a set that was typically composed of a backdrop, perhaps a stairway, and some fixed pieces such as urns or trees. The set unveiled for the October 1916 edition was described in the *Times*:

> Even the most florid adjectives pale in attempting to describe Mr. Urban's radiant color combinations, but those familiar with his art will be able to imagine the beauty of the new background when it is stated in mere words that great crystal columns rise into bowers of gold, from which two huge orange transparencies are suspended, and back of all this through a large circle in a wall of gold is a glimpse of lower Manhattan's illuminated skyscrapers set in an empyrean blue sky.[37]

Ever since his visit to Alexandria as a young man, Urban had been fascinated with the color blue. Those fortunate enough to have seen Urban's settings invariably recall the special shade of blue he used, which eventually came to be called "Urban blue." For the April 1917 *Frolic* he created a new shade that was described in the *New York Telegram*: "a shade of blue more beautiful even than his previous blues characteristic of his artistic color schemes." [38]

In December 1918, patrons who ventured to the top of the New Amsterdam were treated to a roof redecorated and redesigned by Urban, which the *Telegram* claimed was "even a more intimate place than heretofore, and glowing with warm and attractive colorings, in which cerise and red dominate. Also there are plentiful splashes of gilt, the proscenium being resplendent in glittering gold." [39] The star of the show was the great Lillian Leitzel, whom the *Telegram* described as a "veritable wonder of the rope and rings." [40]

In a 1923 series of interviews with Oliver Saylor, Urban revealed his disappointment with the latest version of the *Follies*, which he felt had been "subordinated to a desire for over-gorgeousness," [41] but he went on to spell out what he saw as his great accomplishment in collaborating with Ziegfeld:

> Since 1915, there have been many ups and downs with the "Follies" but there has been one result of which I cannot help feeling proud. Americans

A rare photo of the New Amsterdam Theatre's roof, showing part of an Urban setting for an edition of Ziegfeld's *Midnight Frolic*. Ca. 1920. Columbia University.

today realize that only artists, and really good artists with a wide range of experience, can design scenery. I believe that partially through my efforts the standards of stage production and scenic setting has been brought up to such a level that every producer who can afford to do so will try to employ real artists for his productions.[42]

Time has proven Urban's assessment overly modest. No social and cultural history of the United States that covers the second two decades of the twentieth century would be complete without at least a mention of the *Follies*. Naughty without being offensive, the *Follies* represented the very image of a young America striving to attain sophistication and elegance while indulging in a bit of frivolity. The talent Ziegfeld assembled over the years for the shows that bore his name is staggering: Urban and Lady Duff Gordon, of course, and directors such as Ned Wayburn and Ben Ali Haggin, who staged the tableaux. Among performers the roster includes many stars who have passed into the realm of legend: Fanny Brice, Eddie Cantor, W. C. Fields, Ed Wynn, Will Rogers, Joe Frisco, Bert Williams, Sophie Tucker, Marion Davies, George White, the Dolly Sisters, Ruth Etting, Helen Morgan, opera's Grace Moore, and Nora Bayes. Music played a great part in each edition of the revue, and some of the composers Ziegfeld employed were Rudolf Friml, Victor Herbert, Sigmund Romberg, Irving Berlin, and Dmitri Tiomkin. In the 1923 edition, the Paul Whiteman orchestra was presented.

The *Follies* were indeed the very symbol of America in the years preceding the Great Depression. The person most responsible for elevating them to the level of art, beauty, and sophistication they ultimately attained was Joseph Urban.

Opposite top. The Singer Midgets was a popular vaudeville troupe during the 1920s. Urban designed several settings for the act. 1919.
Columbia University.
Bottom. The influence of Art Deco was noticeable in all the settings for the 1930 musical *Flying High*. This scene of a New York City rooftop included a replica of the Chrysler Building, one of the masterpieces of the Art Deco style.
Columbia University.

SETEBOS

INTO THE TWENTIES: FAMILY MATTERS AND RETURN TO VIENNA

Inspired by Urban's success with the 1915 *Follies*—and not to be outdone by Ziegfeld—Marc Klaw and Abe Erlanger, owners of the New Amsterdam Theatre, engaged Urban to design an extravaganza that opened on November 1, 1915, under the title *Around the Map*. On November 2 Renold Wolf of the *Morning Telegraph* observed:

> Under the guidance of Joseph Urban, who seems to be revolutionizing stage design, this musical globetrot spread before the onlookers sixteen scenes in a dazzling array of colors. The favorite shades of Urban blue, yellows, greens, delicate pink and variations new to stage splendor were woven into one another and further set off by combinations in harmonious tints until it seemed as if the theatre could yield up nothing more entrancing.[1]

The 1916 *Follies* opened to even greater acclaim than the previous edition. It also sparked one of the most arresting love stories of the century as William Randolph Hearst sat transfixed at successive performances while Marion Davies cavorted in "I Left Her on the Beach in Hawaii." The impact of the Russian ballet on New York was felt when Fanny Brice sang "Nijinsky" and Carl Randall danced "*Spectre de la Rose*" on a stage filled with Ziegfeld Girls as roses. Jerome Kern had his first *Follies* song hit with "Have a Heart," and Irving Berlin was represented with "In Florida Among the Palms." Will Rogers made his initial appearance in the 1916 edition, and others in the superb cast included Ina Claire and Bert Williams. For a travesty of *Antony and Cleopatra*, Urban projected a fabulous gray sphinx against one of his midnight blue skies. In a closing scene pink roses streamed from massive vases and Lady Duff Gordon's chiffons ran riot in "My Lady of the Nile."

Fresh from such frivolity, Urban turned his talents to a project of more lofty artistic pretensions. In 1916 New York celebrated the three-hundredth anniversary of Shakespeare's death by mounting a gala spectacle in City College's Lewissohn Stadium. Percy MacKaye wrote a play for it called *Caliban*

Urban's design for the Setebos scene in Percy Mackaye's *Caliban of the Yellow Sands,* the presentation of which marked the tercentenary of Shakespeare's death. 1916. Columbia University.

Photo portrait of Joseph Urban from the late 1920s or early 1930s. Gretl Urban collection.

that traced the progress of drama from ancient to modern times. For this ambitious production the fabric of the stadium had to be radically altered so that the expected audience of thousands would be able to follow the action. This task was assigned to Urban, who saw it as "more than theatrical work; it is theatre plus architecture. The problem was to transform an athletic field and stadium into a fairy theatre for a single week, on a scale so huge, as to hold the attention of twenty thousand pairs of eyes through two and a half hours of performance." [2]

The solution Urban devised was an altarlike stage in the middle of the field where the pageantry would take place while the spoken drama was to be performed on another, larger stage. Two forty-foot towers were used for the lights, which were unusually powerful in theatre terms and not properly adjusted until the break of dawn on opening day. The young designer Robert Edmund Jones was responsible for the settings, and it was he who introduced Urban to Mary Porter Beegle, a dance instructor at Barnard College and student of Isadora Duncan's, who was also chairman of the committee that sponsored the event. Gretl describes Meary Beegle as

. . . tall and Junoesque, with an almost classical face and lovely color of skin and hair. Father was very captivated by her poise, her lovely speaking voice, her dedication to the dance, and above all her virtue. Buschi told me later that this was a hard time for him. He wanted Mary desperately, but he did not really want to marry her. Having a wife in Boston made a casual affair, free of obligations, desirable to him, but Mary was adamant and marriage finally became the only solution. He held out for a year, but in the spring of 1917 Father finally asked for a divorce.

Buschi did not go to Mother because he always hated to hurt anybody and he knew that she would have hysterics, so he came to me and told me that he had met the only woman he could ever love and that I had to help him get a divorce. I remember I threw my arms around him and said, "Oh, Buschi! I don't want to lose you. I don't want to lose you." And I cried bitterly. Buschi said, "You and Elly will never lose me," and he kept that promise.

Top. Urban's design for the main stage used in presenting *Caliban*. 1916. Columbia University. *Bottom:* Performed in the City University's Lewissohn Stadium, New York, *Caliban* required an elaborate lighting system and stage facilities, all provided by Urban. Photograph of the main stage area. 1916. Columbia University.

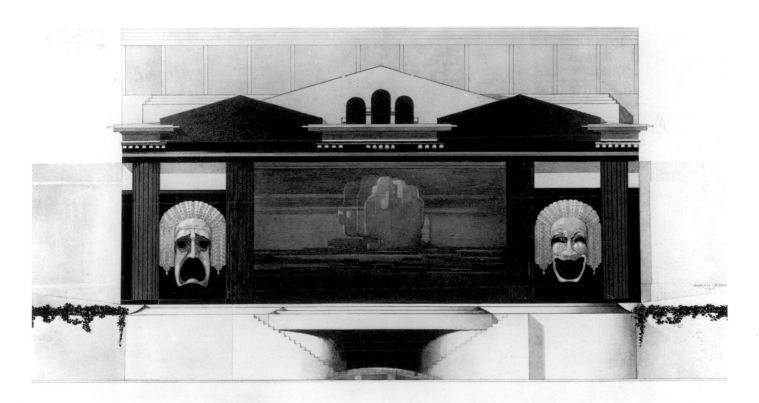

101

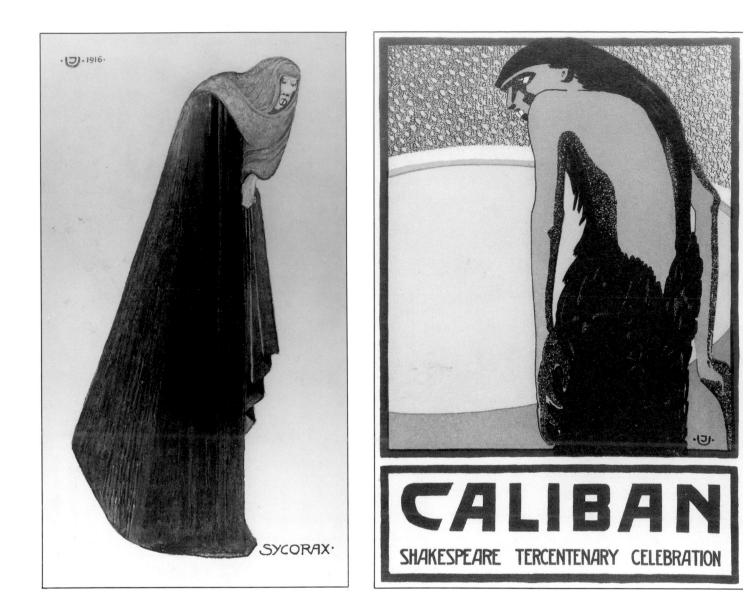

SYCORAX·

CALIBAN
SHAKESPEARE TERCENTENARY CELEBRATION

Top left. Urban's costume sketch for Sycorax, Caliban's mother. 1916. Columbia University.
Top right. Cover of the souvenir album designed by Urban. While working on *Caliban,* Urban met his second wife, Mary Porter Beegle, head of the committee that presented the pageant. 1916. Columbia University.

I don't really know how I managed, but I cajoled and argued, appealing to Mother's pride—surely she did not want to hang on to Buschi against his will. I think she came near to hating me, but I really didn't care. Finally I phoned the good news to Buschi. He asked me to come to New York immediately to plan the divorce as easily as we could for Mother. He met me in New York and took me to Yonkers, where I saw the house he had bought from Edward Sheldon [playwright of *The Garden of Paradise*]. It was a mess, as the interior was being completely redesigned. We had a lovely evening together and finally decided to leave the matter in the hands of a lawyer friend of Mother's, who, incidentally, was one of the beaux she had acquired aboard ship on our first voyage to America.

Everything was arranged to make the proceeding easy for Mother. We girls did not attend the court hearing, but we gathered that all went well because Mother came back quite calm and collected. The lawyer had gotten a more-than-generous alimony settlement, and there was also a proviso for a large settlement in case Father died before her.

Buschi and Mary were married in 1919 not long after my own marriage on November 3, 1918.

In the autumn of 1917, Urban designed the settings for *Faust,* which was the first of his more than fifty productions for the Metropolitan Opera. He also redesigned the house in Yonkers and took over an abandoned ice-skating rink that he converted into a production studio. The sets for the *Follies* of 1915, 1916, and 1917 had all been constructed and painted in Swampscott, but that had entailed a great deal of commuting for Urban. Although he enjoyed the visits with his family in Boston (after initial bitterness on Mizzi's part, she and Urban continued their relationship as close friends), it was obvious that a studio near New York was absolutely necessary. Gretl describes this all-important facility:

> It cost over $50,000 to convert the skating rink in Yonkers into a studio, and it was worth every penny. With the end of the war, Father recruited other Viennese artisans, and for almost two decades the lights never went out as settings for Broadway and the Metropolitan Opera and murals for Father's architectural projects were meticulously crafted.
>
> There was an enormous basement used for storage of canvas and huge rolls of netting for backing, lots of plywood and, of course, hundreds of cans of paint. There were also showers for the men. An annex contained a large kitchen and dining room where they had a delicious big meal every day with Viennese cooking: goulash, Wiener schnitzel, and pastries, and always a little wine. Every once in a while I would have lunch with them, but there really was too much to eat.
>
> Most of the stretching of canvas was done by assistants and students. Father had quite a few young people who came to learn scenic painting, and they were the ones who had to do the rough work, stretching the canvas all the way across what had been the rink and then priming it. This was done so that the canvas would be dry for the painters to start work at eight in the morning. Karl Koeck would take the model of the day and sketch it roughly with charcoal, then designate who was to do what, and the painters would start.
>
> When a setting was finished, which sometimes took two or three days, the men would cut it out with sharp knives, even the most delicate leaves and flowers. Some of them specialized in trees and rocks, while others were best with buildings and architectural details. Finally, the completed sets

Urban's Yonkers studio, where all his scenery was painted and constructed. The building had to be of enormous dimensions, since Urban's artists painted the huge canvases flat on the studio floor. Ca. 1920. Columbia University.

would be attached to netting or plywood, depending on what the piece was. Trees and leaves were attached to netting, while building façades went onto plywood. Sometimes the wives came in and helped out, but the ones from Boston were now rather spoiled ladies and did not care for the work because it meant crawling around on the floor.

Gretl, her mother, and Elly spent the summer of 1918 in a cottage at the Lake Placid Club. As a patriotic gesture Mizzi entertained soldiers from the nearby Plattsburg army training camp, and at one of her informal suppers a young captain, John Thurlow, appeared. To Gretl he was a war hero soon to be shipped off to battle overseas, perhaps never to return. Apparently John acquiesced to the "emergency" and obtained a leave. The wedding took place in Newburyport, Massachusetts, where John's father was president of the small local bank.

Though Gretl refused to wear a wedding gown, the ceremony was formal, concluding with the traditional military departure under crossed sabers. The Armistice was signed during the honeymoon, and shortly thereafter John's father bought his son a seat on the New York Stock Exchange. To Gretl's delight the couple moved to New York and a charming apartment on Fifty-third Street. They were hardly unpacked when Urban, who was designing a show called *Rainbow Girl*, phoned to ask them to supper at Delmonico's:

> Buschi was at his most charming, and Johnny, who knew little or nothing of the arts, was immediately captivated. But Father's wicked grin told me that he did not think much of my choice. He never said so, and even when Johnny and I split up he never said, "I told you so" or "I could have. . . ."
>
> I could not really enter his world, nor he mine. Often when he was giving a dinner party and needed a proper hostess, I would arrive home late and tired and sometimes dirty from the Hearst studio. Those first two years at Cosmopolitan Pictures were tough because the staff was unfamiliar with Father's staging and lighting innovations and had to be constantly supervised. The foreseeable happened. Johnny moved to the Harvard Club and I to an apartment in Gramercy Park.

Urban's marriage to Mary Beegle took place on January 23, 1919. That summer, the Urbans, in various combinations, returned to Vienna. Mizzi

Top. Gretl Urban and her mother, Mizzi, in 1935. Gretl Urban collection. *Bottom*. Mary and Joseph Urban on a transatlantic steamer. Ca. 1920s. Gretl Urban collection.

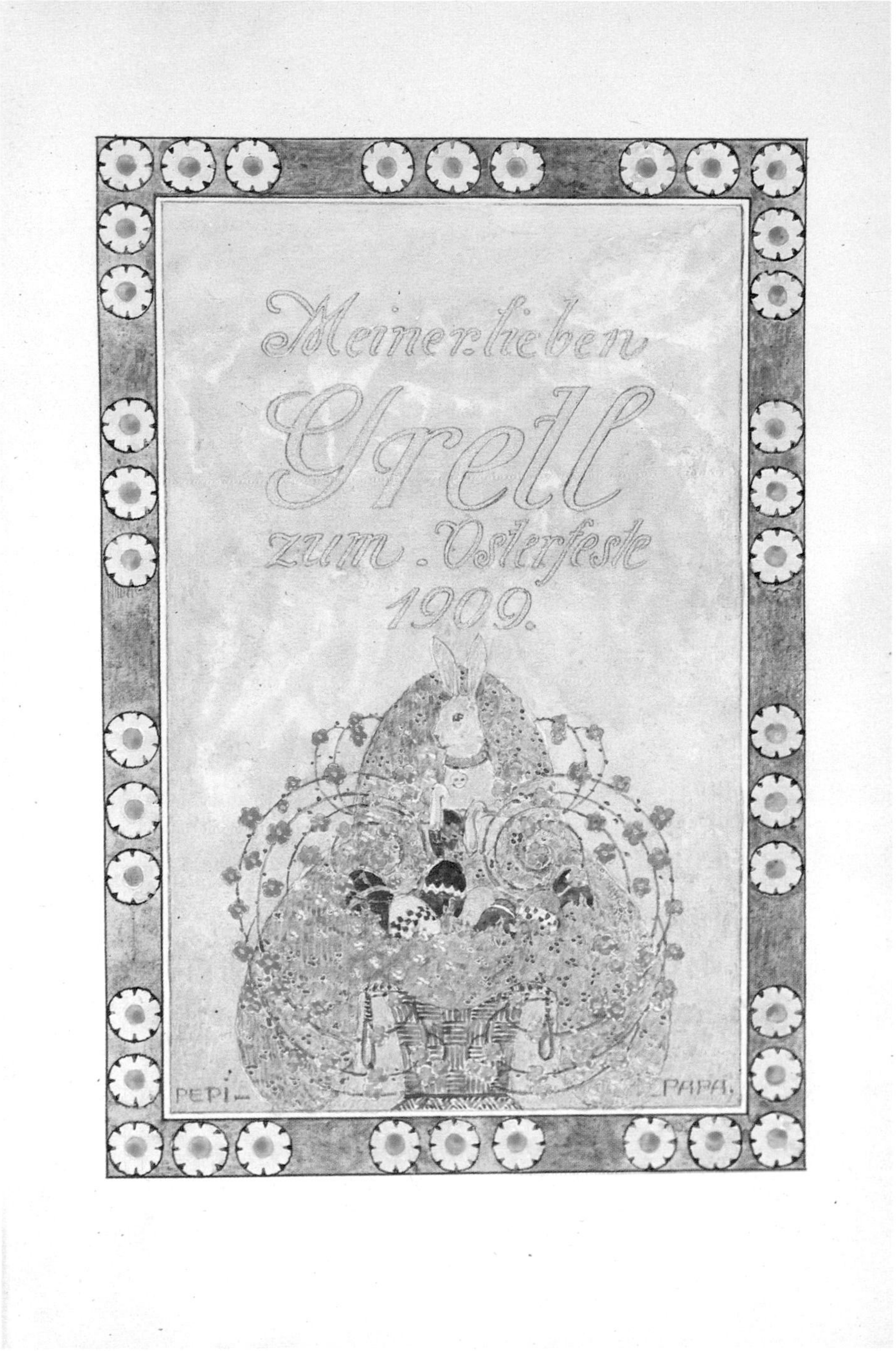

Meiner lieben
Grell
zum . Osterfeste
1909.
PEPI—
PAPA.

Cover of a diary Urban made for Gretl at Easter in 1909. It is still one of her most cherished possessions. Gretl Urban collection.

stayed with her two daughters, while Urban was with Mary. Through complicated maneuvering he managed to keep the two parties separate, afraid that Gretl and Mary would not get along. It was his daughters who accompanied him when Urban paid a visit to Lefler's grave.

Heinrich Lefler had died of a heart attack on March 14, 1919. During the war years he had continued to work in the Viennese theatre. He wrote to Urban: "Although I am carrying a heavier load than ever, because most of my assistants are now in the army, I am working harder than ever, because . . . I am desperately trying to keep the arts we love alive in a city that is dying." His funeral was one of dignity and warm affection, and he was buried in a section of the cemetery reserved for Vienna's great. Everyone who could make it was there, even if in wheelchairs or on crutches. Since no wreath could be found in all of Vienna, friends and pupils fashioned one of pine branches from the Vienna Woods and bound it with gold ribbon from a prewar ball gown that belonged to his widow. On it they wrote: "TO OUR HEINRICH WITH GRATITUDE AND AFFECTION, ALL VIENNA."

Urban and Mary received a warm welcome, part curiosity, part affection, when they arrived in Vienna in the summer of 1919. Urban admitted that he put on a bit of a show—an automobile, expensive American clothes, a suite at the Hotel Bristol—but his slightly malicious pleasure in putting down his former antagonists turned to chagrin when he realized the misery and want in which most of the artists were forced to live. By 1919 the once-glittering capital of a mighty empire had truly become a dead city.

Urban dreaded visiting Heinrich's apartment, but all the furniture and carpets he had designed were still there, looking much the same as when he had last seen them, a lifetime ago. Lefler's widow, Minna, gave Urban a letter her husband had written a few weeks before he died. The only time Gretl saw her father weep was while reading that letter to her and Elly; he would always carry the letter with him, until the cheap wartime paper crumbled. In it, Heinrich, after expressing his pleasure at Urban's success in New York and recalling fond memories in Vienna, said farewell to his friend and collaborator:

> My *Dickes*, you and I have shared a perfect friendship and a perfect artistic understanding which made us as one. A gift not often granted to mere mortals. For this, my *Dickes*, my loving thanks are yours forever.
> *Servus*, my *Dickes*, and *Vale!*
> Your old, old Heinrich

"*Dickes*," meaning "Plump One," was Heinrich's affectionate nickname for Urban. Out of respect for Heinrich, Urban asked Mary and her family also to call him "*Dickes*," which they always did.

Urban's visit to his mother and sister at their cottage was emotionally charged; Mary, self-conscious and inundated by torrents of German, put on what Urban called her "Isadora Act," which failed to endear her to Frau Urban. Due to the money and regular food packages Urban sent during the war years, they had suffered few hardships except a lack of cigarettes, both being, like Urban, heavy smokers.

Knowing that proud starving artists would never accept outright gifts of food, Urban arranged elaborate banquets at the Bristol that afforded his friends the face-saving pretext of reliving old times. Mary declared that had she not been along, they would have been bankrupted. Urban could not bear the suffering he saw, the lack of food, the threadbare clothes, homes without heat, some artists literally starving in back alleys, too proud to beg. Added to the devastation of war was the toll exacted by the Spanish flu epidemic of 1918 that had decimated the population and cast a deathly pall over the city. Egon Schiele, whose talent was finally being recognized after years of neglect, had succumbed to influenza late in 1918, a year that saw the end of the war but also a grim harvest among leading artists of the modern Viennese movement: Gustav Klimt dead of a stroke and Otto Wagner and Kolomon Moser dead from cancer. Fritz Warndorfer and Otto Primavesi, backers of the Wiener Werkstätte, were bankrupt, but the artists, spurred on by Josef Hoffmann and Dagobert Peche, had still gone on producing lovely lamps, figurines, wallpapers and silks, ceramics, boxes with decorative inlay, silver vases—all handcrafted, each unique. Using his own money, Urban bought as

The home Urban bought in Yonkers, New York, previously belonged to playwright Ned Sheldon, author of Urban's first Broadway production, *The Garden of Paradise*. *Top.* A section of the living room of the Yonkers home. The large chair on the left was covered in emerald green silk. Ca. 1920. Gretl Urban collection. *Bottom.* A bedroom in the Heinrich Lefler home in Vienna, with furniture and fabrics designed by Urban under the influence of the Wiener Werkstätte. Ca. 1910. Gretl Urban collection.

many items as he could afford so that the artists would not have to wait for their share of the sales.

The New York Wiener Werkstätte shop that Urban opened at 581 Fifth Avenue in June of 1922 was less a store than an exhibition space. Around a central room with a domed ceiling, smaller rooms were grouped, providing intimate display areas. At first it seemed as though the enterprise would be successful. Gretl recalls:

> People were cautious but curious. Expensive pieces did not sell, but smaller items did quite well, and it was funny to see Father upset when one of his favorite pieces was being looked at by a possible purchaser. There were, in particular, two fantastic birds about twelve inches high, wrought in silver and gold and decorated with semiprecious stones, as well as two obelisks about fifteen inches high, also pure fantasy with jewels and silver. Buschi could not stand the idea of a possible purchaser, so he bought them for the Yonkers house.
>
> There was a gold man over six feet tall, nude and only slightly stylized. He was shipped with great care, and the box he arrived in was so large that it had to be unpacked on the sidewalk; it was impossible to get it into the elevator. The box looked an awful lot like a giant's coffin and attracted quite a crowd. A couple of Father's painters were helping, and Mary declared that the naked man could not be unpacked in public.
>
> Father thought it would be great fun, but we had to agree that the gold man had better not be exposed on Fifth Avenue at high noon. So the boys got a tarpaulin, wrapped up the figure, and carried it upstairs while disappointed people on the sidewalk kept saying, "Let's see it!" The gold man was put in a niche in the shop where he looked perfectly stunning, though causing many averted glances. I wonder what became of him?

Although the Wiener Werkstätte exhibits that Urban arranged in several major cities were highly praised, in the long run the venture proved unsuccessful. The Klimt and Schiele paintings, the Hoffmann and Peche silver, the Powolny ceramics, as well as the jewelry, were all too new and foreign for American tastes, and there were still wartime memories and prejudices lingering in the minds of potential customers. The failure of the Wiener Werkstätte branch resulted in a personal loss to Urban of $150,000 (Otto Kahn was a silent partner in the venture), but the Klimt and Schiele canvases and drawings were lovingly displayed in the Yonkers house. Though sold after Urban's death for a fraction of their value today, they proved useful in helping to cover Mary's stock market losses during the Depression. Some American museums were able to acquire important pieces at bargain prices.

Urban had been nervous about a meeting between Gretl and Mary, and it was not until the summer of 1920 that one took place. In 1919 he had signed with William Randolph Hearst's Cosmopolitan Productions to design films, and Gretl, as his assistant, was creating costumes for the orgy scene in *Enemies of Women*, starring Lionel Barrymore, while Mary was to do the choreography. Bowing to the inevitable, Urban agreed to let Gretl drive up to the Yonkers house:

> Mary was waiting for me in the garden. My legs were shaking, and Mary later told me that she could hardly stand up. I guess I felt I was in a way deserting Mother, and Mary knew how much Father wanted us to like each other. Anyway, we went inside and had a drink and afterward lunch on the terrace facing the Hudson and the Palisades, and we talked and decided we could manage.

I think we responded to each other because we both loved the same man. After that I went to Yonkers practically every weekend, and we got to be quite good friends. Often I spent the whole week there working with Buschi, and that's when I really got to admire her. There is no doubt that she was jealous of the artistic closeness between us, and Father liked to talk to me in German, which she never could master though she tried. She tried to fit in, too, but sometimes Father would say, "Please, dear, go leave us alone," and she would have to go sit in the living room. I knew it made her unhappy, but she never showed any real animosity.

The Yonkers house that Gretl found such a mess in 1917 was completely transformed when Gretl saw it again in 1920 on her first meeting with Mary. The architecturally undistinguished exterior, a vaguely Victorian affair of gables and verandas, was unaltered, but the interior had been entirely transformed in delicate pastel tints, distinctly Viennese, exquisite in detail, somewhat formal but thoroughly unpretentious. Gretl recalls:

> The Yonkers house was built on a terrace bluff facing the Hudson. It descended four stories into a garden area. At the very bottom was an old-fashioned kitchen that even contained an original coal stove. Fortunately, there was a dumbwaiter that worked by pulling ropes.

The interior of the New York branch of the Wiener Werkstätte store had furniture designed by Urban and a Klimt painting on the rear wall. Urban opened the store to help his fellow artists in Vienna who were literally starving to death after World War I. Few items were sold, and Urban suffered a major financial loss as a result. 1922.
Columbia University.

The living and dining rooms on the first floor were separated by gold curtains and by a three-cornered room called the "throne room" because it held two large golden chairs in which Father and Mary presided at parties. There were windows on all three sides and a panoramic view over the Hudson to the Palisades. As the dining room ceiling was low, Father had it and the walls papered in a gay Wiener Werkstätte design that made the room appear very bright and cheerful. At one end was a ceramic figure connected to a tiny fountain, which Father regretted having put there because the tinkling water reminded him of the bathroom.

Fastidious as Father was about himself, he was even more so about everything around him, and he could make a real nuisance of himself. Everything in the house had to be just so. A lamp or a ceramic half an inch out of the way made him move it, and pictures slightly tilted were not tolerated.

All through the house were lovely vases and lamps and silver and ceramic boxes with cigarettes and candy. In the summer every window box had bright red geraniums that were particularly effective in the "throne room" and the "view room" at the top of the house. There were always flowers, even in winter, from the greenhouse where a huge bougainvillea bloomed in December.

There were six or seven sheep dogs, lovely animals. The kennels were in the lower part of the garden with wisteria and ivy growing over them. Occasionally there were puppies, and quite often they got into Father's studio. Although Father really loved them, they made little drops here and there, so he designed a special carpet with flowers on it so the spots wouldn't show. He said the flowers were there for the dogs to smell.

Of course, the big dogs should not have been in the house, but one or two of them always got in, and Father was very unhappy when they shed,

111

Drawing room of Burkeley
Crest, the Hastings, New York,
home of the Florenz Ziegfelds.
Columbia University.

Undated profile drawing by
Urban for an armchair, for
which he also designed
the fabric pattern.
Columbia University.

Chair Of Heavy Black Rep.
Emerald Green Piping.
White Silk Painted With
Washable Colors.
Wood Parts Stained
Black With Waxed Finish.

· Arm Chair ·

which they did even though they were always extremely well groomed. I used to laugh when Father picked white and gray hairs off his immaculate suit.

Father cherished his dogs, his house, and his garden. I shall always see him wandering around in the garden, admiring and enjoying every bush and tree and little plant, although he always wanted to rearrange the rambling roses and ivy. People would say to him, "Nature has to be as Nature will," but he was fond of using flowers on stage and could never get used to nature going its own way.

In Hastings, a couple of miles up the river from Yonkers, Urban's modest efforts at making a home for himself were dwarfed by those of Ziegfeld. He had turned his lordly attention to Burkely Crest and planted twenty-two towering blue spruces on either side of the driveway, laid out tennis courts, and commissioned Urban to design a swimming pool that proved large enough for canoeing. The main house (there was another for Billie's mother, as well as several Japanese teahouses) had been completely redecorated by Sloan Farley, New York's most fashionable decorator, and a playhouse was constructed for Billie and Flo's daughter, Patricia, complete with library, bedroom, and a story-and-a-half living room. A herd of deer, ten in all, was turned loose in the seeded meadows, and two bears and three lion cubs were introduced, along with partridges and pheasants, all of which had their own special preserves. Two buffalo, one of which immediately gave birth, moved in with a baby elephant weighing 250 pounds. There were numerous cats, goats, geese, lambs, three monkeys, ducks, three hundred chickens, and fifteen dogs. Though flowers grew everywhere, Ziegfeld had dozens of long-stemmed roses delivered daily from two local florists. The estate was maintained by a staff of eighteen, augmented, of course, for entertainment, especially for dinner parties that numbered as many as sixty. Of the famous Sunday dinners Gretl recalls:

> The long dining room table was lavishly laid, and there were always a lot of famous guests, all looking their best, while uniformed lackeys solemnly served food and drink under the golden candelabra. Flo sat at the head of the table smiling benignly, very much the lord of the manor; at the other end was Billie, warmly hospitable, completely ignoring the pomp and ceremony and refusing to play the chatelaine.
>
> We had a standing invitation to these Sunday affairs, but Father went as rarely as possible, just often enough not to hurt Flo's feelings. Buschi liked to spend his Sundays at home, at work or with intimate friends. He did not like large dinner parties, and further, Mary had to be talked out of a bad humor whenever she had to go there.
>
> Straightlaced Mary did not approve of Flo and also felt he was taking up too much of Father's time with the *Follies*. Worst of all, he was way behind in paying his bills.

THE METROPOLITAN OPERA

I cherish a deeper affection for my work at the Metropolitan ... than for anything else I have ever done for the theatre," [1] Urban told Oliver Saylor in a 1923 interview. His association with the Met had begun in 1917 and ended only with his death in 1933. During this sixteen-year span not only did Urban design more than fifty productions but he directed his studio in actually building the scenery, oversaw its installation, lighting, and, at least in the early years of his tenure, performed some of the duties of stage director.

Wherever Urban worked in America, there seems to have been one dominant individual guiding the enterprise: Russell in Boston, Ziegfeld on Broadway, and Otto Kahn at the Met. Kahn was born in Germany in 1867 and moved to the United States in 1893. Four years later he joined the banking firm of Kuhn, Loeb in New York, taking a role in numerous international financial organizations as well as in war relief charities during World War I.

A man of tremendous financial resources, Kahn was a great patron of the arts, even helping underwrite American tours of foreign performing companies, including Max Reinhardt's troupe in *The Miracle*. Although he was most closely identified with the performing arts, his generosity extended into other fields. Hart Crane, for example, probably never would have been able to complete *The Bridge* without Kahn's assistance.

Otto Kahn joined the board of the Metropolitan Opera in 1903 and soon became its president. From that point until his death in 1934, he was its prime benefactor. He poured massive amounts of his own money into the Met's coffers and oversaw virtually every detail of its operations. A man of impeccable manners and cultivated learning, he closely followed the artistic scene in Europe and in 1908 brought Giulio Gatti-Casazza, as well as a young conductor named Arturo Toscanini, from Milan's La Scala to the Metropolitan. Gatti served as the company's general manager all during Urban's years with the Met.

Detail of an unused set design by Urban for a garden scene in the Metropolitan Opera production of *Parsifal*. 1920. Columbia University.

Program from the first performance of an Urban production at the Metropolitan Opera. Previously, no designer's name had ever appeared in a Met program. 1917. Metropolitan Opera Archives.

The new impresario found the Met's existing scenery in appalling condition. In his autobiography Gatti comments on his initial inspection of some items then being used onstage:

> I remember that when I came to the Metropolitan I asked to be shown some of the sets used for different operas. They impressed me as being mediocre; old stuff of little importance. Some were actually incredible, particularly a certain set that represented an ugly court and a door in the rear, opening on the sea.
>
> "But what set is this?" I asked.
>
> "It's used interchangeably," was the reply, "for the first act of 'Mignon' and the first act of 'Otello.'"
>
> This certainly may seem an exaggeration, but I can assure my readers it is true.[2]

Gatti found that the Met had good sets only for some of the Wagnerian operas, the *Ring* and *Parsifal* in particular, but for most of the other productions "the company was truly impoverished."[3]

Leo Slezak may have led Gatti to Urban, or it could have been Otto Kahn, who knew the designer from Boston, the *Follies*, and from the 1916 production of *Caliban* staged at Lewissohn Stadium. Before Urban joined the Met, no designer had ever received credit for his work. But for the production of Gounod's *Faust* on November 17, 1917, Urban's name was printed in the program in type as large as that of the composer!

116

After viewing Urban's first three productions at the Met, *Faust*, *Saint Elizabeth*, and *Le Prophète*, a writer for *Vogue* noted that formerly the Met had "placed upon its stage scenes of such fearful and wonderful ugliness that even a whole evening of 'Puccini' could not relieve the strain of their shrieking colour and stupid design."[4] This critic then praised Gatti for selecting the new designer:

> In doing so he cast his vote for beauty against ugliness, for resplendent masses of colour, for balanced and restful design, for accurate and characteristic detail, and for the banishment of the false perspective, the garrulous superfluity, the garish combination of tint and tone which marked the old and backward art of stage craft as it has appeared there.[5]

It was during one of the Met's golden periods that Urban provided settings well worthy of such distinguished artists as Jeritza, Rethberg, Branzell, Bori, Matzenauer, Caruso, Gigli, Chaliapin, Pinza, Lauri-Volpi, Martinelli, Scotti, Melchior, and Schorr. But Urban's achievements at the Met are even more impressive when one considers the facilities provided. Even by standards of the day, the stage was ill-equipped. There were no turntables, lifts, or stage wagons for the swift scene changes required in works such as *Pelléas* and *Don Giovanni*. In addition, there was room backstage only for the opera being presented; after each performance the scenery had to be carted back to the warehouse to make way for the next production. Matinees presented double jeopardy. Piles of stacked scenery draped in soiled tarpaulins were a regular feature of Seventh Avenue near the Met's loading dock.

Urban's relations with the management of the Met were for the most part warm and cordial. He was particularly close to Edward (Neddie) Ziegler,

Costumes by Urban for the 1918 production of von Weber's *Oberon*. Metropolitan Opera Archives.

the assistant general manager. Quaintance Eaton provides us with a portrait of Ziegler and his role at the Met:

> A small man with a firm mouth and cool eyes behind rimless glasses, as taciturn as Gatti and moving as quickly, Ziegler came to be the spinal cord of the nebulous structure. No detail of administrative or financial operations escaped him. He arranged repertoire, scouted for new talent in Europe in the summer and arranged the spring tours.[6]

Gatti, Ziegler, and Urban would meet at the end of each season to plan for the next one. It was not then necessary to schedule singers or conductors years in advance. In the more leisurely era of the steamship, artists would devote a considerable block of time to the Met, and plans were made rather informally. Urban's contract, such as it was, consisted of a single sheet of paper that listed the name of the opera, the composer, the approximate date of the first performance, and the planned cost of the production.

When Gretl finished her art studies in Boston, she joined her father in 1920 as his assistant. She quickly assumed a role in Urban's creative process similar to Lefler's in Vienna. In the first phase of preparation for a new operatic design, there was an intensive period of study of the libretto, the music, and the historical period of the work, as well as the scholarly and critical literature on the opera. Gretl would read some of this material to her father as he sketched, just as her Uncle Heinrich had done. In preparation for *Tristan* she went back to the medieval poem, while for *Pelléas* and *Louise* she translated the original French texts into German, which her father better understood.

Once these background studies were completed, the process of design and construction of the sets was similar to what had been done for the Boston Opera. From the final drawings a model was built for each set. These miniatures were complete even to their own lighting systems, so that they gave a most accurate representation of the actual set. Delivered well in advance of the completed set, they were left at the opera house for inspection by management and stage crew. When the scenery was ready, it was delivered in time for rehearsals. Urban's men helped the Met's stage crew, to show

For the Met's premiere of Mozart's *Così Fan Tutte* in 1922, Urban reduced the size of the Met's huge stage and created a charming baroque setting for the intimate opera. Columbia University.

EGYPTIAN HELEN.

them how the pieces worked and how they should be hung. Some of the larger sections were actually built at the Met to avoid damage in transit.

If, as Urban always contended, architecture was his first love, opera must have been his consuming passion. Otto Kahn, as opera's guardian angel, pumped millions into the Metropolitan, but the Met's archives reveal that Urban's contribution was also substantial. Many of Urban's settings were used for years: *Faust* until 1950, *Parsifal* until 1955, *Tristan* until 1959, and *Elektra* until 1966.[7] He not only designed these settings and built them but also paid the salaries of his scene painters and carpenters as well as the cost of construction materials. Through the early twenties he received $1,500 per scene, but in 1926 he was forced to raise the price to $2,200, having sustained a loss of $9,000 for work done in 1925.[8] For the famous *Elektra* set in 1932 he received only $1,800. On October 29, 1929, the date of the Wall Street crash, the Metropolitan boasted of having two million dollars in the bank. Had Urban, after a decade of work, been paid anything near the equivalent of his contribution, the Met's bank account would have been considerably smaller.

Mary Urban, in a letter to Ziegler, voiced a timid complaint that made Urban furious when he learned of it:

> I should hate to tell you how much we lost on "Cosi Fan Tutte"—where every scene was painted as exquisitely as if it were done for an interior, but the result was so beautiful and charming that I say nothing. We can have our pleasure looking at it. I really think it was the most complete artistic production, from every standpoint, that the Metropolitan has ever had on its stage and we are happy to know we had our part in it.[9]

To which Ziegler replied with impeccable affrontery: "I notice you take pleasure in 'hating' to tell me how much you lost on 'Cosi Fan Tutte.' I think

A figure for Richard Strauss's *Egyptian Helen*. 1928. Author's collection.

119

if I told you how much we lost on it, you might consider yourself fortunate and blessed." [10]

Gretl, who also joined in this labor of love and received seven dollars for some of her most exquisite costume designs, recalled one amusing incident:

> Lily Pons had a lovely figure, and when I designed her costume for *Lakmé*, we conspired to expose her midriff. . . . During the second performance, which I was fortunate to catch, her voluminous skirt, which had been improperly fastened, slipped during the "Bell Song" and slid to the floor, revealing frilled panties and her lovely, shapely legs. There was a muffled gasp from the audience, but without missing a trill, Lily gathered up the skirt and, with a flourish, slipped it, veil-like, firmly in place. The "Bell Song" never received a more resounding ovation.

One of the high points in Urban's long career at the Met was the visit of Richard Strauss in 1921. At that time only two of the composer's works had been presented at the Metropolitan: a single performance of *Salomé* in 1907, following which the opera was withdrawn because of the scandal it provoked, and a premiere of *Der Rosenkavalier* in 1913. *Egyptian Helen* would receive an Urban-designed production in 1928, as would *Elektra* in 1932.

Because Strauss, Frau Strauss, and their son were coming to dinner, the Urban household in Yonkers experienced a tumult of anticipation all one day. Maestro Strauss, much impressed by Urban's work at the Metropolitan, had wanted to see him again socially. They had met casually through Mahler in Vienna, and Urban remembered Strauss as a man who radiated good humor. All afternoon the designer was busy selecting his best sketches and laying them out on a long table under the wall of windows in his studio. Urban's valet, Hans, a baritone, and the family's cook, Elsa, a soprano (both rescued from a stranded German opera company), were quite beside themselves with excitement. Gretl was nervous about Hans's shaky hands, and Mary was nervous about her German. Only Marie the parlor maid, Viennese but not musical, was quite calm. Urban, Mary, Marie, Hans, and Gretl were the reception committee, as Gretl recalls:

> Mrs. Strauss entered first, and we all immediately called her *gnädige Frau*. She was an imposing lady, sumptuously dressed and wearing a hat that could only have been of Parisian origin. Strauss was just as Father had said—quietly relaxed, more like a diplomat, with his neatly trimmed mustache, than a famous musician. Behind him came their son, Franz, a charming six-footer who shook hands shyly.
>
> After the greetings were over, Madame wanted someone to help her with her hat and her hair, so Mary and I showed her upstairs to Mary's small dressing room while the men went on to Buschi's studio to see the sketches. Madame was very gracious, but it was fortunate that Marie spoke German because the hairdo instructions were somewhat complicated.
>
> When we joined the men, Strauss was talking enthusiastically about Buschi's drawings and complimenting him on the miracles he had worked at the old-fashioned Met. He assured us that Father's sketches were far in advance of anything he had seen abroad. Strauss was now an entirely different person; his voice was vibrant, his eyes shone, and his hands made elegant gestures to emphasize points.
>
> Over dinner Father tried hard to get Strauss to speak about his work, but all he could get was pleasant small talk. Over dinner, however, Buschi hit the right note by asking about the Viennese premiere of *Die Frau ohne Schatten*, which had been delayed because of the war. Strauss said he

For Humperdinck's *Hänsel und Gretel*, Urban used an unusual perspective and stage opening. 1927. Columbia University.

preferred the Viennese performance to any other because of the magic of Jeritza as the Empress. She looked the part as none other, and while he always knew she was a superb actress, he hadn't believed she could muster the incredibly difficult demands on her voice. She never faltered, and her highest notes were round and pure and in perfect pitch.

Then there was Hugo von Hofmannsthal, his dear friend and collaborator, the poet and mystic, whose libretti were in beautiful language and style. In *Die Frau* he wanted a modern *Magic Flute*, with deep and warm humanity and the triumph of good over evil. One could never imagine that the author who had written this fairy tale had also written the libretto of *Elektra*, with all its horror and madness.

Buschi here interrupted with "And what about the great composer whose unforgettable music had really created these masterpieces?"

Strauss laughed and said, "My dear Urban, I know I am a good composer, I hope even a great one, just as you are a fine artist and I think a great one, so let's drink to ourselves!" They clinked glasses, and then we all did, with Buschi almost in tears of happiness at this high praise.

When we moved to the living room, Buschi and Strauss started reminiscing about mutual friends—the inimitable Gustav Mahler and the tragedy of his early death, and Slezak of the divine voice and mischievous sense of humor, whose famous "When is the next swan due?" saved the situation at the Vienna opera when the swan in *Lohengrin* failed to arrive. Before he left, Strauss talked about his love for the Alps and the joy he had experienced composing his *Alpine Symphony*.

In saying *auf wiedersehen*, we saw the first smile on the face of the *gnädige Frau*. She had seemed languid and bored during the whole evening and made it clear that she had heard all this before. . . . All through the meal she had picked on poor Franz: he was eating too fast; he shouldn't drink wine with his mouth full; he should run upstairs to fetch her handkerchief. Mary had been distressed to see her looking askance at the food but was glad when she finally ate with restrained gusto. It was clear that while Franz admired his father, he was completely dominated by his mother.

121

After the Strausses left, we were much too exhilarated to go to bed. Father ordered more champagne and said, "I drink to Richard Strauss, who to me is as great a genius as Richard Wagner. I am a very lucky man; most of the artists I know are interpreters rather than creators. This has been a very important and memorable night."

Buschi told Hans to go to bed and asked him how he had managed to keep his hands from shaking. Hans confessed that he had taken a stiff shot of whiskey before starting to serve dinner. Mary, who had only pretended to understand what was being said, confessed that she understood practically nothing and that Madame's boredom had really worried her. "It doesn't seem to worry Strauss," said Father. "He just ignores it. What a woman! How is it that great men have such impossible wives and put up with them?"

The Urbans attended Strauss's final appearance in New York on New Year's Eve of 1921, when the composer conducted the New York Philharmonic in a program at the Hippodrome. He never returned to America.

Settings for the *Follies* had permitted Urban to work with two key elements of his scenic-design palette—color and light—but they did not usually require him to deal with such elements necessary to opera as interiors and exteriors of buildings. Opera called for churches, palaces, city squares, and street scenes. For these Urban's architectural training was invaluable, as was recognized by one of the more astute commentators on American theatre at this time, Kenneth MacGowan:

> It is impossible to overestimate the extent to which Urban's architectural training has helped him to grasp the essence of stage design—the expression of the mood of the play. To the architect it is a doubly familiar problem. His design must express the structure of the building, and must comport with its purposes. That has always been the dual test of great architecture. It applies equally to scenery and the play. It is not beauty that we should seek in a production, but appropriateness. After that is found, the play will provide the emotion which its author conceived.
>
> The complex quality of stage art—an interrelation of light, canvas, form, and meaning—finds an appreciative interpreter in the architect. He knows the multitude of detail, from sewerage to pure design, which goes to make a great building. He comes equipped to the theatre ready to appreciate the many-sided complexity of its finished art. He never makes the mistake of the painter who daubs a giant canvas and calls it a theatrical production.[11]

One of Urban's most-praised operatic settings was the temple in the 1920 production of *Parsifal*. However, not all elements of Urban's installation found acceptance with the public or critics. Urban broke with *Parsifal* tradition when he eliminated the moving panorama that precedes the grail scenes and replaced it with traveler curtains that remained closed until the scene had been changed. Critics protested that one of Wagner's greatest effects had been lost in this violation of his intentions. The dark curtain that Urban used depicted Titurel's vision of Parsifal holding his spear and gazing at the grail. Executed in the best *Jugendstil* manner, it was extremely beautiful in its own right.

Margarete Matzenauer as Kundry had a glorious voice, but unlike Jeritza or Garden, she had a massive figure that was alarming. For the seduction of Parsifal in Klingsor's garden, it had been the custom to wheel her onstage on a portable couch. Urban objected to this spectacle and ultimately convinced Matzenauer that a more alluring effect would be obtained by having the

Opposite top. The temple scene from Wagner's *Parsifal.* 1920. The designs on the columns reappeared on the facade of Urban's Ziegfeld Theatre. Austrian National Library. Gerhard Trumler.
Bottom. The design for the garden scene in *Parsifal* that was actually used. 1920. Austrian National Library. Gerhard Trumler.

This traveler curtain presented an elegant *Jugendstil* interpretation of Titurel's vision for *Parsifal*. 1920. Columbia University.

audience first see her reclining in shadow under a pergola as the curtain rose.

The temple scene was a prime example of Urban's use of his architectural background in creating a stage setting. Gretl always found the scene and its effects moving and impressive, as in her rapturous description:

> He used high, dark columns that vanished to infinity. There were stained-glass windows that were mystical—not of a Middle Ages cathedral, they were not of this earth. The lighting was semi-obscure. . . . As the grail was raised, the lights were dimmed. Just the windows would glow, mystically, magically. Even the stained-glass windows slowly lost their translucent light, and only the Holy Grail, this terrific nimbus of divinity, shone. It was deeply moving . . . the kind of thing that makes the shivers go up and down your back and yet makes you rise in ecstasy.

The *Parsifal* sets in photographs impress one today as being rather simple, straightforward affairs that would not jar anyone's sensibilities. What is most strikingly different, even now, is the designer's colors, which are truly extraordinary: not the dark, brooding hues one associates with Wagnerian operas, but soft, glowing shades of purples, pinks, greens, blues, and yellows. This was a springtime *Parsifal*, seen and interpreted in a fresh new light.

In 1922 Urban recreated medieval Italy for Gounod's *Romeo and Juliet*, and Deems Taylor, both perceptive critic and personal friend of Urban, describes this achievement in the *World*. The importance of architecture in the production is most apparent:

> Joseph Urban provided seven gorgeous sets for the production, the finest of which was the Verona street scene, with its red brick and sandstone

124

church and blazing blue sky seen through shadowed archways. Almost equally good were Friar Lawrence's cell, its groined ceiling, a triumph of deceptive lighting, and Juliet's Romanesque balcony overlooking a moon-drenched garden. The hall of the Capulets, with its tawny walls covered with primitive mosaics, looked stunning in the opening scene, when it was filled with merrymakers, but its design and coloring were overpowering when the young lovers were left alone. Juliet's chamber had wonderful gold walls hung with curious tapestries, and the tomb of the Capulets showed a huge, arched vault, open at the further end, with a fascinating iron grille silhouetted against a somber sky.[12]

Taylor also had kind words for Gretl's costumes, which he wrote "were good in line and sumptuous in texture and color."[13]

In this same review Taylor twice mentions the sky effects Urban created, which were indeed a matter of special pride to the artist. One might have expected Urban to use different backdrops for the full-day sky of the street scene and another for the gloomy final one, but he achieved both effects with a single background, relying on a special combination of painting and lighting techniques that he described for a *Times* interview:

> By this method . . . I am able to get results that would be impossible if we applied our paint in the usual way. The conventional sky drop is given a solid coat of blue paint and that is all that is considered necessary. In painting a sky I apply one color with a stroke in one direction, then on top of that another color in another direction, and above that still another shade. Then when a light is thrown on it, instead of being reflected and

Urban made two unused designs for Klingsor's garden in *Parsifal*, both of which featured unusual color schemes. 1920. Columbia University.

125

giving the drop the appearance of painted canvas, the light is broken up and diffused and you get atmosphere. Different colored lights may be applied giving the sky different tones.[14]

By a similar technique, underpainting with silver, Urban gave rocks he created for settings a mysterious glow when lights focused on them were dimmed.

Spontini's *La Vestale* was presented in the 1925 season and provided Urban with the opportunity to recreate ancient Rome, which he did in splendid fashion. The first-act setting for the Roman Forum reveals many of Urban's favorite scenic devices. First there was the unusual angle at which the audience saw the Forum, which was up and through a massive triumphal arch. Inside the openings in the arch there were natural-looking shadows resulting from the use of overhead lights, which Urban describes: "I light my stage from above so that the light will come down as in nature and will cast shadows. A bridge is placed above the stage and on this the lighting crew, sometimes a dozen or more, are stationed with spotlights."[15] In some of the Met's older scenery, shadows were actually *painted* in and had absolutely no relation to source of light.

By the use of platforms and staircases, the Forum was placed at a higher level than the foreground of the arch. These platforms and staircases allowed for more impressive entrances and exits for lead singers and more realistic groupings for the chorus, which no longer would have to stand in one clump or a straight line.

Finally, we can appreciate to a certain extent how important color was to Urban's work through the *Vestale* drawings. When reproduced in black and white, the Forum scene looks like a Piranesi print, somewhat dark and brooding and certainly massive. In color, however, the same drawing becomes airy, spacious, and light. One can feel the intense Roman sun reflecting off the white marble structures.

The forum scene from Spontini's *La Vestale.* In black and white the drawing looks like a Piranesi print. This same design is printed later in color to show the importance of color in Urban's work. 1925. Columbia University.

Urban's society friends from New York and Palm Beach, among them Anthony Drexel Biddle, were familiar with his work for the *Follies*, but few of them had ever seen a production at the Met. When some expressed interest in experiencing firsthand what they had heard about from operagoing friends,

Overleaf. In this version of a street in Seville created for Rossini's *The Barber of Seville* in 1926, one can sense Urban's architectural training. The buildings as presented onstage appeared to be solid structures made of stone. Columbia University.

Urban carefully selected an event he thought would not be boring: the 1926 Metropolitan premiere of Puccini's *Turandot*. With the glamorous Maria Jeritza in the title role, the elaborate and colorful settings, and Puccini's lush music conducted by Tullio Serafin, *Turandot* was a perfect choice. The production was one of the most spectacular and colorful the Met audience had ever seen. Certainly the libretto allowed for such treatment, as Olin Downes realized when he wrote that it was not Urban's fault if the Riddle Scene looked like a "Chinese Aïda."[16] Lawrence Gilman describes the setting for this scene:

> The second scene of Act II provided one of Mr. Urban's most dazzling inventions—a black and white flame-hued curtain on which a vast peacock spread its tail surmounted by a many-armed idol. The peacock vanishes and we behold the Enigma scene framed in Mr. Urban's most sumptuous Ziegfeld manner, a golden staircase, the Emperor throned in splendor against a blue and orange background and around him banners and multi-colored lanterns and courtiers in yellow and peacock blue. In Turandot Urban has truly surpassed himself.[17]

Urban's friends, and presumably everyone else in the audience, were spellbound by Jeritza in the climactic scene. Her dress, designed by Gretl Urban, carried an elaborate train that she manipulated dramatically. At the top of the glittering staircase, the statuesque soprano began questioning Calaf, sung by Lauri-Volpi, and as she posed each riddle and received the correct answer she dramatically descended a few steps. Urban's friends were duly impressed by his artistry and his triumph, but none would ever become a devotee of the opera.

Otto Kahn tried to present fresh new works to the Met audience, but usually with little success. Since he traveled frequently and extensively throughout Europe, he was well informed about new works performed on the Continent. In March 1927, while in Leipzig, he attended an opera called *Jonny Spielt Auf* (loosely translated as "Jonny Strikes Up the Band") by the Czech composer Ernst Křenek. According to Kahn, the work was a great success, and additional productions were planned for Hamburg and Berlin. So impressed was he with *Jonny* that he sent a cable to Gatti urging a production at the Met. The opera was, in Kahn's words, "Very interesting and some beautiful music. Excellent libretto. Inexpensive to give. Advise serious consideration for next season. Sure to arouse much comment and believe popular success."[18]

The Met public, and the box holders in particular, seldom embraced new or unfamiliar works, staying home instead. Even such a "new" work as *Così Fan Tutte* was a box office disaster, as noted above by Ziegler. For the box holders, rejection of the newer operas Kahn presented was as much a personal slap at him as it was an expression of their displeasure at being deprived of another evening of *Bohème* or *Aïda*. Gatti was only too aware of how the public would react, despite Kahn's glowing account and assurance that it would be "inexpensive to give." He waited almost three weeks before replying to Kahn's initial telegram with a letter. "For want of space and time," the general manager wrote, *Jonny* could not be presented until the 1928–1929 season.[19]

The first performance of *Jonny Spielt Auf* at the Met was given on January 19, 1929, and it provided Urban with the opportunity to create a scenic extravaganza, including a scene on a glacier that Deems Taylor later named

The all-encompassing macanilla tree Urban created for the last scene of Meyerbeer's *L'Africaine* had an integral role in the plot. The heroine, Selika, inhaled its poisonous fragrance and died after watching her lover sail away. 1923. Columbia University.

as one of Urban's best settings, a fatal encounter with a rushing locomotive, and an Art Deco, flag-draped New York finale. During the summer of 1927 Urban had seen a production of *Jonny* in Hamburg. He found that the new German stage machinery and the theatre's desire to show what it could do actually distracted the audience; the spectators were more concerned with how the effects were achieved than with the opera itself. Urban felt that his own practice of simplifying the setting rather than complicating it with machinery to produce effects was the correct approach. Given the total lack of any modern stage equipment at the Met, Urban really had little choice.

The plot of this opera concerns the rise to fame of a black violinist. In Europe the title role was played by a black singer, but since the Met did not yet allow blacks to sing leading roles, Jonny was sung by a German, Michael Bohnen, in blackface. Křenek had introduced elements of jazz into the score, which at the time was quite daring, as were such scenes as a fight in a moving auto and a woman singing while pushing a vacuum cleaner across the stage.

Viewed as little more than a curiosity when it was first given in New York, *Jonny* has had a recent European production, and Křenek's music is being tentatively revived. What is of most appeal today, given the revival of interest in Art Deco, are Urban's sets for the last scenes. For the finale the station clock from the previous scene, the unfortunate encounter with the locomotive, is transformed into a huge globe. Jonny is perched on top playing his violin while the assembled cast dances around him, American flags are unfurled, and the New York skyline appears in the background. The period costumes were designed by Lillian Gaertner.

Sixty years later the absurdity of this opera and production is more apparent. Here was a Czech composer making use of the one native American

Opposite. Otto Kahn saw Křenek's *Jonny Spielt Auf* during his European summer vacation in 1927, and he urged the Met's general manager, Giulio Gatti-Casazza, to mount a production as soon as possible.
Top. The scene with the locomotive in Grand Central Station dissolves into the Art Deco finale, *bottom.* 1929. Columbia University.

musical idiom: jazz. By 1929 Scott Joplin had long been buried in a pauper's grave, but George Gershwin was in the Met audience when *Jonny* had its premiere. Then there was the matter of a white German singing the lead role in blackface, which was reminiscent of Al Jolson or Eddie Cantor. For his efforts Urban received from the critic of *Musical America* the most scathing review of his career:

> The Metropolitan Opera Co's. treatment of the second part of *Jonny Spielt Auf* revealed all the delicate charm of a palsied elephant galloping over a toy counter. Messrs. von Wymetal [stage director] and Joseph Urban and assistants constructed enough heavy props, backdrops of the vintage 1893, elaborate and unconvincing paraphernalia, including automobiles and locomotives, to absolutely ruin the mad crescendo which is designed to rush Jonny to a riotous and final triumph. A few souvenirs of the small time vaudeville houses ought to be called in on occasion like this which apparently finds the Old Guard helpless and panting before stage effects designed since 1900. We've seen railroad wrecks, earthquakes, horse races and fires staged in the town auditorium more convincingly than these clumsy scenes that laid such heavy hands on the accelerating career of Jonny.[20]

The irony is that Urban, who was chiefly responsible for doing away with the stage trappings "of the vintage 1893," was now being called "Old Guard" and accused of not assimilating "stage effects designed since 1900"—techniques that he himself had introduced. It is possible that Urban intentionally designed the *Jonny* production to recall earlier stage effects, or, given the demands of the libretto and the limitations of the Met's stage facilities, he may have felt he could achieve the effects no other way.

Critics of Urban's settings usually focused on two issues: that the sets looked too new and that they were too sumptuous (more suitable for the stage of the *Follies* than for the opera house). The first issue was easily rebutted, for the interiors of palaces, cathedrals, and their related decorations, as in *Romeo and Juliet*, were indeed new when the action in the opera took place five hundred or more years earlier.

TALES·OF·HOFFMANN· ·PROLOGUE AND EPILOGUE· ·METROPOL·OPERA·1924

TALES OF HOFFMANN· ·OLYMPIA· ·METROPOLITAN OPERA·1924

The cottage setting for the first act of Weinberger's *Schwanda the Bagpiper*, which centered around another of Urban's great trees. The angle of the cottage's roof is repeated in the stage opening that dissolves into the tree's upper branches and leaves. 1931.
Columbia University.
Preceding spread. With its arches, this drawing for the 1925 production of Wolf-Ferrari's *The Jewels of the Madonna* could almost be an exercise in perspective.
Columbia University.

As for the elaborateness of Urban's settings, there is no question that he was famous for this particular quality, but it appeared only when required by the libretto. When necessary, Urban could supply a starkly simple set that was in complete accord with the mood of the scene. No finer example than the prison scene in *Don Carlos* need be mentioned. The repeated arches underline the oppressive isolation of the prisoner and seem to be bearing down on him. These arches were later used by the architect in the New School's auditorium and reappeared, from other hands, in the auditorium of Radio City Music Hall.

During the early part of his tenure at the Met, Urban acted as the unofficial stage director and showed cast members how to use his settings more effectively: in particular the platforms, staircases, and solid "built" items that permitted the cast members to use trees, walls, and mantelpieces as props against which to rest or lean naturally. With the arrival of Wilhelm von Wymetal and Herbert Graf as stage directors, Urban found two colleagues who understood his methods and intentions and with whom he could collaborate easily.

Stage director Dr. Ernest Lert had worked with Toscanini at La Scala, and when he declared in 1929 that the three or four rehearsals he was allowed for a Met revival of *La Fanciulla del West* were inadequate, his criticism appeared in the press. Lert was also a problem for Urban, who was working on a production of *Luisa Miller* in the fall of 1929.

The first sign of trouble came when Gatti ordered a backdrop moved sixteen feet closer to the rear of the stage, which required the painting of two large side panels to mask the resulting empty spaces. This meant more work, time needlessly spent by Urban's already busy artists, and an additional expense of five hundred dollars for the Met. Urban offered Edward Ziegler a means of avoiding such problems:

> For the future it would be very advisable if for the first scenery and lighting rehearsals nobody would be in the auditorium who does not know anything about handling of scenery and it would be advisable that the director and his assistants see the scenes after they are completely lighted. The nervous and inexperienced handling of scenery to get certain effects before they ever see it correctly lighted causes these changes which mostly would not be necessary if the director would see the scenes in the completed right light.[21]

One of the principles of the new stagecraft was that scenery had to be viewed only with its proper lighting, and lighting for Urban was all-important.

Urban's Art Deco interpretation of the fires of Hell for the second act of *Schwanda.* 1931. Columbia University.

Gretl recalls with special fondness the time she spent with her father in the near-empty auditorium. Only the lighting crew, some stagehands, and possibly Otto Kahn sitting discreetly and quietly in the back of the dark hall were with them. It was magic to watch the scenes come to life and change before her eyes as her father coaxed the desired lighting effects from the equipment and the crew. So important did Urban consider these technical rehearsals that he never missed one of them, even if it meant traveling by train from his current architectural work in Palm Beach. When Urban achieved the desired effect, he would proclaim to the stage crew in his Viennese accent, "*Cheesus*, it's beautiful!" The stage crew, with great fondness, nicknamed the designer "Cheesus."

We have one brief account from someone who attended these rehearsals:

> Urban, as I watched his lighting rehearsals, would first of all call for a blue light on the scene. Then he would bring other colors into play until he had just the effect he desired. Always, as the curtain rose on the third act of *Aïda,* there would be spontaneous applause from the audience for the beautiful blue moonlight shimmering on the Nile, transforming the old drab setting [which had been built before his time] into a magic scene.[22]

Interference with Urban's work became even worse by the end of October. Dr. Lert refused the fifth model Urban prepared for the third act of *Luisa Miller,* even though Gatti had not seen it. According to the designer, the model was an "exact execution" of a pencil sketch Lert himself had made. Urban went on to list his major complaint against the stage director in a letter to Ziegler: ". . . Dr. Lert is not only changing the ideas for dramatic development but starts to change vases, details for balustrades, perspectives, trees, and things which have nothing to do with him and surely no one can expect me to be told how scenery is to be painted."[23]

The set as Lert wanted it had developed into "an architectonic impossibility and to a weight of construction without any sense to it." So disgusted was Urban with what he saw as a waste of time and money that he urged Ziegler to let someone else execute the scene and asked that his name be taken off the production. Accompanying the letter was a bill for the eight hundred dollars in additional costs the stage director's indecision had caused.

By February of 1930 Urban's displeasure had grown to such proportions that he wrote letters of resignation to Gatti and Ziegler. To Gatti he explained that he was "deeply interested in architecture and everything concerned with modern art. In the last years it has so developed that I find this new field gives me much more happiness and freedom to work unhampered."[24] Urban reminded Ziegler that he well knew of "all the disappointments I have had in the Opera House, and I feel that in spite of my many years association I have not gained the confidence of Gatti and have not reached any influence whatever in the institution."[25]

One has to ask here how much the unsuccessful attempt of Otto Kahn and Urban to build a new Metropolitan Opera House was involved in Urban's "irrevocable decision" to leave the Met. The greatest disappointment of his career in America, according to Gretl, was not being able to build a new Met. The controversy and unpleasantness Urban underwent while the project was being discussed will be taken up in a later chapter. One also suspects that Otto Kahn was instrumental in having Urban change his mind and stay with the company for what turned out to be the remaining three and a half years of his life.

Despite this momentary lapse, Urban's years at the Met were mainly very happy and satisfying. Since at one time in his youth he had seriously considered a singing career, he certainly knew and appreciated the music. The designer's memory has been kept alive by the opera company whenever one of his productions is mentioned in the opera's programs, and more than half a century after Urban's last production, the Met's gift shop sells greeting cards with his drawings of some settings reproduced in color. And several of Gretl's costume designs are similarly available. The Metropolitan Opera still profits from Urban's legacy, and his designs have proved less ephemeral than he could ever have imagined.

FILMS:
NEW YORK AND HOLLYWOOD

Newspaper publisher William Randolph Hearst first became involved in motion pictures through International Film Service, an arm of his International News Service, which for years had been filming newsreels of such notable events as the San Francisco earthquake, industrial riots, and presidential inaugurations. In 1915, irritated by the revolutionary activities of Pancho Villa that threatened his extensive land holdings in Mexico, Hearst began production on a different kind of film, a "patriotic" serial entitled *Patria* that linked two of his persistent bêtes noires. Filmed in Fort Lee, New Jersey, and starring Irene Castle, the plot dealt with a Mexican-Japanese conspiracy to overpower the United States. Ever concerned with the "Yellow Peril," Hearst cast Warner Oland as a sinister Japanese baron in the habit of striking his matches on top of a bust of George Washington—a character designed to send shudders of fear through an American audience. Indeed, Japanese Ambassador Hanrihara expressed such perturbation that President Wilson was moved to send a plaintive appeal to Hearst: "May I say to you that the character of the story disturbed me very much. It is extremely unfair to the Japanese and I fear that it is calculated to stir up a great deal of hostility which will be . . . extremely hurtful. I take the liberty, therefore, of asking whether the company would not be willing to withdraw it." [1]

Joseph Urban on one of his film sets for *When Knighthood Was in Flower*. 1922. Museum of Modern Art/Film Stills Archive.

Patria was not withdrawn, nor did Pancho Villa's irregulars retreat. Hearst's Babicora ranch in Chihuahua was looted of sixty thousand head of cattle and Hearst's manager found it expedient to flee to El Paso. Outraged, Hearst had his *New York Journal* demand: "Is it not time for the soldiers of the United States to do something PERMANENT? . . . The way to IMPRESS the Mexican is to REPRESS the Mexicans." [2] The irony of Hearst's saber-rattling at Mexico while offering the Kaiser an olive branch (even in the face of the *Lusitania* sinking) was not lost on his enemies. As a result of his pro-German, anti-British stance, Hearst became one of the most hated men in America. His hopes for political office, congressional or presidential, were ended.

Relations with his wife, Millicent, who had given Hearst five sons, including a set of twins, had become badly strained. He had met her in 1896 when she was dancing with a group known as "The Merry Maidens," and they were married in 1903. Abandoning the stage, she devoted her considerable energies to good works, benefit teas, the opera, and social and cultural events sponsored on a high level by people whom Hearst described as "asses and stuffed shirts." Though a model hostess and mother, she was somehow less appealing to her husband as Millicent Hearst than she had been as Millicent Willson of "The Merry Maidens."

Marion Cecilia Davies was born either in 1897 or 1900; Hearst was born in 1863. At the time of their first meeting, which took place around 1917, Marion was already a prominent Broadway chorine. She made her debut in 1914 in *Chin Chin* before realizing the dream of almost every girl on Broadway: a place in the *Ziegfeld Follies*. Her name is listed three times in the program of the 1916 edition, her first. In one scene, about Shakespeare's ladies, she played Juliet. Hearst first saw her in the *Follies*, and a relationship was begun that lasted until his death in 1951. The more than thirty-year difference in ages was no deterrent: Marion's predilection for older men was richly rewarded, and Hearst's passion for youth was similarly gratified.

If Hearst felt compelled to transform Marion into a great movie star, no one can blame him. She was radiantly beautiful, vital, charming, and, above all, talented. Unfortunately, he promoted her career with the same relentless hand that directed his empire, and her talents were frequently obscured by the ballyhoo attendant upon the release of her films.

In closing the memoirs she taped in 1951, Davies says:

> When W. R. was really interested in something, he would go in heart and soul. Not just a little bit, but all. He did the same with my pictures as he did with his newspapers.... He had signs all over New York City and pictures in the paper, and I was always meeting people. I thought it got to be a little too much, but W. R. didn't.... I said, "This is irritating to the general public. They read it and then go to see the picture, and then they think it isn't what they thought they were going to see." But I couldn't stop him.[3]

And she concludes somewhat ruefully: "W. R. thought he was building up a star. He saw me, in all his good faith, as an actress, or that I had the ability to be one. I hope, before he died, he found out I wasn't. Still, I think he thought I was."[4]

Marion may have had her doubts, but time has proven Hearst's evaluation of her talents to be correct; contemporary film commentators have come to regard her work highly. Orson Welles described her as "one of the most delightfully accomplished comediennes in the whole history of the screen. She would have been a star if Hearst had never happened."[5]

As the designer of many of Marion's costumes, Gretl Urban became her close friend:

> In everyday life she was not really pretty. Her hair was sometimes carelessly bleached; she was casual with her make-up, and her eyes had that faded blue of the true blonde. She liked frilly clothes and lacked the chic to get away with them.
>
> Indifferent as Marion's looks were offstage, onstage she photographed like a dream. Proper lighting and camera angles and gorgeous costumes, of course, helped, but her face was ideally photogenic.

Portrait of Marion Davies by Rolf Armstrong, on the cover of *Screenland* magazine, February 1924. John Gilman.

Urban achieved this dramatic lighting effect for *The Young Diana*, 1922. Unfortunately, even Marion Davies's biographer, Fred Guiles, had to note that the plot has now become "unavailable." Columbia University.

She was always self-conscious in doing love scenes, and many a director and even Father waxed emotional trying to get a little emotion out of her.

One thing she could do perfectly: she could weep beautifully, drops of real tears rolling down her eyes without spoiling her looks. All that was needed was some romantic music played by the studio violinist, and the tears started coming.

The first film Marion made under Hearst's aegis was the serial *Beatrice Fairfax*, released in 1918. The following year Hearst truly committed himself to Marion's film career when he bought Sulzer's River Park Casino, a massive red-brick structure occupying the entire block on Second Avenue between 126th and 127th streets in New York City. He transformed it into one of the finest motion picture studios of the day. Money was no object; Hearst bought the best equipment and hired the most talented people. To provide the settings for the spectacles he intended to produce, he engaged Joseph Urban under an exclusive contract.

Urban had reservations when first approached about working in motion pictures. Film really was still a new medium and art form; his specialty had always been color, and films were black-and-white. The salary Hearst offered was in the end the deciding factor: that money would eventually enable Urban to open his own architectural studio and return to his first love. In the meanwhile, much of his film work would entail efforts such as reconstructing façades of Parisian streets or the Tower of London for Hearst's historical epics, and that at least was a form of architecture.

Accordingly, Urban signed a contract on February 19, 1920, that gave International Film Service Co., Inc., his exclusive design services at a weekly salary of $1,2442.31. The exception to exclusivity specified in the contract was Urban's right to continue doing productions for the Metropolitan Opera.[6] Urban loved the opera and did not want to give up working in color. In practice, the designer was also allowed to continue working for the *Follies*, probably because that was one of the few types of entertainment the usually dour and reserved Hearst genuinely enjoyed.

Gretl became her father's assistant at the studio and remembers the first time Urban appeared there:

The directors and cameramen received Father warily. Here was this new Hearst favorite, who was famous for theatre design and color, but with no experience in black-and-white film technique. Father greeted them all in his usual warm, gay style and told them he had to get to work right away. Then Father sent word to Marion to let him know when she could receive him. We went to her dressing room. Marion, who was very shy, stammered a little when she told Father how much she admired him and how sure she was that with his help she could become a really good actress. Father put his arms around her and promised he would create beauty and lovely light and be at her disposal whenever she wished. She was delighted with the costumes and settings that Father had sketched, grateful as a child. Marion always remained a little in awe of Father, and she soon started making me the messenger when she wanted to question him. We were the same age. I became her friend and often confidante. She was really very much alone and isolated from most of her co-workers.

Hearst arrived in Father's office the evening of that first day and welcomed Father with as much friendly warmth as his personality permitted. He had Luther Reed, Robert Z. Leonard, the director, and others with him, and told them all that now Joseph Urban would be in complete artistic charge of all productions.

Hearst proved sometimes a difficult man to work with, but Father was constantly amazed that with a little diplomacy and a dash of flattery one could get him to do almost anything. Hearst had practically no sense of humor and was always very dignified, with his somber clothes and white piping on his waistcoat. Father felt rather sorry for Hearst, that in spite of his immense fortune he did not seem to know how to enjoy life, except maybe when he was on horseback.

Stern of the pirate ship Urban designed for *Buried Treasure*. 1921. Columbia University.

There was, nevertheless, at least one major confrontation between Urban and Hearst, which occurred early in the designer's tenure at the studio. One of Hearst's passions was antique furniture, or what was passed off to him as

being antique furniture. Many of his purchases found their way to the studio, where Hearst ordered them to be used in film sets. One particular selection irked the designer because it did not remotely belong to the historical period of the film. A stickler for historical accuracy, Urban refused to permit the piece on the set.

Hearst exploded. Urban started yelling. Marion fled to the safety of her dressing room, and Gretl hid behind the room's half-opened door. The rest of the cast and crew did a vanishing act. Soon there was laughter and a cheery "good night." Urban had reminded Hearst that he was hired to oversee the artistic perfection of the film and could not tolerate such a conglomeration of furniture. Hearst capitulated.

In the Urban archives is a two-page, undated manuscript entitled "Real Screen Drama Greatest Need, Declares Joseph Urban." [7] There is no evidence it was ever published, but if it had been it would hardly have endeared this film novice to those with more experience in the medium. Notably idealistic and critical, the piece does present Urban's views of the current development in films:

> To the public—and especially the American public—must be attributed more cleverness and good taste than many men in the motion picture industry are inclined to grant it. That touches the sore point of the screen— that the public is not sufficiently the judge of the quality of our pictures; that before the picture is exhibited, others decide for the public whether or not that public will approve.
>
> There is little hope for the future of pictures unless there is greater intelligence displayed by some of those who concern themselves with the industry.
>
> So far, we have borrowed more or less from the stage and have largely overlooked that we lacked spoken words, space, and color. . . .
>
> Art has always been aristocratic and exclusive. Each art hitherto developed secretly behind closed doors and with only a few people to watch and be satisfied. But this new art of the motion picture must not be the interest of the few; it must talk the language and express the feelings of millions. . . .
>
> Before we can really advance there must be a vast improvement in the writing of stories for the screen. That is the weakest point of all. The crux of the situation is that the screen needs a screen drama and has none. [8]

The first thing Urban did at the studio after his initial period as observer was to completely redesign the lighting system. If he could not actually use color, he was confident that "with proper backgrounds, furniture that belongs to those backgrounds and decorations that suggest color, the mind of the spectator can be made to think in colors even when they are not shown." [9] When the cameramen and directors saw the results, they offered their enthusiastic cooperation. Urban, however, found film-making tedious. A man of immense energy, he had no patience for the long waits between shots. Since smoking on the set was not allowed, he stayed in his office and appeared on the set only when called.

Hearst, however, often watched from an upper balcony where the wardrobe was located. He remained in the shadows while the filming was done, but everyone knew he was there. Though he rarely made comments during the actual shooting, he could be merciless in his comments and criticism of actors and directors when he watched the rushes. Often Marion was reduced to tears.

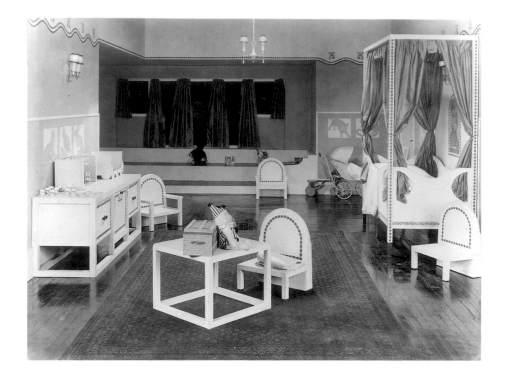

Before his initial contract expired, Urban designed three films, *The Restless Sex* (1920), *Buried Treasure* (1921), and *Enchantment* (1921). Although none of these films was successful at the box office, Urban was informed by George van Cleve, vice president and general manager of Cosmopolitan Productions (and coincidentally Marion's brother-in-law), that Hearst was exercising his option to renew the contract for three more years.

One of the ways Hearst expressed his friendship to Urban was to invite Gretl, Mary, and the designer aboard his yacht for weekend cruises. The 225-foot *Oneida* was sumptuously furnished and suitably palatial, reflecting the fortune its owner had poured into it. Almost every summer weekend the Urbans, Marion, director Bill LeBaron, and scriptwriter Luther Reed, along with the director of the film currently being shot, were invited on board to view the latest rushes of the studio's efforts.

Urban rather begrudged these enforced weekends at sea because of the time they took away from his other work. He did, however, like to swim. Sensing Urban's restiveness and wishing to please, Hearst had the captain rig up a huge net with enormous beams that could be lowered into the ocean. A pool was thereby provided so that Urban could safely swim even in the middle of the ocean. Gretl remembers that "Hearst presented it to Buschi as a special surprise and was childishly pleased when Father dived into it with a joyous shout."

For Gretl, the yachting weekends were an unalloyed delight. A launch would pick up the party after work at the studio on Fridays, and since life on board was casual, an overnight bag sufficed until return late Sunday. On one Friday evening in the fall of 1921, with Long Island Sound smooth as glass, Hearst suggested they put out to sea. It was much cooler on the open Atlantic, and all day Saturday the company, rested and refreshed by a leisurely swim, lolled on deck. But on Sunday Urban remarked to Gretl and Marion: "We're way out in the ocean and I think we are headed in the wrong direction." At cocktails Urban repeated his observation, to which Hearst gave one of his rare toothy grins and said: "Surprise, surprise! The weather's ideal for a nice sea voyage. I have decided we're all going to Mexico." Gretl continues the account of this unexpected expedition:

> We were speechless, but Father finally choked out, "I've got better things to do than to go joy-riding in the clothes I'm wearing and only an extra pair of BVD's." Hearst calmed him down, promising to stop somewhere and get everything he might need, and to further mollify Father, told the head steward to go to Urban for orders.
>
> Consequently there was champagne at dinner and liqueurs after and all the best food the chef could provide. Every morning the boat was stopped so we could swim, and Luther and Bill sang "Anchors Aweigh" while the crew struggled with the monstrous net. The wireless hummed, and Hearst spent hours buried in mountains of papers. Considering the unusual amount of food aboard, Buschi was convinced the old fox had planned this trip all along. The stewards washed our spare robes overnight, and Hearst had them hand out a lot of bathrobes that were much too large for Marion and me.
>
> Father began to grumble again, and Hearst told the captain to dock at New Orleans for a shopping trip. The harbor was not deep enough, so we had to come in by motorboat. The city was steaming hot, and while Luther and Bill found what they needed, Father could find nothing big enough except two pairs of pajamas. Hearst had given Marion money, so she and I bought some nice underwear, but the two dresses we bought lacked any kind of style.
>
> We were all dripping with perspiration, and Hearst, who was as bad as Father about wearing a jacket, looked grim as we rushed back to the speedboat. Disaster! In the middle of the harbor the boat broke down, and the only flashlight aboard soon conked out. There we were, practically invisible in the river, with mosquitoes eating us alive. Hearst was in a white fury, and the poor sailors were scared to death. The siren with which they tried to send an SOS to the yacht was so weak that Buschi claimed it sounded like the bleat of a small sheep. It seemed forever before the captain

finally decided to send out another boat. With the disabled craft in tow we finally made it to the *Oneida*, where we all disappeared into showers.

Refreshed and on deck with drinks, Father observed the incredible enchantment of the river limned by far-off spectral trees milky white under the full moon. "We must remember it for a future setting for some mysterious fairy tale." And during supper Father said to Hearst: "You know I was furious, because if there are two things I hate they are inefficiency and discomfort, but the beauty of the Mississippi tonight has made up for all of it." The scene was never realized on film, but Father got some of it into the setting on the Ziegfeld stage for the love scene in *Show Boat.*

The *Oneida* ran into heavy weather in the Gulf, but when they docked at Veracruz a private train that Hearst had ordered by wireless awaited. Old-fashioned but elegant, it consisted of a lounge car with a drawing room for Hearst and Marion, a dining car, and sleeping cars with showers at either end. Hearst announced that they were going to Guadalajara to visit the cathedral, then south to Colima to inspect certain properties, and thence to Mexico City where a meeting with President Alvara Obregón was projected. Gretl continues her narrative:

The trip through Mexico was gorgeous and unforgettable. "Imagine," Buschi would say, "traveling on your own train and being able to stop wherever you find something of interest." There were vast stretches of desert on which you could see a lone man, or a donkey with a laden-down woman traipsing along behind. . . . Town followed town and windowless adobe huts with dozens of children staring at us from the open doors. After the desert came scenery reminiscent of Switzerland with forests and waterfalls. And there were whistle-stops with bands playing and Hearst buying more spicy Mexican food from withered old women, and a couple of times he triumphantly bought some fresh strawberries. And so to Colima: primitive, lush, enchanting. It had a small park, and it was the custom of an evening for men to circle its small fountain in one direction and the eligible girls in the other. If a man liked the looks of a girl, he would slap her derrière with his cane; she would walk over to him, and they would go away together. Buschi, of course, had to get into the act. He had bought a cane and tapped one of the girls on the rear. He almost got into a fight, but someone explained to the young men that we were foreigners and did not know any better. While this was going on, someone slapped my rear end, and we got out of there fast. Bill said to Father, "That was a damned fool thing to do!" Luckily Hearst did not see his famous studio director acting like a juvenile. Buschi was contrite but explained he wanted to find out if it would work. "Not for you it didn't," I told him, and we returned to the safety of our train and a cooling drink.

Hearst did not permit Marion off the train for fear of gossip even when we went to stretch our legs in some godforsaken tiny hamlet. In those days Marion was kept under wraps, albeit rather elaborate ones. In New York she and her mother, Rose, and sisters were domiciled in a sumptuously decorated Riverside Drive townhouse, while her father, Bernard J. Douras, who found Rose incompatible, lived in an adjacent brownstone. Hearst himself maintained a hideaway in the Beaux Arts Hotel in the East Forties. It was a rather depressing place, cluttered with Victorian furniture and dark red velvet. When, on occasion, we watched the rushes there, Marion would come with us, to be whisked up in the private elevator, all very dignified and hush-hush. Hearst always arrived later. While we were watching the

Director Bill LeBaron, Joseph Urban, and Marion Davies on trip to Mexico with William Randolph Hearst. 1921. Gretl Urban collection.

152

screenings, projected by Joseph Willicombe, Hearst's superdiscreet secretary, Marion and Hearst sat together, but we never observed the least sign of intimacy between them. Marion always addressed him as W. R.

Marion got a fabulous salary but derived little pleasure from it. Hearst invested most of her money for her in real estate in the Fifties around Park Avenue, which was good planning for the future, but Marion could have used a bit more of it in the present. Nor did he shower her with gifts. She had a magnificent marquis-cut diamond and a perfectly matched string of pearls, but most of the gifts that Hearst used to bring her in triumph Father called junk. He made her buy her own clothes, telling her she must learn to save money. Father was outraged by this, being extravagant himself and knowing the reckless way Hearst squandered money, especially on fake antiques.

Urban's stay in Mexico City was punctuated by Montezuma's revenge, an annoyance other members of the party were spared. Marion was unveiled briefly for the audience with newly elected President Obregón, who from then on was lauded in the Hearst press. Upon his return Hearst stated that his "properties were in continual trouble and turmoil during the several preceding administrations, but have been in complete peace and security during the administration of Pres. Obregon." [10]

When Knighthood Was in Flower, released in September 1922, was Marion's first big motion picture success. The film itself won praise as one of the finest spectacles ever produced, but Marion's performance as Mary Tudor was hailed by the critic of the *New York Review* as a new breakthrough in her career:

> Miss Davies's persistence in pursuit of her ambition has at last borne genuine fruit—she does not rely mainly on her beauty in this picture but really acts. She agreeably astonished her first night audience with a carefully wrought and easily expressed characterization. It looks as if Miss Davies will have to be reckoned with for herself alone hereafter. [11]

The film was a vast undertaking for Urban. To meet the demands of the script, he reproduced two blocks of a street in old Paris, a Gothic cathedral, part of London's Billingsgate district, and the Tower of London. The set for the Paris scenes was at the time the largest indoor set ever built, consisting of thirty-two complete buildings, or at least their façades. All of the shooting was done indoors, using the facilities of three studios: Cosmopolitan's own, the Jackson Studio in the Bronx, and Famous Players on Long Island.

Urban's innovative use of artificial light allowed the film to be finished more quickly than otherwise possible, since there were no delays due to weather conditions. Nevertheless, the film still took 160 days to make. With its three thousand extras, it cost $1,500,000 to produce. [12] Urban was praised for his historical accuracy, the architectural solidity of the sets, and the contribution his work made to the story. The *New York Times* reviewer wrote:

> . . . though you may have your doubts about the historicity of the story, you are bound to be impressed with the authenticity of the settings. Surely Joseph Urban, who is responsible for them, has been true as well as magnificent. His scenes are splendid or simple, according to the character they should have, and, while they often impress the eye by their size and finished composition, they never seem present merely to be impressive. They are part of the story and they are ultimately successful in enriching it. [13]

When Knighthood Was in Flower, 1922, was Davies's first real hit. She played Mary Tudor, Henry VIII's younger sister.

Top. A play of light and shadow on one section of a street scene for *Knighthood*. 1922.
Columbia University.

Center. An unusual photo that shows Urban on one of the sets of *Knighthood* with the cast. 1922.
Museum of Modern Art.

Bottom. Dressed as a boy to escape from England, Davies, as Mary Tudor, acknowledges a pledge of loyalty from her supporters. 1922.
Columbia University.

In addition to designing the film, Hearst also commissioned Urban to redecorate the Criterion Theatre in New York for the film's premiere. The lobby was fittingly redone in Tudor style, and twelve new loges patterned after the royal boxes in the film's tournament scene were installed in the auditorium. In those early days of film, the screen was not yet commonly covered by a simple traveler curtain. Instead, actual stage settings were prepared for the area in front of the screen, which was concealed at the rear of the set. Urban also designed such a setting for *When Knighthood Was in Flower*.

One of the film's unforeseen results was the start of Louella Q. Parsons's rise to fame and influence as a Hollywood gossip columnist. At the time of *Knighthood*'s opening, she was a columnist for the *Morning Telegraph* in New York. Not finding anything about Marion's performance to criticize, she wrote an editorial blasting Hearst: "Why don't you give Marion Davies a chance? She is a good actress, a beauty and a comedy starring bet. Why talk about how much was spent on the lovely costumes and the production cost?" [14]

Hearst later met Louella and told her that he had read her editorial: "... it was good. You should write more things like that." [15] And he saw to it that Louella did, for shortly afterward she was given a contract to work for Hearst at $250 a week.

Louella tried to interview Urban on many occasions, but unfortunately for posterity he proved elusive. Gretl recalls Louella as "a rather odd lady. She wore the strangest out-of-date clothes, loaded with pins and chains. She affected a motherly air, beaming with sweetness. Aware that Father was one of Hearst's favorites, she did her best to endear herself. Her approach was one of simpering admiration. When she loomed in his vicinity, Father would mutter, 'Keep that woman away from me, or I'll be rude as hell to her.' "

The next great success for Marion and Urban came with *Little Old New York*, which opened on August 1, 1923. For this gala event Urban redecorated the Cosmopolitan Theatre on Columbus Circle, the rechristened Park Theatre where Urban's first New York production, *The Garden of Paradise*, had played. This Herculean endeavor was barely completed in time for the screening. To brighten the auditorium, Urban had ordered gold slipcovers for the orchestra seats. They were late in arriving, so Gretl, with all the help she could muster, was frantically putting them on the seats. Victor Herbert, leading the orchestra through a rehearsal of his score for the silent film, even dismissed the musicians so that they could aid Gretl.

A more life-threatening problem, however, was the hanging of an enormous five-tiered chandelier. While displaying the apparent delicacy of a spiderweb, it was, nevertheless, extremely heavy. The crew had great difficulty securing it to the ceiling, and they continued at their labors even while the fashionably dressed audience was assembling in the lobby. Finally it was adjudged safely attached, or at least safely enough for the audience to be allowed to enter. Marion revealed in her memoirs the thoughts that ran through her mind during the course of the evening: "I didn't look at the picture, because I was looking at that chandelier all the time. It was an enormous thing, and all the audience down below would've been killed if it had fallen." [16] After the film, Marion took a few quick bows and hurried out of the theatre, hoping the audience would follow her to safety.

Arts and Decoration hailed the theatre as Urban's first architectural work in America and described Urban's stage setting:

Top. The chandelier Urban installed in 1923 at Hearst's Cosmopolitan Theatre, his first architectural work in New York. Formerly the Park Theatre, it was where Urban's first Broadway production, *The Garden of Paradise*, was presented in 1914.
Center. View from the stage to the balcony. 1923. Columbia University.
Bottom. The stage with the movie screen hidden behind sliding panels. 1923. Columbia University.

The stage is lighted solely by crystal chandeliers without the addition of colored illumination or any obvious stage "effects." A small fountain occupies the center of the stage, and the flowers, small pale roses—natural ones—contribute neutral color. It was the intention of Mr. Urban in undertaking this, his first architectural work in America, to create a concert setting rather than anything approaching a conventional movie stage.[17]

The *New York Times* critic praised the film: "For costumes and settings and photography, 'Little Old New York' is one of the most exquisite productions ever thrown on a screen." [18] In this film Marion's real gift for comedy was revealed. Instead of extravagant costumes, she wore boys' clothes with a straight pageboy hairdo. *Little Old New York*, a delightful romantic comedy, was expertly directed by Sidney Olcott with none of the ingratiating coyness typical of so many films of that day.

Hearst missed the premiere, being "stuck," as he said, out in San Simeon, where he was in daily conference with his architect, Julia Morgan. He was also anxiously awaiting a check for one million dollars from his inheritance, upon which Pheobe Hearst, his mother, had wisely imposed restrictions (Hearst was chronically in financial difficulties). Hearst forwarded to Marion a wire he received from Zicgfcld:

MY DEAR HEARST

I HAD THE GREAT PLEASURE OF WITNESSING THE OPENING OF THE COSMOPOLITAN THEATRE WIIICII YOU HAVE MADE ONE OF THE FINEST THEATRES IN NEW YORK. JOSEPH URBAN HAS DONE HIS FINEST WORK IS THE UNANIMOUS OPINION OF LAST NIGHTS AUDIENCE. THE PICTURE LITTLE OLD NEW YORK WAS EXCELLENT AND MARION DAVIES PERFORMANCE WAS PERFECTION. MY WIFE WAS ENTHRALLED WITH MISS DAVIES WORK ON THE SCREEN. AS MARION SAYS I AM A HARD BOILED EGG I CAN FRANKLY SAY THAT YOU ARE TO BE CONGRATULATED ON THE UNQUALIFIED HIT OF EVERYTHING IN CONNECTION WITH LAST NIGHTS OPENING. I WAS PROUD OF THE FACT THAT I WAS RESPONSIBLE FOR BRINGING JOSEPH URBAN TO NEW YORK AND THAT MISS DAVIES WAS ONCE A MEMBER OF MY COMPANY.

REGARDS AND CONGRATULATIONS. TOO BAD YOU WERE NOT HERE.[19]

On the bottom of the telegram Hearst wrote: "He thinks he will claim some credit now. I told you that when you once succeed everybody begins to tell how they found you. W. R."

One of the reasons for Hearst's current financial distress was a disastrous fire that occurred at Cosmopolitan Studios during the filming of *Little Old New York*, destroying Urban's elaborate reconstruction of an early-nineteenth-century New York street scene, Fulton's steamboat, and most of the costumes for the production. Urban's personal library was also destroyed. Gretl recalls the devastation, the burned-out stages, and Hearst's antiques and paintings all damaged beyond repair:

We all stood around sort of dumbfounded. Marion's dressing room and most of our offices had not been touched by the fire, but the water damage was frightful. Father and Sidney Olcott took command and we all pitched in—directors, seamstresses, stagehands, actors—to save and dry what we could. Fortunately Father's designs were undamaged. When Hearst arrived with a group of reporters and photographers, he looked ravaged and old. We could not help feeling sorry for him. Many naturally were worried about what their future might be.

The filming of *Little Old New York* was completed in Fort Lee, New Jersey, and two more films were shot in New York. *Janice Meredith* was released in August 1924 and was another spectacle. It covered American history from the Boston Tea Party to the end of the Revolution. Along the way, the plot gave Urban the opportunity to recreate the Hall of Mirrors at Versailles for the scene where Ben Franklin is received by Louis XVI and Marie Antoinette. Another major scene was of Washington's crossing of the Delaware.

Yolanda, a romantic drama set in the France of Louis XI, was released in November 1924 and was also a spectacle. Victor Herbert wrote an overture for the film, one of the last things he completed before his death. Gretl designed the costumes, and she told a newspaper interviewer, "Of all the many costumes I have designed, I think I like these the best." [20] Marion, who played Mary of Burgundy, supposedly contributed hours of research, as reported in the *Newark Star Eagle*, to make sure costumes and settings were accurate:

> Before beginning actual work on the picture, the Cosmopolitan Star herself studied diligently the history of that time. For weeks she plumbed the character of Princess Mary. She buried herself in the study of old prints in the library and in the Metropolitan Museum in order that the costumes that she wears in the photoplay might be absolutely authentic. Before starting work on the picture Miss Davies made a trip to Europe where she continued her research. All this was in the nature of checking up on the research department.[21]

Lobby card for *Yolanda*, starring Marion Davies, one of the last films Urban designed in New York. 1924. Ira Resnick

Hearst took Bill LeBaron, Luther Reed, and the Urbans with him when the film operations were moved to Los Angeles. The rest of his staff was fired. As a result of a deal Hearst had struck with Louis B. Mayer, the new M-G-M studio would finance Marion's pictures and pay her a $10,000-a-week salary. In return, Mayer hoped to benefit from favorable publicity in Hearst's papers.

Mary Urban, though somewhat patronizing, was secretly delighted about being in Hollywood. Gretl was enthusiastic:

> I got a big thrill out of meeting Douglas Fairbanks and Mary Pickford, the Talmadge Sisters, John Gilbert, and all the motion picture moguls. Buschi remained unimpressed when I told him he wasn't giving Hollywood a chance. He agreed with me but assured me he had made up his mind to dislike it, and the less said about it the better.
>
> "Those people aren't real. They're acting all the time—even to themselves for each other," he said. He did get to like Charlie Chaplin very much and was impressed by the man's versatility and comedic genius. He cast a roving eye on Gloria Swanson and Florence Vidor, but unfortunately they were both otherwise occupied and only paid him tribute as a famous artist, not a figure of romance.

Hearst spent much of his time at San Simeon, but his visits to Hollywood were frequent. Gretl recalls:

> Hearst and Marion loved amusement parks, especially one called Venice to which Hearst took us several times. On one memorable occasion Elinor Glyn, Lady Duff Gordon's sister, came along. Elinor was known as "The Lady of the Tiger Skin" because of a famous portrait of herself stretched out on one that appeared on dust jackets of her books. They included such titles as *It* and *Three Weeks*. Her novels, quite daring for the day were avidly read, but Father called them kitsch.

Elinor was anxious for Hearst to film her stories (Hearst considered them too daring for Marion), so she did her damnedest to charm him. She was no longer young, but Buschi said she was a woman never to have beguiled any man at any age. At the instigation of Marion and Alma Rubens, and to please Hearst, Elinor consented to enter the fun house. She couldn't have known what she was in for. Luther came rushing to Father with the news that The Glyn was in the fun house and we must come and watch her exit down the chute. What a sight she was when she arrived, landing all askew, her hitched-up skirt revealing old-fashioned bloomers and her regal red wig over one ear! I'm afraid we laughed uproariously, but Father's Austrian courtesy got the better of him; he offered his arm and escorted her to one of the cars. We all followed rather sheepishly, all except Hearst, who went shooting clay pigeons, which he was very good at.

On the West Coast our yachting weekends continued as before, but we never stayed at sea more than a few days. If we had, Buschi told one and all, he would have swum ashore. On one weekend cruise to Catalina with Bill, Luther, Mary, Marion, Anita Stewart, and Charlie Chaplin aboard, we had to have a costume party. So we were to find what outfits we could in Catalina for the party the next night. Everyone except Marion was utterly bored at the idea. Marion and Anita bought themselves some little-girl dresses in which even Father had to admit they looked very cute. Charlie Chaplin put on one of my dresses, and I put on one of his suits. Bill LeBaron wore a dark robe and said he was a monk. Luther Reed borrowed a rather fancy negligee of Mary's, while Father and Mary just wrapped themselves in blankets and said they were Indians.

Hearst, not in costume, had the boat decorated with Japanese lanterns, and, crackpot idea or not, we all had a good time as we sailed along. Unexpectedly, Charlie Chaplin suddenly stood up in the prow of the lounge where we were sitting and started reciting "To be, or not to be. . . ." He had us all spellbound, his handsome head silhouetted against the evening sky. It was an extraordinary, deeply moving experience, everybody forgetting that he was wearing a dress. We all applauded, much impressed, and Buschi

said that if it were not for his lack of height, he would have made a great dramatic actor. Charlie told Father he would always dream of doing Hamlet one day, but that he would never attempt it. Pathetic comedy was his real talent and would remain his life's work.

That was the night I caught him making love to Marion in my cabin. To ease the embarrassment I laughed and told Marion I was glad she was having a little playacting fun. I never saw them near each other again, but from what Marion told me, they did have a frustrating, even frightening affair. During one of our visits to San Simeon, when, as usual, Marion was left behind, she planned to spend a weekend with Charlie in some hideaway. Hearst found out about it even though he was with us in San Simeon. The unobtrusive Mr. Willicombe followed their tracks, and Marion was brought back to the fold without fuss or scandal. According to her, the incident was never mentioned by Hearst.

It was Hearst's almost paranoid preoccupation with avoiding scandal that motivated him to deny the presence of Thomas Ince as a member of a yachting party on board the *Oneida* in November 1924. Thomas H. Ince was a very successful independent producer in Hollywood with such major films to his credit as *Civilization* and *Anna Christie.* Hearst was interested in forming an alliance with him for future Davies productions. The party included, besides the Urbans, Marion, the actress Seena Owen, ballet-master Theodore Kosloff, Elinor Glyn, Joseph Willicombe, Marion's sister, and the medical doctor and Hearst executive Dr. Daniel Carson Goodman. Gretl recalls the fateful night:

> The mood on the yacht was pleasant and relaxed. The food and drink were the best, as they always were when Father was on board. The sea was smooth and the night balmy. We sat on deck until about midnight, then all went to bed. Mary and Father occupied one of the large staterooms aft. During the night Mary heard groans from the adjoining cabin, and while Father went to Ince's room Mary woke Dr. Goodman. Ince was in great pain and vomiting profusely. I don't know whether Dr. Goodman was much of a doctor, but he diagnosed it as a severe heart attack.
>
> We headed immediately for San Diego. When the anchor was dropped, we all stood around as a launch was lowered. In front of us, Hearst warned Dr. Goodman not to let anyone ashore know that his patient had come from the *Oneida.*

Ince died at his Hollywood home the next day. His death must be placed against the background of Prohibition and the scandals that rocked the film capital in the 1920s. The death of a young actress at a wild party attended by Fatty Arbuckle ruined his career. The murder of William Desmond and the death of Mabel Normand only added to the public's perception of Hollywood as a modern-day Sodom and Gomorrah. To counteract this image, the Hays office was established to maintain at least the semblance of morality both on and off the screen.

Gretl attributes Hearst's almost paranoic aversion to scandal to his intention of keeping the full extent of his relationship with Marion from the public. After Ince was taken from the yacht, Hearst did his best to avoid any connection with Ince's death. First reports in the press stated that Ince was suddenly stricken while on a train to San Diego.[22] Unfortunately for Hearst, however, Ince had told a doctor and a nurse that his distress resulted from liquor consumed on the *Oneida.*

161

When this information was revealed, Hollywood gossip ranged from stories of a wild party on the yacht to Hearst's shooting Ince because of the producer's romantic overtures to Marion. Despite a statement from the San Diego district attorney that he was satisfied Ince died from "heart failure as a result of an attack of acute indigestion" [23] (Ince did have ulcers), W. A. Swanberg noted that rumors about Ince's death were still circulating when he began work on Hearst's biography, which was published in 1961.[24]

It is hardly surprising that *Zander the Great*, Marion's first Hollywood picture (and Urban's last for Hearst), was not one of her triumphs. The Ince incident, which occurred in the midst of filming, was disturbing enough, but the round of parties in the new ballroom of her palatial beach "cottage" proved even more distracting. Marion remembered, "It was gay. I didn't mind it so much, but I thought, 'Oh, Lord! I've gotta join the party, and if I do, I won't be on the set in the morning.' " [25] Indeed, she did not always make it. In *Zander* Marion was cast as an orphan with pigtails and freckles who flees the cruel authorities with another orphan, a boy of ten, to encounter alarming adventures on the road and at the hands of bandits near the Mexican border. Marion, who was pushing at least twenty-four and perhaps twenty-seven, shows distinct evidence of maturity, and the story, which teeters perilously between comedy and outrageous melodrama, was not helped by Hearst's constant interference. When he was at San Simeon, daily rushes were sent to him by special messenger, resulting in explosive telegrams, sometimes ten or twelve pages long, outlining his latest revelations. They were likely to call for big effects such as a huge sandstorm with stampeding cattle and things blowing away, or little touches like filming Marion in a Mary Pickford–type wig, her eyes saucer-wide as she anticipates new perils.

For the film Urban created a rather operatic hacienda, said to have been borrowed from one of the most famous estates in Mexico. A newspaper describes the architect's creation:

> Of solid concrete, stained a dull yellowish pink, the house was scaled to the usual dimensions of a domicile of eight rooms, consisting of three wings, an upper and lower verandah and a wide patio, Spanish doors and barred windows, arches, pillars and courtyard, all having the charm of early Moorish architecture, while desert vegetation transplanted from the actual desert sixty miles from Los Angeles, gave the place the desired effect of a ranch house far removed from city life.
>
> So unusual was the design of this house, and so delightful its conception, three Los Angeles architects copied it for use in building Western residences, which are more and more adopting the Spanish style of architecture.[26]

Unfortunately, one is not able to appreciate Urban's efforts in regard to the hacienda, since the film does not provide any clear view of the structure. Mrs. Dennis Camp, wife of a Texas millionaire, must have seen the actual set because she commissioned Urban to recreate it for her as a real house in Dallas. Although the plans were completed, specially designed carpet ordered, and arrangements made to import adobe workers from Mexico, the house was never built.

For a man who thrived on great activity and needed an outlet for his enormous creativity, Urban had little to do in Hollywood. Hearst's film activities had been greatly curtailed, and Urban begged to be released from the short time remaining on his contract. Hearst refused, hoping he could entice the architect to stay in California by offering the opportunity to build

Opposite. Marion Davies played brides from two different eras in *The Bride's Play.* 1922.
Top. A set for the contemporary segment of *Bride's Play.* 1922. Columbia University.
Bottom. Davies in the section of *Bride's Play* that was set in ancient Ireland. 1922. Columbia University.

something on the grounds of San Simeon and an office tower in San Francisco.
Urban proved to be as unyielding as Hearst.

Hearst's great preoccupation in California was San Simeon, his baronial
home perched above the Pacific Ocean. It is one of the great houses in
America, along with Biltmore in Asheville, North Carolina, and Mar-a-Lago
in Palm Beach, and the Urbans were fortunate to have visited the mountaintop
several times. Gretl describes their first visit:

> The scenery on the way to San Luis Obispo was beautiful and varied,
> and even Buschi enjoyed the trip with his usual enthusiasm, until we hit
> the incredibly bumpy road that climbed higher and higher to Hearst's Santa
> Lucia mountain domain. There was not yet a smoothly paved road. We were
> jostled from side to side, and sometimes the road looked downright
> dangerous.
>
> As we neared the top, Buschi groaned, "Cheesus, what's this monstros-
> ity!" He was referring to Hearst's pride and joy, the main building, which
> Father said reminded him of a constipated cathedral. However, as we got
> into the garden and saw the incredible, majestic view, we all got out of our
> car, enthralled by the primeval splendor of the mountains and the Pacific
> Ocean. Buschi said he could forgive Hearst his monstrosity for having given
> him this moment of complete and unexpected rapture. While we went
> walking or horseback riding, he would sit on the terrace hour by hour in
> what he called "prayerful contemplation," finding inspiration in every
> magnificent change of light.
>
> Hearst was not unaware of Father's disenchantment with Hollywood;
> on each visit he hoped that the beauty of San Simeon would induce him to
> stay. He showed Father where he wanted to build a swimming pool, perhaps
> in the Roman manner with columns and statuary, and a temple to art, or
> whatever else might be suitable to the setting. Father would have liked

nothing better than to blend architectural beauty with the beauty of nature, but he was firm in refusing to renew his contract and sign an exclusive agreement. For all of this and a new office building in San Francisco that Hearst threw in for good measure, the two played the game back and forth, with Hearst never giving up hope.

Hearst took enormous pride in the wild country surrounding the estate and wanted Urban to see it. There was no way of getting into the wilderness except by horse, and on Urban's final visit, in April 1925, Hearst persuaded him to make the trip. Urban had never been on a horse; he claimed that once someone had tried to hoist him onto one, and he had fallen off the other side. Given Urban's size and inexperience, Gretl was naturally concerned:

Poster for *Quality Street*, 1927, starring Marion Davies, now in the employ of M-G-M through a deal Hearst struck with Louis B. Mayer. Ira Resnick.

> I was truly worried about Father. Hearst assured me there was no danger. He picked a very steady horse and had one of the very best cowboys at Father's side, and one for Mary, too. Hearst led the way, followed by me and Marion, who was also nervous. Suddenly we were in another world. The pristine beauty of the country carpeted with flowers and dotted with antelope was intoxicating in the spring air.
>
> Father, clinging to his western saddle, began to think it wasn't going to be so bad until we hit wild, craggy terrain, ravines with rocks rising to perilous heights, then up a path so narrow there was just room for the horses, which dislodged rocks that plummeted down into a raging torrent.
>
> Hearst, a centaur on a horse, was oblivious to our terror. Finally, miraculously, the scene changed to cultivated fields with magnificent cattle grazing, and, as in a fairy tale, we found ourselves at a neat farmhouse where the farmer and his wife received us like royalty.
>
> Father said, "I can't get off the horse or I'll never get on again!" The cowboys managed to haul him down. He said it wasn't so bad, especially when he saw the delicious picnic Hearst's chef had prepared with caviar and iced champagne. Afterward we relaxed, and Hearst discussed cattle feeding and breeding.

Urban drew on his
architectural training to
reconstruct seventeenth-
century Paris for *Under the
Red Robe.* 1924.
Columbia University.

The party returned by a less dangerous route, and though Urban affected the expressions of an abused boy, he recovered with the aid of a salt bath and rubdown. He never, however, got on a horse again.

Urban commuted regularly to New York by the elegant and fast trains of the day, while ostensibly working under a near-exclusive contract for Hearst. For the 1924 season he designed *Pelléas et Mélisande*, *La Vida Breve*, *Tales of Hoffmann*, and *Falstaff* for the Met, an edition of the *Follies* for Ziegfeld, and four other Broadway shows. That Urban was able, season after season, to juggle multiple projects simultaneously is a tribute not only to his genius as an artist and organizer, but also to the staunch assistance rendered by Gretl, his Viennese staff at the Yonkers studio, his dedicated secretary, Sue Goldklang, and to Mary, who ran the Yonkers estate like clockwork and persevered in the collection of bills from such dilatory debtors as Flo Ziegfeld and the Metropolitan Opera.

On one of his last trips east while the company was on location in the Mojave Desert filming *Zander*, Urban found office space on Fifty-seventh Street, just off Fifth Avenue, which was perfect for the architectural firm he intended to establish once his contract with Hearst expired. With the assistance of Edward Ziegler from the Metropolitan, and relying on the capital he had accumulated by working in films, he signed a lease. Not having told anyone about his intentions, he arrived back in California in a radiant mood; he could hardly wait to break the news. He spent all his free time planning every last detail of the office. When all was ready, he sent Sue Goldklang, who had once worked for Hearst, to New York with the plans so that work could begin.

While Urban did play an important role in the development of new lighting techniques and set new standards for authenticity and realism in settings, his work in films is now all but forgotten. This is due both to the eclipse his career underwent after his death and the fact that the films themselves are not often shown beyond the confines of a film festival or a museum's screening room. What is important about the five years Urban spent in films are his contact with another figure of great wealth and power, William Randolph Hearst, and the ultimate use to which he put the money earned as a film designer, which is the subject of the next chapter.

The contract with Cosmopolitan expired on February 19, 1925, and the Urbans left soon thereafter for New York. Urban must have been jubilant, knowing that for the first time since 1908 and the *Festzug* scandal he would return to his architectural career and fulfill his dream. Gretl describes the farewell to California:

> Marion wept when we left, and a whole procession of people came to the train to say farewell. Hearst, although not present in person, sent flowers to the train, and we got so many we did not know what to do with them. I felt rather sad to leave the lovely climate and the leisurely, luxurious life, but Father, the old renegade, said everything looked more desirable, including the people, the farther the train took us away.

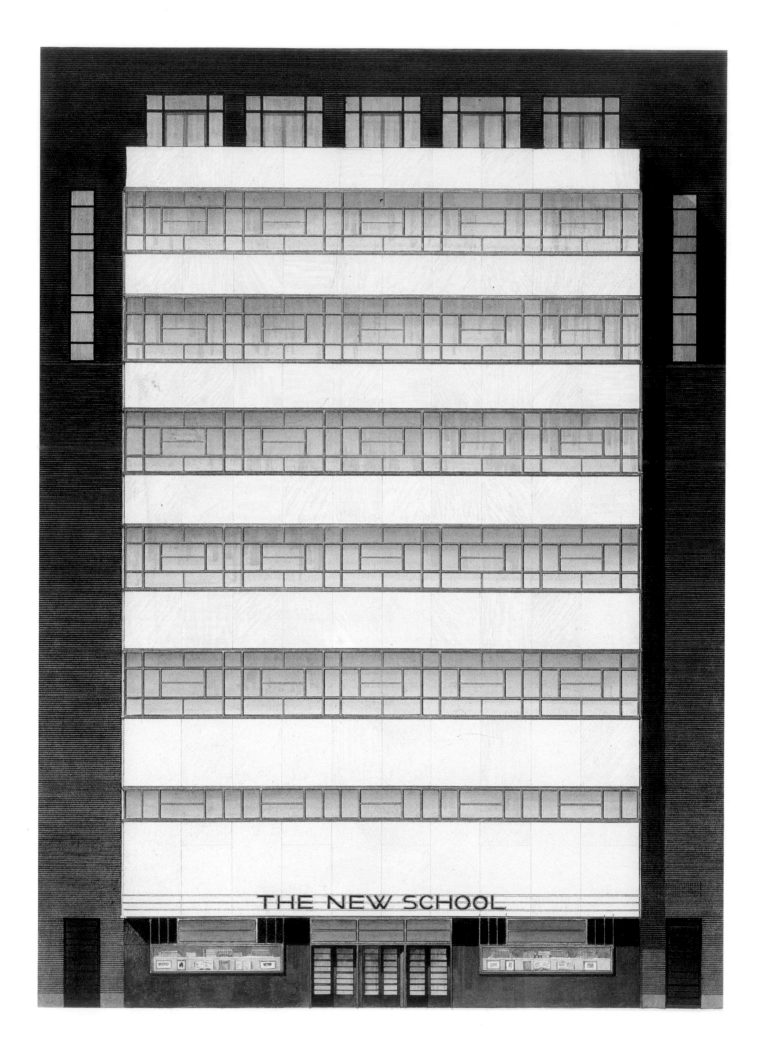

ARCHITECTURE:
PALM BEACH AND NEW YORK

Urban's decision to abandon Hollywood and the security of Hearst's encirclement for an uncertain future as an architect was profoundly disturbing to Mary. The Metropolitan Opera had proved more a financial liability than a sinecure, and Ziegfeld's payments, though lavish, were frequently deferred. On their return to Yonkers in 1925, Mary had observed, "Well, my dear, we certainly have burned our bridges. I don't quite see our future." But Urban did. Inspired by the prospect of being his own boss and of building more than hollow façades, he poured out to her his hopes for leaving a permanent legacy, one that might endure longer than just a season or even a generation.

Urban was later to summarize his conception of the range and depth of an architect's function:

> The trouble with our modern architecture . . . is that too much of it is piece work without sufficient conformity to one general design. If a building is to reflect the efforts of artistic planning, it must be harmonious to the minutest detail.
>
> It is artistic blasphemy to entrust the ventilation, plumbing, decoration and even fittings to separate contractors. The result of such rashness is bound to be a clashing of effect which practically cries aloud for adjustment. Personally, I could not live, work or breathe in such a home.
>
> An architect, to do justice to his constructions, must do as much as he can himself and personally supervise whatever is beyond his powers. He must know the problems of ventilation. He must intimidate the plumber until that wretch distributes his pipes in keeping with the general scheme. He must sketch, plan and consult on every detail, and the more of an expert he is in all related fields, the more unity he will achieve.
>
> This is where the experience of my early days [in Vienna] comes in handy. I do all the decorating and ornamentation myself. Frequently I select the furniture and fittings, personally, and I should even like to choose not only the people who live in my houses, but the clothes they wear and the things they do. Then I would be certain to exclude all jarring notes.[1]

An early design by Joseph Urban for the façade of the New School in New York City, which was superseded by one with a more simple arrangement of the window panes. Ca. 1928–1929. Columbia University.

Views of Urban's architectural office in New York City. Urban used the money he earned working on films to set up his own firm and to return to his first love, architecture. 1925. Columbia University and Gretl Urban collection.

Palm Beach was at the height of its building boom in 1925, and it turned out to be the ideal place for Urban to resume his architectural career. Once more he was asked to design dream houses and pleasure palaces. It had all begun because of the First World War. For years wealthy Americans had swarmed to the French Riviera, but with that playground inaccessible, attention was turned to Florida. As early as 1917, Paris Singer, of the sewing machine family, had recognized Palm Beach's potential and had turned to architect Addison Mizner for help, with the idea that together they could make Palm Beach the winter capital of the world. In 1918, financed by Singer, Mizner built the Everglades Club, and the same year he constructed a palatial mansion, El Mirasol, for Mrs. Edward Stotesbury of Philadelphia and another, Amado, for Charles Munn, who raced greyhounds.

It was Singer who launched Urban's career at the resort by hiring him to do work on the Everglades Club, work that attracted the attention of Anthony Drexel Biddle, Jr., the well-known socialite and sportsman. When Biddle asked Singer to arrange a meeting with the architect, the result was a lifelong friendship between the two men and a good many subsequent architectural commissions for Urban. One might not have expected that a man who worked constantly and devoted his life to his career would become the close friend of a person who never worked a day in his life, but Gretl remembers that "Tony was someone very special in Buschi's life. There was a great deal of hero worship in Tony's love for Buschi, and Buschi loved Tony with the sort of tenderness one gives to a younger brother." Here is Gretl's account of the first meeting between Biddle and Urban:

> Tony said that my father greeted him most cordially and asked him to sit down for a few minutes while he finished putting his things away, explaining that he had been working and had not noticed that it was already six o'clock. Buschi went on, and Tony said he felt as if he had known him for a long time, he was that easygoing and friendly.
>
> Tony watched with interest while Buschi rinsed his brushes in a glass of water, carefully dried them, and put them into a tray. And when he wiped the palette side of the paint box, Tony asked if he might have a look at the box because he knew nothing about art and had never seen such a box before. So Buschi let him see the little square containers, each holding a different color, and told him some of their interesting names. When he put the box away, Tony said Joe gave him a lovely smile and said, "I'm ready for a dry martini now; how about you?" Tony answered that he would be glad to have a cocktail, and they went downstairs and found a quiet corner.
>
> When the drinks were served, Buschi looked directly at Tony and said, "How can I help you, Mr. Biddle?" Tony was somewhat taken aback. He had come to offer the man a job, but the man did not seem to be thinking about a job at all but only about helping him. So Tony plunged right into an explanation of how he and a group of his friends liked Palm Beach so much that they wanted a clubhouse of their own and would Mr. Urban be interested in building it for them.

Marjorie Merriweather Post's Mar-a-Lago under construction in Palm Beach, Florida. One of America's greatest homes, it was substantially enlarged and extensively redesigned by Urban and redecorated both inside and out. 1926. Columbia University.

Left. A gracefully curved wing of Mar-a-Lago. 1926. *Right.* A staircase with a macaw at Mar-a-Lago. Urban invited a friend from his Hagenbund days in Vienna, sculptor Franz Barwig, to work on the home. Barwig readily agreed since there was little work for artists in Vienna, and brought his son to help him. 1926. Columbia University.

Urban would not commit himself without having seen the site, so next morning architect and potential client inspected the proposed location and agreed that it was indeed perfect. The architect envisaged a simple yet elegant building, airy and spacious, where people could be happy in the sun, and the client found this concept more than agreeable. Assured that money was not a problem, Urban admitted that he liked the idea of building a club in Palm Beach: "Now we have a contract, Mr. Biddle. I will work on an estimate of the cost while you prepare the necessary papers, but you can count on me that I consider our understanding legally binding."

As the two men went back to the car, Biddle informed Urban of one potential problem. Quite near the site of the proposed club was the palatial residence of Marjorie Merriweather Post, who was convinced that a new building would ruin the view from her home, Mar-a-Lago, whose name meant "from the sea to the lake." Indeed, her property extended from the Atlantic on the east to Lake Worth on the west.

Marjorie Post was another of the very wealthy and influential people Urban would work for and come to know well. Her father, C. W. Post, had invented Postum, a popular grain-based substitute for coffee, and, later, Grape Nuts breakfast cereal. Mr. Post was never to have the son he had hoped would inherit his company, so he started training his daughter in its workings. Not only did she inherit the company when her father died, but by her own acumen she turned it into one of the world's major food-processing operations. A woman of immense influence in Palm Beach and elsewhere, Marjorie Post, now Mrs. E. F. Hutton, had no legal right to block the building of the club, but her opposition might have made it difficult to recruit members. Biddle asked if Urban would meet Mrs. Hutton and describe what he planned to build. A lunch was arranged for the following day, and by the time Urban had finished describing the clubhouse, Mrs. Hutton was sold on the idea. In fact, she subsequently so enjoyed the club that she had a tunnel dug under the highway so that her friends could use it without crossing the busy coastal road.

After lunch Mrs. Hutton led her guests on a tour of the works of art displayed throughout the ground-floor rooms of Mar-a-Lago. When asked his opinion of her collection, Urban frankly told her that it was indeed comprised of treasures, but many were obscured and sometimes even obliterated by poor placement, detracting decoration, and poor lighting. Much to Biddle's astonishment, Mrs. Hutton not only did not get angry but even thanked Urban for his sincerity.

The outcome of this luncheon for Urban was commissions for two Palm Beach landmarks. He was hired to design and decorate the Bath and Tennis Club, to which he was named an honorary member, and to redesign and redecorate Mar-a-Lago's first floor and add space for an expanded staff of servants. What Urban ultimately did was to convert the original servants' quarters into additional guest rooms and to build a new wing for the staff. Mar-a-Lago became a true pleasure palace once Urban applied his hand to it.

Top. Examples of the Barwig's work appear throughout the home. 1926. *Bottom.* Another exterior view of Mar-a-Lago. To accommodate Mrs. Post's many guests and the staff required to attend them, Urban added more bedrooms and a wing for servants' quarters. 1926. Columbia University.

173

The most spectacular room in the house is the two-story grand salon or drawing room that was especially designed to display seven antique Venetian tapestries. Its elaborately carved and gilded ceiling was copied from the Accademia in Venice, and first-time visitors were understandably overwhelmed when they entered the room. Delighted by the impact the room made, Marjorie Post sometimes concealed herself on a small balcony high against the gilded ceiling to observe guests' reaction on first entering. Not all reactions were favorable. Mrs. Edward Shearson, an established figure in Palm Beach since 1920, was the one purported to have remarked that the decorations would be more suitable to a powder room in the Vatican, to which Marjorie Post enjoined, "She should know; that's undoubtedly where she had her audience."

For Marjorie Post's daughter Nedenia (the future actress Dina Merrill), Urban designed a bedroom suite that was both a child's fantasy and pure Urban. The focal point of the oval bedroom was a fireplace in the shape of an outsized beehive, and a plaster relief of twisted vine and pink roses trailed around the room, with bright yellow canaries peeking out. Lefler-Urban fairy-tale illustrations were used as a motif for a specially designed carpet, and a fairy princess's bed was crowned with a canopy that terminated in a finial of carved squirrels.

Urban never forgot the plight of his artist friends in Vienna after World War I, and although the New York branch of the Wiener Werkstätte was a failure, he continued to buy Viennese fabrics, wall coverings, lamps, and various other decorative items to use wherever appropriate in his commissions. For Mar-a-Lago he brought sculptor Franz Barwig and his son from Vienna to create the many sculptural pieces that were incorporated into the decoration, including the squirrels in the child's bedroom.

Urban was happy to be reunited with his friend who in Vienna had inspired him to try sculpture. He designed an alluring coupling of Salomé and John the Baptist, but he found working the wood tedious; so Barwig finished it and Urban added touches of gold leaf. Today, quite fittingly, it graces the rare book and manuscript section of Columbia University's library, which houses the Urban archives.

When Mrs. Hutton died in 1973 at the age of eighty-six, Mar-a-Lago was offered to the state of Florida, which promptly declined the gift. President Nixon then persuaded Congress to have the National Park Service maintain the property as a winter White House and guest facility for visiting dignitaries, but it proved unsuitable for security reasons. From time to time there were reports that Mar-a-Lago was about to be demolished to make way for a subdivision, a casino, or a condominium. However, in 1986 the estate was purchased by New York real-estate tycoon Donald Trump, who restored the home to its former glory.

Mar-a-Lago, though opulent, is that rare creation: a private fantasy grounded in the taste and style of an era and executed with craftsmanship that never could be duplicated today. It must be counted among the great estates in the country, ranking with Marble House in Newport, Biltmore in Asheville, and, of course, William Randolph Hearst's San Simeon.

Design elevation and photo of the exterior of the Oasis Club in Palm Beach with the double staircase Urban would later use in the New School. 1926. Columbia University.

TIO · OF · THE · OASIS · CLUBHOUSE · IN · PALM · BEACH · FLORIDA · JOSEPH · URBAN · ARCHITECT

175

A 1927 newspaper article described Urban's efforts at the Bath and
Tennis Club: "He has put into the design a moderate amount of Spain and
combined it with gorgeously comfortable trappings." [2] These "trappings"
included more than a hundred orange-and-blue continental-style cabanas,
similar to what Urban knew from the Lido in Venice, each of which contained
a main room, two dressing rooms, and a shower.

Both the Oasis Club, which Urban also designed (it was to be a residence
for bachelors at the resort), and the Bath and Tennis Club were used for
charity balls and galas during the Palm Beach winter social season. For many
of these evenings Urban acted the role of an artist attached to some
seventeenth-century monarch's court: he provided elaborate decorations for
the soirées of local nobility. One can gain some measure of Urban's hectic
activity through newspaper reports from a single week in March 1927. The
New York American reported on the fifth that he had turned a club room at
the Oasis into a "coconut grove of exquisite beauty on the moonlit shore of
an azure sea." [3] On the same day the *New York Evening Post* reported that
the Bath and Tennis Club and its grounds had been transformed into "a
gorgeous panorama depicting the splendor and glory of ancient Babylon and
Nineveh." [4] Seven days later the same paper described a St. Patrick's Day
dance at the Bath and Tennis Club:

> Under the magical artistry of Mr. Joseph Urban the club was transformed
> into a dazzling scene of splendor, depicting scenes from "A Thousand and
> One Nights," a street scene of Bagdad, and colorful and beautiful vistas of
> the orient.
>
> The patio represented a harem with the guests seated on large satin
> cushions of brilliant colors. At one side was the golden throne of the prince
> and at the far end of the patio was a golden stairway.[5]

At the end of April 1927, Urban found himself recreating the Bath and
Tennis Club on the roof of New York's Ritz Carlton for a party given by
William Randolph Hearst. Urban simulated the waters of Lake Worth, the
jungles of the Everglades, and the ocean beach itself by way of huge canvases

that covered the walls. To achieve a moonlight effect he draped blue gauze combined with silver net over the entire space. Striped orange-and-blue cabanas and palm trees specially imported from Florida completed the impression of the Palm Beach club.[6] When Marjorie Post's stepdaughter, Barbara Hutton, made her debut during the 1930 Christmas season, it was Urban who decorated the Ritz in a garden theme complete with white birches, poinsettias, and palms.[7]

Tony Biddle enjoyed the Bath and Tennis Club so much that he suggested the creation of a northern counterpart that he and his friends could use during hot New York summers. The result was the Atlantic Beach Club on Long Island, which Urban designed in a newly refined, crisp style. It was completed in 1930, but only a few tantalizing photographs remain to show the club's long, horizontal lines, terraces, and lack of extraneous decorative detail. The apartment block Urban designed in 1931 to accompany the Atlantic Beach Club was never built.

Edward Hutton, Marjorie Post's husband, and Tony Biddle were among the investors in the Palm Beach Paramount Theatre, which Urban designed. It is best described by the architect himself:

Urban's friends wanted to have a beach club near New York that would serve as a northern counterpart to the Bath and Tennis Club in Palm Beach. The Atlantic Beach Club on Long Island was the result, and its design reflects the architect's move toward a simpler, more geometric style. 1929. Columbia University.

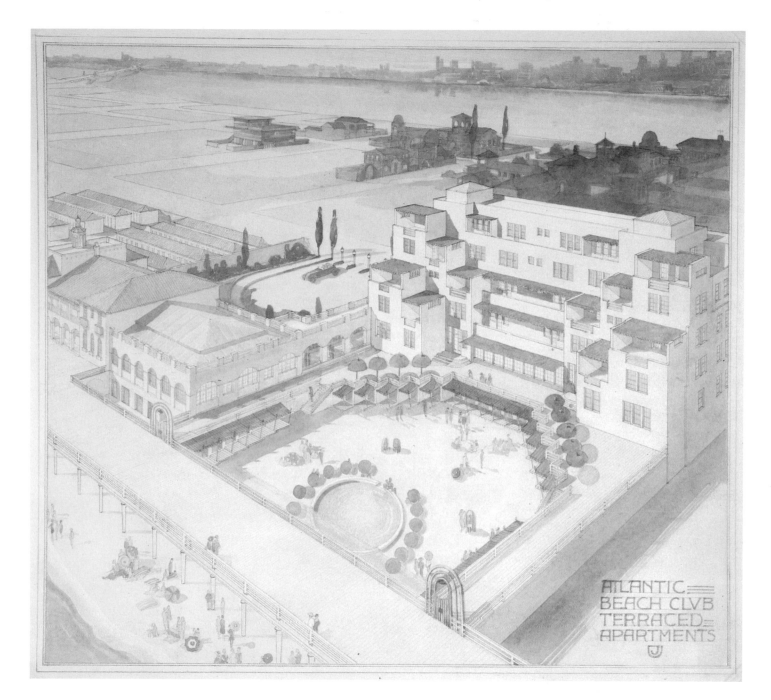

ATLANTIC
BEACH CLVB
TERRACED
APARTMENTS

Opposite top left. The bold patterns of the deck area of the Atlantic Beach Club. 1929.
Top right. A sun lounge in the club. 1929.
Bottom. Library-lounge in the Atlantic Beach Club. As always, Urban designed all the interior furnishings and appointments. 1929. Columbia University.

Above. Urban planned an apartment complex for the Atlantic Beach Club, but, as with many of his proposed projects in the early years of the Depression, it was never built. 1931. Columbia University.

The Paramount Theatre at Palm Beach is for a life almost the opposite of that in New York City. Life itself, there, is leisured and sunny. Real estate is not at such a premium and the architect who is fortunate enough to build there may still count on some of the beauties of nature—the palms, distances, the deep blue sky—as part of his architectural scheme. Moreover, the theatre there is not an escape from the life around, but a part of it, fitting into its rhythm. The architecture of the Paramount Theatre at Palm Beach is accordingly simple, spacious, Southern. It is approached through an arcade and patio which invite loitering in their shade to inspect the elegant shops around it. The exterior is warmly sunlit; the interior, dark green and silver—cool and comfortable. Because a moving picture screen requires no depth behind it, as does the regular stage, and because a suitable and economic use of the lot suggested the form, the auditorium was built fan-shape with the screen at the handle of the fan. Aside from providing good vision, this shape has such fine acoustic properties that the hall is often pressed into service for concerts.[8]

The theatre was built into the Sunrise Building, also financed by Hutton and Biddle, but no longer survives, although the building recently has been restored. Gretl designed the curtain and the charming murals that the *New York Times* described as consisting of "strange fish and feathery seaweed in languid waters."[9]

For his friend Tony Biddle, Urban built a lavish home in Palm Beach called the Villa del Sarmiento. The dining room could accommodate eighty under a ceiling copied from the Alhambra, and a black marble stage at one end could be converted into a fountain when no theatricals were planned.

Urban lived lavishly in the Florida resort, as he did everywhere else. During his first season there, he rented a yacht, complete with captain and crew, to live on and to use as his studio. When Mary learned that her husband was paying $1,000 a month for this seaworthy abode, she immediately left New York to try to find him a less expensive residence. Ultimately Urban did move to land, but not because of Mary's cries of financial ruin. For Urban work always came first, and he simply could not work on the yacht. Such was his popularity among the Palm Beach younger set, essentially Tony Biddle's friends, that at the end of an evening's formal festivities they would often descend on "Joe's yacht" and stay on deck until dawn to watch the sunrise.

Urban commuted regularly between New York and Florida, mainly to attend the all-important lighting and dress rehearsals at the Metropolitan, for Otto Teegen was overseeing the New York architectural work and Gretl was handling the scenic commissions. Except for the extended period she worked on the mural in the Paramount Theatre, Gretl spent little time in the resort, but she has effectively summarized her father's work and play there:

> I was kept pretty busy in New York between business at the office and supervision of the Yonkers studio. Father commuted frequently, and he would tell me about the Palm Beach festivities and Mary's joy at being lionized by the social elite. He did not like the snobbery but said, "Poor Mary, let her have her fun."
>
> With all the parties, Buschi remained adamant about not staying up late more than one night a week. Mary often stayed on at parties alone and never stopped talking about them, much to Father's amusement.
>
> Father tried to make his friends more aware of art and his joy in it. Most of them knew nothing about modern interior design. He showed them how well antique and modern furniture could blend, and some of them learned to appreciate modern sculpture and painting.

Buschi used to laugh when they begged him to indicate where to put things, and then they never dared to place them anywhere else, although he told them it was their home and they should arrange everything to suit themselves.

When Father's work was done in Florida and spring brought his Palm Beach friends back to New York, he and Mary gave a dinner at the St. Regis to show his appreciation for their hospitality. There were about two hundred guests, and I never danced with any man I did not know. Buschi never danced but sat comfortably with his mocha and brandy and cigarettes, delighted with the good time everyone seemed to be having, occasionally bursting into song with the orchestra and tossing off affectionate remarks to the dancers as they passed.

Urban's elevation for the Sunrise Building in Palm Beach, which incorporated his Paramount Theatre. 1925. Columbia University.

181

Courtyard of the home Urban built for Anthony Biddle in Palm Beach. 1927. Socialite "Tony" Biddle became one of Urban's closest friends after they met in Palm Beach. With his own great financial resources and social contacts, Biddle was influential in directing many important architectural commissions to Urban.
Columbia University.

William Randolph Hearst could not persuade Urban to work for him as an architect in California, but New York City was another matter entirely. Urban already had remodeled the Cosmopolitan Theatre at Columbus Circle for Hearst and his films, and Hearst was aware that discussions were under way with Urban about designing a new Metropolitan Opera House destined for property owned by Otto Kahn on Fifty-seventh Street near Eighth Avenue. Believing that Eighth Avenue was on its way to redevelopment and improvement, Hearst decided to ask Urban to design a headquarters building to consolidate the offices of his twelve magazines. Had all gone according to plan, Urban would have had three completed projects within three blocks of each other.

The new Met was never built, but the Hearst building is one of the two surviving examples of Urban's architectural work in New York City—a subtle joke made at the expense of a client always talking about his "newspaper empire." His architect, born in the most imperial of cities, provided Hearst with something suitably imperial, but as in an operetta.

The International Magazine Building, as it was called, fills the blockfront of Eighth Avenue between West Fifty-sixth and Fifty-seventh streets. While it may look like a solid box from the street, it was designed as a "U" shape with arms surrounding a central court. Unfortunately, the six-story building has an air of incompleteness since the additional seven stories Urban provided for were never added. No plans appear to survive that show the completed work as conceived.

A critic writing for the *New Yorker* characterized what was built with the facile term "theatric architecture." [10] However, when the building opened in April 1928, front-page coverage in the *New York American* (a Hearst paper, to be sure) gave a more favorable assessment. The architect himself wrote a long essay in which he set down the underlying intentions of his plan:

> A more or less public building of the character of the International Magazine Building should easily be located in the hurry and bustle and crowds of the city, and it should be distinctive and tell to the passerby in the best possible manner in its exterior what is going on on the inside.[11]

The building's façade has a series of purely decorative columns that rise from the third story and terminate above the roofline in the garland-draped urns Urban used so frequently in his scenic designs. What took place inside the building was symbolized at the base of the columns by statues that represented some of the subjects in Hearst's magazines. All but overwhelmed today by the towers surrounding it, the building remains pretty much as it was except for air-conditioning units in many windows and different signs for the retail areas on the ground floor. The Hearst building is by no means a masterwork, as Urban himself realized, but the architect never actually disowned it.

About this same time, Urban received a commission to build what was, in fact, the life-size, solid, three-dimensional realization of one of his fairy-tale drawings. In 1926, after attending a production of *Hänsel und Gretel* at

In his design for the International Magazine Building in New York City, Urban poked gentle fun at William Randolph Hearst's imperial pretensions. 1927. Columbia University.

The Gingerbread House Urban built in Hamburg, New Jersey, for Wheatsworth Biscuits was an early prototype of a theme amusement park. 1928. Columbia University.

the Metropolitan Opera, the president of Wheatsworth Biscuit Company was inspired to have Urban reconstruct the witch's house on a hill adjacent to his Hamburg, New Jersey, flour mill. Although intended as a publicity stunt, this Gingerbread House was an enchanting pavilion of brightly colored poured-stone walls, strawberry-tinted turrets, and vanilla-icing roofs. Inside, a cantilevered staircase ascended to a Birthday Cake Room, a Plum Pudding Room studded with cookies, and then to a dome dominated by a huge wire spiderweb from which dangled an alluring arachnid with enormous glass eyes. On the lawn outside the castle was a witch's cauldron (capacity eleven children), and nearby there loomed a grotto with goblins lurking inside. It took Urban two years to conjure up this bewitching structure, but for generations it delighted the children of the New York metropolitan area.

Art Deco, the artistic style that succeeded Art Nouveau, took its name from the *Exposition des Arts Décoratifs et Industriels Modernes*, which was held in Paris in 1925. The new style used mechanistic and geometric designs in place of the old florid lines derived from naturalistic elements. It emphasized the use of modern materials such as stainless steel and aluminum, as well as precious wood veneers inlaid in geometric patterns on furniture or fixtures such as elevator doors. New York City is fortunate in having two prime examples of the style, both of which have recently been meticulously restored: the Chrysler Building and Radio City Music Hall, located in the Rockefeller Center complex, which itself features many superb examples of the style. Urban made use of the Art Deco style in his Bedell and Kaufmann stores projects, the interiors of the Central Park Casino, his 1933 apartment for Katharine Brush, and some of his club and hotel rooms.

The exhibitions Urban arranged at the start of the century for the Hagenbund were both artistic and promotional in purpose. Member artists and craftsmen wished to display their art but also attract patrons and purchasers. With his establishment of the New York branch of the Wiener Werkstätte, Urban was again involved in marketing, this time designing his first store. He had some experience, therefore, when he received commissions to remodel the Bedell store in New York and the Kaufmann store in Pittsburgh.

It is difficult to believe, but the art of decorating retail store windows with a view to attracting customers is a relatively recent development, dating just from the 1920s. Until then stores simply put as much of their merchandise on display as possible, in no ordered or decorative arrangement—an effect similar to what one sees today in the windows of discount drugstores. The redesigned façade and display windows that Urban created for the Bedell ladies' fashions store on West Thirty-fourth Street were important enough to receive coverage in several architectural magazines when it reopened in 1929.

Urban used one-third of the depth of the original store to create an enclosed vestibule that featured a series of roomy and brightly illuminated display cases. Except for the entrance to the vestibule and the entrance to the store proper, the walls were all show windows, and in the center of the open area was a large rectangular, free-standing display case.

The commentator for *Architectural Forum*, Arthur North, described Urban's work: "These show windows are very deep and permit the display of merchandise without crowding, giving also spaciousness that is befitting the display of beautiful merchandise. The display vestibule is brilliantly illuminated." [12] *Architecture and Building* tells of Urban's all-important use of color: "The color scheme is black, ranging from brilliant polished black to mat shades. The ceilings are deep blue giving an effect of height, aided by the brilliant illumination." [13]

The redesigned two-story entrance was partially covered by a metal grille that on first glance appeared to be simply a geometric pattern. On closer inspection, however, one could see that female figures dressed in fashions

A photograph of the entryway to the Bedell Store in New York City shows Urban's innovative arrangement of display cases and windows within the courtlike entrance. 1928. Columbia University.

The grille over the Bedell store's entrance begins as a geometric design at the bottom and develops into an illustrated history of women's fashions. 1928. Columbia University.

185

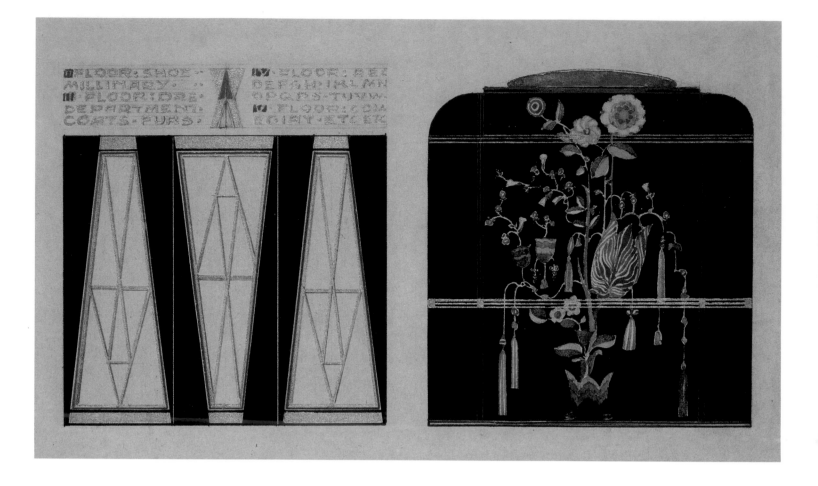

Urban's designs for the elevators in the Bedell store, showing both the doors and the interior decoration. 1928. Columbia University.

from different historical periods were incorporated into the design. Urban was here applying his own dictum that a public building's façade should give an indication of its function. Otto Teegan, Urban's successor in his firm, provided the Bonwit Teller store on Fifth Avenue with a similar, though simpler, grille, which was destroyed when the building was demolished to make way for the Trump Tower.

Whereas Urban's stage designs were greatly influenced by his architectural background, his architectural work was equally indebted to his theatrical experience. He was trained, after all, in Vienna, where theatre played such an important part in the city's life, and he had lived with the theatricality of the public buildings on the Ringstrasse. In a sense many of Urban's buildings and interiors were extensions of his stage designs: backgrounds against which wealthy and prominent clients could display themselves and their treasures, and settings in which merchandise could be displayed to attract purchasers.

An element so simple in shape as an elevator car was turned into a work of art as well as a theatrical experience in the Bedell store. In an article entitled "Store Elevators and Escalators," which appeared in the June 1929 issue of *Architectural Forum*, Theodor Muller describes what Urban placed behind Art Deco elevator doors: "[Joseph Urban] has designed an extremely decorative car, the effect of which is only suggested in these illustrations, since the colors of the stylized flowers are brilliant against the black lacquered steel. Picture this car operated by a small Japanese girl in jade green pajamas. . . ." [14] Urban applied the ancient art of lacquer to new materials in creating something beautiful that could be enjoyed by thousands of people. The original designs he made are miniature gems, and fortunately they have been preserved in the Urban archives.

Today one can see the effects of Urban's store designs in such great retailing successes as Henri Bendel and Bloomingdale's, with their highly original interior layouts and displays. At least one of Urban's contemporary critics, Lewis Mumford, saw his work in the Bedell store as another example of the hucksterism in American life, as characterized by Sinclair Lewis in his 1922 novel, *Babbitt*:

> To be "modern" is . . . to be at the opposite pole from being "modernist."
> The latter represents the esthetic collywobbles of the pusher, the advertiser,
> the booster; one sees it at its worst in shop fronts like those of Bedell on
> Thirty-fourth Street and the Gotham Hosiery Company of Fifth Avenue; and
> it is, if anything, an even lower and deadlier stage of architecture than the
> archaism of the past generation.[15]

The unsigned critic of *Architecture and Building* was more appreciative of the architect's intentions:

> The modern development of store fronts with a view to their advertising
> value finds a very fine example in the Bedell store front on West 34th Street.
> It stands out from any point of approach and its striking artistry is worthy
> of close examination. . . . The design is a well thought out scheme to attract

The designs in the Bedell store elevators were created in lacquer over stainless steel. Japanese women wearing green pajamalike uniforms operated the elevators. 1928. Columbia University.

187

attention and to display merchandise. It is distinctive, appropriate to its particular purpose and of beauty both in design and selection of materials.[16]

Although department store owner Edgar J. Kaufmann commissioned Urban to redesign and redecorate his establishment in Pittsburgh, the plans, with all their exquisite colors and Art Deco details, were never carried out. Kaufmann was later to commission Frank Lloyd Wright to design a country house for him at Bear Run, Pennsylvania. Known as Fallingwater, the house is one the great landmarks of twentieth-century architecture.

In 1926 Mayor Jimmy Walker decided that New York City should have a suitable setting in which to receive and entertain foreign guests, just as major European cities had. He and a group of prominent citizens thought the old Central Park Casino at Fifth Avenue and Seventy-second Street would be an ideal location and announced plans for the structure's renovation. The building was the work of Calvert Vaux, one of the original designers of Central Park, and was popular in the 1890s when it had been known as the Ladies' Refreshment Salon. Not a casino in the sense of a gambling hall, it was more of a pavilion, or, as described by *Architectural Record*: "It was a compromise between a road house and a sort of Coney Island Winter Garden."[17]

Since Flo Ziegfeld and Tony Biddle were on the project's board of governors, it is not surprising that Joseph Urban was the man chosen to rejuvenate the building. Before work could start on the project, however, there was a legal dispute to be resolved. The Casino had come to be known as "Jimmy Walker's rustic palace in Central Park,"[18] and a taxpayers' suit was brought to stop it from being turned into a private club for the mayor and his cronies. Biddle, as chairman of the Casino's board, publicly denied that a facility closed to the public had ever been contemplated. A New York State Supreme Court justice ultimately found that the Parks Commission had done nothing illegal, that no city property was being wasted, and that the project could therefore begin.

Urban transformed the old Victorian building into an elegant pleasure palace that reflected both the spirit of the twenties and the administration of "Gentleman Jimmy." The Casino's management described the building as "the most beautiful and elegant restaurant in the world." [19] The black-and-white photographs and the one color drawing that survives can only approximate the effects Urban achieved. To fully appreciate the Casino, one had to see its rooms peopled with elegant couples in evening clothes and hear in the background a society orchestra or the young, then unknown, Eddie Duchin playing the piano.

The Casino opened in June 1929 with the irrepressible René Black, later of the Waldorf, as maître d'hôtel. The interior consisted of four major rooms: a small dining room, the main dining room, the ballroom, and the pavilion, which opened onto a terrace. The pavilion was decorated with a bright floral motif that appeared on the walls, the carpets, the ceiling, and even on the fabric that covered the chairs. In keeping with his own dictum, Urban designed all the furniture and appointments for the Casino; the cretonnes used in the pavilion were even blocked in Urban's own studio. The proud architect told the *New York Times* that the pavilion's decor had been inspired by "the freshness of spring flowers and joyousness of a wind among young leaves." [20] The paper went on to describe the small dining room as comprised of "fumed knotty pine, a ruddy ceiling and materials of vigorous texture and pattern." [21] In describing the main dining room, Urban said that the "broad surfaces of silver give a living neutral background to a pulsating rhythm of maroon and green." [22]

The original color design for the mural in the ballroom is the only surviving sketch for the project. It presents a floral fantasy set against a soft

190

Top. The Tulip Room at the Casino. Urban unified the design of the pavilion by using a floral motif throughout. 1929. Columbia University. *Bottom.* The Casino's Ballroom. The black glass ceiling panels reflected both the light from Urban's chandeliers and the elegantly clad couples on the dance floor beneath it. 1929. Columbia University.

Top. The central feature in the Casino's Ballroom was a floral mural reminiscent of Gustav Klimt's gold-period paintings. 1929. Columbia University.
Bottom. A lounge area in the Casino for which Urban designed both the furniture and the fabrics that covered it. 1929. Columbia University.

192

gold background. Urban used a black glass ceiling to reflect the huge chandeliers and the people dancing beneath them. Once more, Urban provided a vivid description of the Art Deco gem: "In the ballroom, the line of the mural composition is like the wave of a conductor's baton beginning dance music, while dim reflections in the black glass ballroom ceiling give space and movement in sympathy to the life of the room." [23]

The Casino proved to be immensely popular. In the words of Robert Caro, the biographer of Robert Moses, "the Casino was more than a restaurant or a night club. It was Jimmy Walker's Versailles. Friends joked that the Mayor spent more time there than at City Hall." [24] The mayor held court in a secret set of rooms that Caro describes:

> . . . in a duplex upstairs retreat, closed to the public, its very existence concealed by the building's lowering Mansard roof, Tammany politicians were entertained by Broadway chorus lines—rushed to the Casino *en masse* by motorcycle escort. And all the while, in a small adjoining office, its walls covered with green moiré and its ceiling with gold leaf, its heavy door carefully soundproofed, Walker held court for favor seekers and politicians, and it was there, insiders said, that much of the city's business was transacted. [25]

The Casino became one of the symbols of Jimmy Walker's corrupt administration, and it was this identification with the mayor that brought about its destruction.

When Fiorello La Guardia successfully led his reform movement to power and was elected mayor in 1934, Robert Moses became the parks commissioner. Under a broad grant of power given the commissioner by the legislature to tear down buildings incidental to the park's use (and restaurants came within this category), Moses sought to avenge a slight his friend Governor Al Smith suffered at the hands of Jimmy Walker. Not only did the commissioner have this power, but he could apply it without his actions being subjected to judicial review unless they were clearly abusive exercises of his authority. It was obvious that Moses's motives for wanting the Casino destroyed hinged on his dislike of Walker, and an injunction was sought to prevent him from obstinately demolishing something much beloved by the public, designed by two prominent artists, and still in good condition. Nevertheless, the state court in Albany upheld the parks commissioner's power, and before that decision could be appealed the Casino had been demolished and replaced by a playground.[26]

Both Gretl and her father had delighted in the Casino:

> Buschi had much affection for the Casino because he was able to design it for the lush natural beauty in which it stood. He felt very strongly that New York deserved an elegant restaurant in Central Park, the type that abounded in the Prater in Vienna and the Bois de Boulogne in Paris.
>
> While he kept the building simple, he gave its interior class and charm and a feeling of airy comfort. When the Casino was finished in 1929, he loved to go there not so much for the delicious food but for its ambiance, which reminded him of [the Hotel] Sacher and Ronacher's [a popular night club for aristocrats], where you knew you would find some of your friends.
>
> In the Central Park Casino, Buschi's separate worlds met. You would find the Bodanzkys or the Biddles, the Gaertners and the Ziegfelds, the Lunts or the Schorrs, etc. And as in the golden days of the *Kaiserstadt*, Buschi enjoyed moving from table to table for a brief visit and some gay talk about work or play.

Like the Urban Ziegfeld Theatre, it too is gone, and with it much of the *chic* and distinction that were such attractive characteristics of New York City before World War II . . . a New York that was rich and elegant and gay.

Urban's use of murals in decorating public rooms goes back to his work with Lefler in Vienna's *Rathauskeller* at the turn of the century. Just as he used a mural for the key to his design in one of the rooms in the Central Park Casino, he used murals in the many hotel rooms he decorated. The theme for a typical Urban room was provided by a mural that he designed and had painted in the Yonkers studio. All of the room's appointments—carpets, drapes, upholstery or slipcover fabrics, and lighting fixtures—were then designed to coordinate with the mural. Fortunately, many of the original color drawings for these rooms survive, leaving good account of how dramatic Urban's unusual color schemes were.

Themes for murals ran from tigers in the eponymous Tiger Room installation at Chicago's Hotel Sherman to an undersea motif for the Seaglade Grille of New York's St. Regis Hotel, in which Tony Biddle had a major financial interest. Urban also decorated the St. Regis Roof Garden.

The Metropolitan Museum of Art in 1929 organized an exhibition to display what leading American designers and manufacturers were creating in the new Art Deco style. By this time Urban was very much involved in industrial design, having created pieces for the Baker Furniture Company, fabric designs, a line of luggage for Hartman, and the color combinations for the Ruxton automobile, which never actually went into production.

Urban had two rooms on display at the Metropolitan during the exhibition. One was a garden terrace intended for the roof or setback of a city apartment building. It is strikingly similar to a room of his that appeared in the 1906 issue of *The Studio* dedicated to the art revival in Austria. The other room was a handsome study or den for a man. Working closely with the manufacturers, Urban designed every item on display, including the carpet.

What is of more significance today than Urban's rooms is who his fellow exhibitors were. With the exception of one ceramicist, they were mostly prominent architects of the day whose reputations, unlike Urban's, survive to the present: Ely Jacques Kahn, John Wellborn Root, Ralph T. Walker, Eugene Schoen, and Raymond Hood. A major cultural institution had ranked Urban as one of the top practitioners in his field, but it was still too easy for some to dismiss his work as that of a stage designer. As evidenced below, this facile characterization occasionally appeared in print. Raymond Hood's biographer, Walter H. Kilham, Jr., identifies Urban through his designs for the Metropolitan Opera, but he does, however, reveal Urban's relationship with some of his fellow architects and how they unquestionably accepted him as one of their own.

Opposite. Designs for remodeling the Hotel Gibson in Cincinnati, Ohio. 1929. Columbia University.

The "Four-Hour Lunch Club" that met at Mori's Restaurant on Fridays was almost an institution. In addition to Raymond Hood there was his closest friend, Joseph Urban, a Viennese architect who had come to New York, initially achieving success as a designer of sets for the Metropolitan Opera. He finally had the opportunity he wanted to design buildings as well, perhaps through people he met at the luncheons. . . . Ely Jacques Kahn was also a regular member and Ralph Walker frequently joined them. They are said to have tuned up over a cocktail dubbed "Nipple Spray" by Urban, followed by crab flake pancakes with cheese sauce, prepared by Mori's best

·LOBBY·

·BALL·ROOM·

OVAL CUPOLA: Canvas Painted In Oil Colors, Bronze And Gold Leaf.·· STRAIGHT SIDE WALLS OF MAIN FLOOR AND BALCONY: Canvas Painted In Anilin Colors, Bronze and Gold Leaf.·· PILASTERS & BALCONY FRONT: Highly Polished Artificial Marble.·· MOULDING ON PILASTERS: Cast Iron Gold Leafed.·· BALCONY RAIL: Wrought Iron Gold Leafed.·· FLAT CEILING OF MAIN FLOOR & BALCONY: Plaster Silver Leafed Highly Glossed. WAINSCOT: Selected Clear White Maple Stained. At Top Of Each Panel A Rosette Of Bevelled Mirrors With Gilded Metal Frames.·· WINDOWS: To Have Opalescent Glass.·· FLOOR: Center Dance Floor Maple Strip. With Surrounding Floor Laid Herring bone, Covered With Carpet.·· LIGHTING FIXTURES: Silk Shades With Three Circuits Of Lights.·· NOTE: If Elliptical Form Of Ball Room Is Adopted, The Side Walls On Sixth Avenue Front Can Be Moved Back To The Line Of The Inside Column Face Gaining Room For Additional Tables And Utilizing Exterior Windows As Interior Windows.

·ELEVATION SHOWING SCREENS OPENED·   ·ELEVATION SHOWING SCREENS CLOSED.

·ELEVATION OF FOUNTAIN WALL WITH SCREENS OPENED·
Scale 1/2"=1'o"

PROPOSED SCHEME OF DECORATION PERMITS OF TWO EFFECTS: FIXED PAINTED PANELS WITH HINGED SCREENS WHEN OPENED MAKES COLORFUL INTERIOR FOR AFTERNOON TEA OR EVENING ENTERTAINMENT.

FOR LUNCH TIME SCREENS MAY BE FOLDED UP REVEALING GREEN LEATHER COVERED WALL AND LEATHER COVERED BACK OF SCREENS MAKING COMPLETE GREEN INTERIOR.

·ELEVATION OF END WALL WITH SCREENS OPENED·
·Date July 20, 1928· ·Drawing No·
·JOSEPH URBAN, Architect·
·5 East 57th St New York City·

196

A view of the roof garden in New York City's St. Regis Hotel and, above, one of the original design sketches. 1927. Columbia University.

Opposite. Two original drawings for the Hotel Gibson. The bottom design includes elements Urban would employ in a 1931 *Follies* setting. 1928. Columbia University.

Overleaf spread. Urban was one of several prominent American architects invited to participate in the Metropolitan Museum of Art's 1929 exhibition, "The Architect and the Industrial Arts." He displayed two complete, full-scale rooms. *Top.* A gentleman's study very much in keeping with the exhibit's intention of presenting American examples of the "Modernist" or Art Deco style. 1929. *Bottom.* A terrace roof garden for a city apartment. 1929. Columbia University. *Right.* Undated proposed office building for New York City. Columbia University.

Italian cook. There were nearly always guests like Tony Sarg, the artist, Frank Lloyd Wright, as Ely Jacques Kahn described him "damned positive about everything," and Alvin Johnson.[27]

At a much earlier period in his life, Urban was a member of a similar group of artists and architects who met at a Viennese coffeehouse to discuss their work. Urban's participation in the Siebener Club brought him to the attention of that ultimate patron of the time and place: the Habsburg Empire itself. One can only speculate on what influence or impact the discussions at the Four-Hour Lunch Club had on the members' work. Raymond Hood, for example, designed the McGraw-Hill Building on West Forty-second Street in New York and sheathed it in glazed blue-green blocks. Did this reflect the influence of Urban, the master of color?

The New School for Social Research was founded in 1918 by such distinguished American scholars as Charles Beard, James Harvey Robinson, Thorstein Veblen, and John Dewey. The founders intended to reinvigorate higher education as it had developed in the United States with an institution, clearly experimental, based on their own principles and theories.[28]

In 1928 the school was forced to leave a building on West Twenty-third Street it had leased for the previous ten years. After a search for suitable rental space proved unsuccessful, the administration decided that the school should erect its own building. The location would have to be accessible to mass transit because most of the school's students depended on it to get to class. And because the school's treasury contained only $37,000, all costs would have to be kept to a minimum, including purchase of the land, architectural fees, and construction costs.

Alvin Johnson, the school's president, immediately visited Daniel Crawford Smith, one of the institution's students and benefactors, whom he described as a "partly retired business man, a passionately loyal friend of the New School." [29] Smith owned three town houses on Twelfth Street between Fifth and Sixth avenues; living in the center one, he kept those on either side as protection. He loved flowers and tried unsuccessfully to have a garden in his damp and dark backyard.

Johnson and Smith agreed that the school should have its own building, and Johnson quickly set out to convince "Uncle Dan," as he was affectionately known, that his three lots would provide the ideal location. To make his appeal more attractive, Johnson proposed that an apartment be built for Smith and his wife on the sixth story of the new structure to rent at a modest fee for as long as they lived. Since it would be well above the neighboring brownstones, the apartment would be quiet, and it would have a sun-drenched terrace ideal for a flower garden. Uncle Dan was convinced; the school was built; and the Smiths lived happily in their penthouse.

A lot adjacent to one of Smith's was subsequently purchased, and this provided eighty feet of frontage on Twelfth Street. With the help of friends in real estate and construction, the necessary mortgages and financing were arranged. To raise the additional money needed for construction, bonds were sold to supporters of the school.

Johnson had two men under consideration as architect for his project: Frank Lloyd Wright and Joseph Urban. Although Wright's career was experiencing a dry spell from which it did not emerge until he built Fallingwater in 1936, Urban was being considered alongside the man generally regarded even then as America's greatest architect. Brendan Gill, Wright's most recent biographer, tells how a group of Wright's friends, including "the designer Joseph Urban," invested $75,000 in a corporation called Wright, Incorporated, "the purpose of which was to free him [Wright] from the Great Dismal Swamp of financial misery into which his repeated extravaganzas invariably led him." [30] Gretl remembers that her father once made an outright gift to Wright of $5,000 and would have given more if Mary had not intervened. Urban was never repaid.

While Johnson admired Wright, he thought that he and the strong-willed, highly opinionated architect would disagree on what type of building would best serve the purposes of the school. He felt he might work better with Urban, but he could not imagine how he would pay the enormous fees Urban was reported to earn. A fellow trustee who was also a member of the building

committee arranged a luncheon meeting for Johnson and Urban, which Johnson later described:

> I expected to be struck dumb when face to face with the great man. But with all his visible power, he was so understanding, so charming, that I found myself almost eloquent in describing the New School, its character, its aspirations, its meaning for education and society. I dwelt on the imperative need of a building that should express the ideals of the School, give visible form to its personality.[31]

Urban was enthusiastic about the project even though he had been advised that the school could not afford his usual fees. His eagerness to accept the commission under such financial stringencies was a puzzle to Johnson. The two men went on, however, to work very closely together during the initial planning stages of the project. They would first discuss floor plans or color schemes and then adjourn to the Plaza for lunch or dinner. In the course of this close collaboration, Johnson learned why his new friend was so dedicated to the New School building: "He had come to feel that the sand in his life glass was running low and he wanted to present the future with an example of the art he loved most, architecture, from which he had been drawn away to the ephemeral splendor of the stage."[32]

For Urban, the New School was truly a special project and his masterpiece. Fortunately it survives, although the interior has been greatly altered and an addition has subsequently been attached, but respectfully set back from the original building. The school marked a new mastery in Urban's skills: more disciplined, restrained, and refined than ever before. Here is the ultimate expression of the three key elements Urban applied throughout his career: simplicity, light, and color. He gave meticulous consideration to every detail, even designing his own exit signs. The specially created bronze handrails in the stairways are functional, elegant, and even pleasant to the touch. Despite the architect's reputation for extravagance and expense, the building cost only $500,000. Some quite remarkable effects were achieved with a great economy of means.

Opposite top left. The entrance foyer of the New School, with the doors to the auditorium–theatre to the left.
Top right and bottom. Two views of the New School's library and its double staircase. 1930. Columbia University.

The building that Urban designed was the first in New York to employ some of the principles and techniques of the new International Style, which had been developed in Europe by Mies van der Rohe, among others. Once more Urban had adopted a new, simpler style of design, for in Vienna he had moved from the Historical Style to Art Nouveau, or *Jugendstil*. With the New School he introduced the style that would dominate architecture until the advent of Postmodernism in the 1980s.

Philip Johnson was one of the earliest advocates in America of the International Style, which he himself would later use as an architect. In his lengthy critique of the New School, Johnson set down the style's principles.

> What may reasonably be considered the elements of the new style? (1) The purpose or function of the building as restricted by the exigencies of purely structural requirements is the major factor in the plan. The architect employs this plan as a starting point for the ultimate design of the whole building which thus develops rationally from within. The interior arrangement inevitably determines the general formation of the façade. (2) The building relies chiefly on this functional and structural arrangement for its decorative effect. Ornament is not employed. (3) The genius of the architect coordinates the practical needs in such a way that fine proportions and simple design create the beauty of the building.[33]

One of the finest examples of the International Style is Mies's Seagram Building in New York City, for which Philip Johnson created the magnificent Four Seasons restaurant.

Before considering Philip Johnson's critique in more detail, a description of the building is in order. The school, despite its size and style, did not radically upset the scale of other buildings, mainly brownstones, on its block. The cantilevered façade, a carefully considered study in black and white, was composed of alternating strips of white brick and bands of windows. Fenestration was designed to allow the maximum amount of natural light to pour into each room.

Light and color received a great deal of consideration in this project, and color, in the form of painted surfaces, was the chief decorative element of the building. In Urban's hands it was both inexpensive and greatly effective. Each room had its own color scheme, which is preserved only in Urban's original drawings or contemporary descriptions. The architect discussed the color schemes and their relation to lighting conditions and structural features in an article in *Parnassus* magazine:

> Warm colors . . . are located where they receive the most light, cold where there is most shadow, a change of plane is generally emphasized by a change of color, thus the walls have one set of colors, the ceiling another. By thus modeling the wall surfaces of a room the boxlike property of four walls is given an expression of contrasting filled spaces and void space; the monotony of the enclosing areas is transformed to an imaginative statement of the space enclosed and given a character by the emotional statement of color.[34]

Shepard Vogelgesang was a frequent commentator on all phases of Urban's work, and his essay in *Architectural Record* on the New School provides additional rationale for Urban's use of color. He wrote that in addition to white some ninety colors were applied, and explained that there were considerations behind Urban's choice of colors other than their relation to lighting, among them:

> . . . balance of accent, focusing attention at a desired point in the room, maintenance of a diagrammatic scheme to add to the legibility of planning where needed, and selection of colors for their emotionally reactive values. By confining color to the actual planes of the building accenting structural features—columns, for example, are generally kept white—architectural values are enhanced and color given its proper function in building.[35]

Vogelgesang left a description of how the color scheme appeared to someone looking from outside through the windows of the façade: "It shows in blocks of red, blue, green, yellow, orange, white, purple, brown, dark blue, as it occurs in the rooms behind the glass."[36]

Edmund Wilson expressed his opinion of Urban's work in an essay whose title reflects the writer's view of the whole project: "Aladdin's Lecture Palace."[37] His summation of the project must have stung Urban:

> Joseph Urban, the architect of the New School, is a brilliant theatrical designer—at least as far as the Ziegfeld "Follies" go. But when he tries to produce a functional lecture building, he merely turns out a set of fancy Ziegfeld settings which charmingly mimic offices and factories where we keep expecting to see pretty girls in blue, yellow and cinnamon dresses to match the gaiety of the ceilings and walls.[38]

Opposite. The dance studio provides a splendid example of Urban's use of color as the prime decorative and unifying element in the design of the New School. Urban's second wife, Mary, was a dancer with Isadora Duncan's troupe and taught dance at Barnard College. Her influence is felt in the studio with its circular, sunken dance floor.
Top. A photograph of the dance studio. 1930.
Center. Urban's color study of the studio. Ca. 1929–1930.
Bottom. The studio's color scheme as prepared by the architect. Ca. 1929–1930. Columbia University.

THE NEW SCHOOL FOR SOCIAL RESEARCH · STUDY FOR COLOR TREATMENT OF THE DANCE STUDIO · NEW YORK CITY · MAY 1930 · L

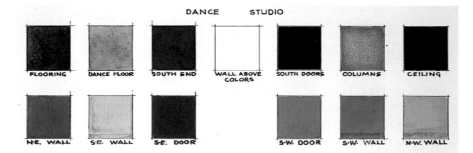

DANCE STUDIO

FLOORING DANCE FLOOR SOUTH END WALL ABOVE COLORS SOUTH DOORS COLUMNS CEILING

N·E· WALL S·E· WALL S·E· DOOR S·W· DOOR S·W· WALL N·W· WALL

Wilson conveniently fails to mention work Urban did at the Metropolitan Opera that was universally praised as great artistic achievement, which is not to suggest that his sets for the *Follies* or Broadway were of lesser quality.

While Urban gave his attention to every last detail of the building, three rooms were of special importance to him: the library, the dance studio, and the auditorium. The library occupied the fourth and fifth floors of the school, and it was to be the social home of the students, a lounge on one floor joined by a grand staircase to a reading room on the floor below. The double staircase that turns back upon itself was used several times by Urban: the Oasis Club in Palm Beach had one on its exterior, and the one at the Park Avenue Restaurant was bordered by gleaming metal railings.

Unfortunately, the Urban library had to be sacrificed as the school grew and its requirements changed. The alterations were difficult for Alvin Johnson to accept:

> To me the New School building is sacred to the memory of Joe Urban. For good practical reasons some changes have been made in the layout since the building was erected, but I must confess that every one has caused me acute pain. The most important change was the removal of the noble stairways from the lounge floor to the library floor, and closing of the well in between the floors. The change was necessitated not because of any flaw in Urban's functional conceptions, but because of a shift in the functional requirements of the Graduate Faculty and its students, which could not have been foreseen when the building was designed.[39]

One of the requirements to which Johnson referred was the need for a quiet library where scholars who had fled Nazi persecution in Europe could work undisturbed, one not joined to an inevitably noisy student lounge. This influx of refugee scholars and artists caused the New School to become known as the "University in Exile."

Alvin Johnson describes the origin of Urban's plan for the dance studio, with its sunken maple floor, in the school's basement:

> According to Mr. Urban in the periods of history before the dance really meant something, religiously and socially, the dance floor was a circle with a space for the spectators to sit or stand all around. The spectators felt themselves part of the performance; often a spectator would be inspired to join in the dance, or groups would dance in circles adjacent to the central circle. A decadent aristocracy thrust the dancers up on a stage, with the spectators viewing them from below, fixing their attention on a show of legs no more edifying than the trays of frogs' legs in a fish market. We would sink our dance floor instead of elevating it, and the spectators, seated or standing, would get a sense of the grace and beauty of movement of the dancers' whole bodies.[40]

Since Mary had once been an Isadora Duncan dancer, she may have given some input while Urban was creating the dance studio.

Eugene Clute described the lighting throughout the school and has left a vivid description of the colors applied in the studio:

> The ceiling is painted dull black, excepting the reflecting areas in the center and around the walls which are white. To the level of the tops of the doors, the walls are painted in colors, one section being orange and the next yellow with blue next to that and so on. The floor [the aisles, not the dance floor itself, which was highly polished maple] is dark blue. The entrance doors

are light green and one of the two doors opposite the entrance is in vermillion and the other in light emerald green.[41]

Cove lighting set a little way back from the walls all around the ceiling brought the colors to life. There was an additional source of light, a rectangle illuminated by coves on all sides, above the circular dance floor.

The most striking room in the building, one that survives and is still capable of astonishing those who see it for the first time, is the theatre, or auditorium. Edmund Wilson called the room "a gray oval igloo-like cave."[42] Alvin Johnson describes how the unusual shape came into being:

> Our most serious problem of construction was presented by the auditorium. I wanted to have it shaped like the inside of a half egg shell, with the rostrum at the small end of the egg. I hate a large, quadrilateral room, like a Masonic hall. A shy lecturer—and most lecturers who have anything to say are shy—is embarrassed by the huge empty space overhead and by the undigested audience groups in the near and far corners. If the capacity of the room is 600, the audience looks enormous, formidable; if there happens to be a small attendance—say 100—they scatter about in small groups or as individuals. . . . An oval room tends to draw the audience together. A hundred hearers do not seem so few and six hundred do not seem distressingly many.
>
> Mr. Urban said nothing when I suggested the egg shell. He put his palm to his chin and the glow in his eyes turned inward in thought. He would encounter acoustic problems, and he would be pounded by the cub

More than sixty years after its completion, the New School's auditorium-theatre is still fully capable of astonishing those who experience it for the first time. 1930. Columbia University.

207

architectural critics for designing a non-functional room. But a few days later he said:

"You shall have your egg." [43]

Acoustical problems were lessened by perforating the ceiling to absorb some of the sound. There was indeed criticism that the room was "non-functional"—not that it did not work but that there was no reason related to the room's purpose or function that led directly to its form. The criticism in one instance did not come from a "cub" critic but from Philip Johnson.

With its gray-and-red color scheme and motif of repeated arches, the six-hundred-seat theatre is as fresh today as it was more than sixty years ago. The arches seem reminiscent of Urban's great arch in the prison scene of *Don Carlos* and quite obviously influenced the interior of Radio City Music Hall (which was designed by Edward Durell Stone, although Raymond Hood was also involved, as he had been for the entire Rockefeller Center project[44]). The stage opening was made as wide as possible, so it could be used for plays, chamber music, recitals, and films. By closing off the stage, the apron was suitable for lectures, with the speaker thrust out into, and surrounded by, the audience.

Just as specially commissioned works of art would grace the interiors and façades of the buildings in Rockefeller Center, two murals were installed in the New School. In the red-and-black directors' room Urban mounted Thomas Hart Benton's *America Today*, which presented scenes of industrial America. Benton's work now graces the lobby of the new Equitable Building on Seventh Avenue in New York City.

Mexican artist José Orozco's only work in New York City can be found in a classroom and adjacent hallway on the seventh floor of the New School. Orozco based his frescoes on the themes of revolution, oppression, and brotherhood. With "strong, deep colors, a palette of closely pitched red, oranges and browns dramatically highlighted by occasional uses of blue and green," the panels greatly pleased Urban.[45] The Orozco frescoes were restored in 1988 to their original brilliance, and the *New York Times* said of them that "they may . . . rank as the city's most outstanding examples of mural art." [46]

Having dealt with the main features of the building in some detail, we may now fairly consider Philip Johnson's criticism. Johnson's definition of the International Style has been given earlier; in what follows he states to what extent Urban has applied the principles of the new style:

> Viewed in its location on Twelfth Street, the New School, at first, gives the impression that many of these elements have been embodied here. But a closer inspection suggests that the architect has produced the illusion of a building in the International Style rather than a building resulting from a genuine application of the new principles.[47]

Johnson first cites as an example the cantilevered façade for which there was no functional justification. Rather than creating additional usable space, the cantilever actually wasted it. The rooms at both ends of the façade were oddly shaped because part of each projected out three feet from the corner sections that were not cantilevered. The three-foot overhang was intended to provide shelter on the busy street for the school's students, but a simple canopy would have been less expensive if not so visually striking. To create the effect on the exterior of unbroken panels of windows, the interior support columns were set back from the walls. However, this resulted in unusable space since the columns were still too near the windows to allow anything to go on between them and the walls.

The façade, according to Johnson, was not devoid of ornament since the arrangement of the windows and mullions did not derive from any structural consideration but was "worked upon in order to provide ornament." [48] In sum, according to the principles of the International Style, the form of the façade did not result from or reflect the function of the building's interior: "The real procedure of modern architecture was reversed—the façade design arbitrarily controls the interior." [49]

Johnson's analysis of the interior is based on the same functional principles. Urban knew that he would be criticized for the shape of the theatre, and Johnson obliged. Aside from the client's desire to have an egg-shaped auditorium, no mean consideration, there was no structural justification for its design. The theatre's dome in particular consumes a great deal of space, which given a different configuration of the auditorium could have been used more effectively.

Despite his detailed criticism, Johnson does appreciate Urban's achievement, which he duly and quite fairly recognizes in the last paragraph of his review. One must again take note of Urban's work as it related to a "new style":

> In the New School we have the anomaly of a building supposed to be in a style of architecture based on the development of the plan from function and facade from plan but which is as formally and pretentiously conceived as a Renaissance palace. Urban's admiration for the New Style is more complete than his understanding. But the very fact that the School can be subjected to analysis from the point of view of the new elements of building shows how far the architect has been influenced by the New Style. His work is an outstanding piece of pioneering in New York. Although it diverges . . . in many respects from the best work that has already been done here and abroad, it is on the whole a most important evidence that the International Style is creating an increasingly permanent place for itself in America. The use of ribbon windows, to emphasize the horizontality of the facade, the fundamental simplicity of design, and the successful use of color in the interior are all features that are real contributions to better architecture. The New School for Social Research is an encouraging sign that soon there will be many more buildings in this country similar in spirit but which will come closer to a true mastery of the International Style.[50]

The library, the dance studio, and the Benton mural are gone. Urban's brilliant arrangement of colors, applied when labor and maintenance costs were a minor consideration, is gone. The façade remains. The auditorium remains. The New School itself, with its long tradition of innovation in education, continues to be a vital part of the intellectual life of New York.

Asked to identify the earliest example of the International Style in New York, today's architectural student, or even architectural historian, would probably name Gordon Bunshaft's Lever House, finished in 1952, and completely overlook Urban's building, which opened on New Year's Day in 1931. Had the New School been two or three times its height or located in midtown Manhattan—on Park Avenue in the Fifties, for example—Urban's role as a "pioneer" would have been well known and appreciated today.

In addition to the New School, Urban designed in 1931 three other significant projects (only one of which was built) that provide further examples

of his new, leaner style. The Park Avenue Restaurant in New York was described by columnist Ed Sullivan as the "most gorgeous spot in New York." [51] In this project the murals Urban used so frequently were replaced by beveled mirrors that reflected the room and its occupants at unexpected angles. On the first floor the main feature was a bar that was circular, a theme carried through in the huge round mirrors and a decorative device Urban made use of again in his last completed project, the Katharine Brush apartment of 1933. In the restaurant a double stairway similar to the one in the New School's library led to a mezzanine. The total effect was one of cool, glittering elegance. Unfortunately, the circular bar proved to be the undoing of the short-lived restaurant. Prohibition was in effect, after all, and zealous federal agents destroyed the room in a raid. Teegen and Schott, the successor firm to Urban's, designed a restaurant with a similar circular bar and mirrors (called the House of Morgan) once Prohibition was repealed.

The concept of a movie theatre in a shopping mall was once again explored by Urban in a plan published in *Architectural Record* in 1931. [52] Intended for suburban Westchester County, New York, the plan included space for six retail stores on either side of the 1,200-seat theatre. This design of more than sixty years ago could be built today without seeming the least bit dated, although the cinema would no doubt be converted into a twin or triplex.

The third project dating from 1931 was also planned for the suburbs: a small private home estimated to cost about $11,000.[53] The building was a perfect cube completely devoid of decoration and rather resembles the work of Le Corbusier, whom Urban greatly admired. It consisted of three levels, and its ground floor contained the basement and garage; the second had a maid's room, dining room, and kitchen; and on the third were four bedrooms including the master bedroom with its own balcony. On the roof was a

Two views of the Park Avenue Restaurant in New York City. Once again Urban achieved a brilliant effect with a simplicity of means. The walls were painted black and the ceiling green. The club was closed and its mirrors were smashed when federal agents enforcing Prohibition raided the place. 1931. Columbia University.

211

FACADE·OF·THE·PROPOSED·MAX·REINHARDT·THEATRE·IN·NEW·YORK·CITY

FOUR THEATRES

Theatre had an unusual prominence in the social and cultural life of Vienna, where Urban lived the first forty years of his life. From his initial stage design at the Burgtheater in 1905 until his death in 1933, Urban centered his life on the theatre: as a scenic designer and as an architect. In the last year of his life, he reflected on the relationship between architect and stage designer:

> Architecture—great architecture—is always representative of its own age, and the theatre artist is forced to adjust himself to the physical limitations the architect sets for him. He must at the same time also make a record of his own times and a prophecy of the times to come. The whole history of the theatre shows the close relation between the scene designer and the theatre architect. The scene designer has always been primarily infected with a desire to give his players all possible space in which to act; the architect in keeping his theatre in harmony with the architecture of his time. It has been the give and take between the theatre architect and the scenic designer which has made the theatre what it was in every age. All the architectural changes of the generations have been reflected in scene design and in costume design and the problems which are the problems of architecture of one age are the theatres' problems in the age succeeding.[1]

Urban's original drawing for the proposed Reinhardt Theatre in New York City. Urban very effectively incorporated the fire escapes required by the city into the overall design of the façade. 1927. Columbia University.

In 1929 Urban published his only book, *Theatres*, which contains the plans for six theatres, only two of which were actually built.[2] He offered a brief commentary on each theatre and included a study of the historical development of the theatre and of the relationship between theatre design and the social order. Ten years earlier he had written a short piece simply entitled "The Stage," which appeared in *Theatre Arts* magazine. That essay offers an almost poetic view of the modern theatre that influenced all the projects in *Theatres*, and it is given here in its entirety:

> The stage brings us the greatest thoughts, the most beautiful phantasies and dreams; from many of the biggest thinkers, poets and artists of the

world. We learn the things of life and beauty that we did not know, that we did not imagine existed.

The theatre of the future must become:

The carrier of the culture of its nation.

The altar to which the best and greatest of a nation offer their energy and beauty, strength and knowledge.

The institution which receives equally the gift of genius and the force of the workman.

The shrine of beauty so democratic that every new cultural element coming finds there cooperation.

The future stage must be so big and general in its influence that the strength of its conviction goes out to the very frontier and knocks off the door of its neighbor. Who refuses this gift hurts himself and impoverishes his life.

In our future life the stage must have the same influence that the Christian church has had in the past.[3]

The architect–scenic designer, with his unique perspective, places the beginnings of theatre in ancient Greece, where plays and dance evolved from rituals performed in the vicinity of temples. The first theatres were primarily circular spaces for the stage surrounded by wooden stands for the audience. Eventually the rows of wooden seats were replaced by tiers of marble that enclosed the performing area on three sides and created what is now called an "arena" stage. Urban wrote that in these classical theatres, both Greek and Roman, "there was always one first and supreme law—to hear well and see well."[4] The architect continues his description of the classic theatre:

> Always the players were surrounded on three sides by the spectators, the action unfolding within the same space in which the audience sat. There was no picture-frame division, such as our present day theatre knows. The Greek Theatre held the emotions of actor and audience as in a cup. So perfectly could one hear that the rustle of garments in the stillness was audible to the last of 17,000 persons. Every individual sat in a direct line of vision. There was no strain either on actor or audience but instead an overwhelming sense of spiritual contact, due to the presence of the actor and audience within the same undivided space.

In the Baroque era, jaded courtiers demanded more elaborate entertainment, combining music, dance, and incredible scenic effects that would lead to the creation of opera. The courts no longer looked favorably on the democratic seating arrangements of the antique theatre, and to accommodate new scenic effects a different kind of theatre was called for. Urban credits the architect Giovanni Aleotti with providing the design that met these new requirements:

> Aleotti, in 1639, invented the deep, narrow wing stage and created the theatre with tiers of loges. It was a radical departure in construction, ignoring of course the two main laws of the antique theatre, those of good vision and good hearing. It also destroyed the intimate connection between performer and spectator, disregarding the fundamental spatial principle that in the classic theatre had created the spiritual connection between actor and audience. This theatre was the child of a frivolous society which came not to see, but to be seen.

The so-called "Italian" theatre reflected both the needs of the new forms of entertainment and those of the social order, just as the antique theatres did. In court theatres there was always a central box for the local noble figure and his immediate retinue. Fanning out from both sides of the royal box in a "horseshoe" were boxes for other members of the court. Only those in the very center of the horseshoe actually enjoyed a full view of the stage, but the configuration did afford courtiers an excellent view of each other.

When Shakespeare opened his Globe Theatre on the banks of the Thames in 1599, Urban points out that

> ... the importance of the connection between actor and audience was recognized once again. Here they filled one-third of the pit with a sceneless platform surrounded on three sides by the audience.... On this stage Shakespeare played his undying dramas and here the art of acting was brought to a state of perfection which never, from the time of the classic drama to our own day, has been excelled.... Like a sleeping poison, the remodelling of the Italian stage sickened and crippled the whole theatre body, drama, action, stage and auditorium.

Convinced that no existing theatre was adequate to meet the artistic demands of his four-opera *Ring* cycle, Richard Wagner decided to create a special theatre. The *Festspielhaus* that opened in Bayreuth in 1876 was intended to be only temporary, but fortunately, through more than a hundred years and two world wars, it has survived to the present day. So that the audience could fully appreciate all the elements of art, music, and drama that were fused into his *Ring*, Wagner built his auditorium in the shape of a fan, enabling the spectators to see and hear everything taking place onstage. To lessen the separation between audience and singers, he covered the orchestra pit with a black acoustical shell and sloped it beneath the stage. The result was a miracle of acoustics and perfect sight lines. For the stage director, the enormous size of the performance area offers virtually unlimited resources.

Architects of later opera houses experimented very little with the theatrical conventions of proscenium stage and orchestra pit and concerned themselves with the configuration of the auditorium, seating arrangements, and fresh designs for balconies and boxes. For Urban, however, any reform that started with the auditorium was wrong:

> ... a reform to be successful, must start only with the stage, never with the auditorium. So long as the stage is not widened to dimensions which will embrace the audience, so long as the stage does not offer full communication between actor and audience, any reform is only a compromise, not a real solution of the problem.

Most reforms carried out in the years between the world wars were directed toward theatres for dramatic performance rather than opera. Directors and architects sought first to eliminate the strictly defined separation between players and spectators imposed by the proscenium stage. Their initial attempt at modification was to install in front of the proscenium a lip that created a new playing space thrust out into the audience. This led to changes in seating arrangements that placed the audience, arena fashion, around the newly expanded stage. The next logical development was a rethinking of traditional stage settings.

Not surprisingly, leading European directors with their own performing companies, notably Max Reinhardt, engaged prominent architects to create new theatres. The *Grosses Schauspielhaus* in Berlin, once a circus, was remodeled in 1919 into an arena-style theatre fully suited to the needs of

THE · AUDITORIUM · OF · THE · REINHARDT · THEATRE

Left. Floor plan showing the arrangement of the boxes in the Reinhardt Theatre. 1927. *Theatres.*
Right. The auditorium of the Reinhardt Theatre was designed to create an intimate atmosphere bridging audience and actors. Scenery was to be kept to a minimum, placing greater emphasis on lighting effects and the technique of the actors.
Columbia University.

Reinhardt. Designed by Hans Poelzig, the 3,500-seat auditorium is featured in many commentaries on the development of theatre in this century.

One of Reinhardt's most famous productions was a spectacle called *The Miracle*, which Otto Kahn tried for years to bring to New York after seeing its original staging. It opened in London in 1911, but World War I prevented the production from appearing in New York until 1924, when Kahn put up $400,000 of the $600,000 required to mount it. Since Urban and Lefler had designed the sets for the German and Austrian productions, Urban was understandably disappointed when Reinhardt selected Norman Bel Geddes, who had briefly been a student in Urban's studio, to create the single massive setting. Reinhardt explained to Urban that he hoped *The Miracle* would be a great popular success and lead to his own company in America and he therefore felt it necessary to have a native-born designer. Bel Geddes transformed the Century Theatre into the interior of a Gothic cathedral, where a cast of five hundred performed the pantomime spectacle and the audience sat in pews. When Bel Geddes asked for assistance with the set, the ever-generous Urban was glad to help.

A great success, *The Miracle* ran for almost three hundred performances in New York and toured the rest of the country for five years. Reinhardt returned to the city in 1927 with his Deutsches Theatre company, which performed, in German, *A Midsummer Night's Dream*, *Danton's Death*, and Hofmannsthal's *Everyman*. During this stay Reinhardt asked Urban to design a theatre for him. Since their ideas about the modern theatre coincided, Urban went ahead, made the designs, and presented them at a farewell dinner party for Reinhardt at the St. Regis, an event for which Gretl was responsible:

> Father was rather nervous because I had to make all the arrangements, but everything went well: flower arrangements on the table, boutonnieres for the men, orchid corsages for the ladies, the best of wines. There were about twenty guests, and Father's designs were celebrated by much toasting, but fortunately no speeches.
>
> Max had told Father that he had never heard any Negro spirituals, so with the help of Gene Buck [songwriter, librettist, founder of ASCAP, and longtime friend] a superb quartet was found, and the evening ended on a glorious note.

The theatre Urban designed for Reinhardt was unlike any of the five theatres the director occupied in Europe. It was, in fact, unlike anything recently built on the Continent. The stage was, of course, the central concern in Urban's theatre design, but for this project he lavished a good deal of attention on the façade. His goal was to meet any theatre's need for advertising current presentations and also provide for the fire escapes required by New York's fire code. The resulting solution was daring, modern, sophisticated, and elegant. In an article for the Sunday magazine section of the *New York Times*, Urban described his intentions for the façade:

> In designing the theatre Max Reinhardt is expected to occupy in New York I have brought the fire escape out of the alleyways and tried to make a base for the electric signs as well as a decorative feature of the facade. The face of the house is to be of vitrolite, a gleaming black glass. At various levels across the front stretch the horizontal lines of the fire escape balconies in golden metal work. Down the centre runs a grilled tower containing the emergency stairways, and this tower is continued high in air as a kind of pinnacle. Thus I have tried to apply the fire escapes as a golden arabesque against the shining black of the facade itself.
>
> To accommodate the advertising signs to this design I have inserted long panels of interchangeable letters across the front of the various levels of the fire escape balconies. And I have also, of course, provided a frame for the name of the theatre running up one corner of the building.[5]

In *Theatres* Urban justified a "decorative scheme of such force" for the façade because it was "a necessity when the theatre has to compete with the sheer bulk and height of surrounding skyscrapers. It is far too easy for a low façade to be crushed and lost in the crowding and the confusion of metropolitan building." Intended for West Fiftieth Street, the theatre would have had other buildings on either side of it.

219

Urban wrote in *Theatres* that while the Reinhardt Theatre was conceived for a producer, it was actually designed for the actor:

> Entire emphasis is on a form that will put the actor in immediate harmony with his audience. . . . The theatre of the actor separates itself from the life of the community. The audience approaches the actor as an artist. The theatre is dedicated to him and his art. It is designed to give him the utmost luxury in the exercise of his powers. . . . To create a theatre which shall bring the audience to the actor is an interesting problem for the architect, full of fascination and of opportunity—the special problem of this Reinhardt Theatre.

The oval auditorium Urban planned was only eighty feet deep, half the usual depth of other New York theatres, but its size and shape guaranteed intimacy and perfect sight lines. There were to be five tiers of boxes, which in the floor plans strongly resemble the toboggan-shaped boxes of the post–World War II opera houses in Hamburg and Cologne. The boxes in these opera houses, however, protrude into the auditorium while those in Urban's design are flush with the walls of the house. They were designed to provide full view of the stage, but each box was to be hidden from the view of any others. The audience was to focus on the actors and not on each other, as in a horseshoe-shaped court-style theatre.

The walls were to be hung with heavy red curtains that were intended to deaden sound, to separate the boxes from each other, and to provide a single decorative element that would not distract attention from the performers. Above the tiers of boxes was a gallery for musicians and actors. Reinhardt loved to have actors approach the stage from all parts of the house, and Urban designed this theatre so that players could enter from the aisles, the gallery, and the orchestra pit, which was hidden under the steps of the stage.

Urban described the stage facilities and the emphasis this theatre's design placed on the actor:

> The entire plan for the backstage is of the simplest, even the cyclorama, if one is used, will be portable. It is planned for playing with no scenery, or as little as possible. The color of the costumes to be relieved against a black background, some figures to merge with the background till like a Rembrandt portrait the gesture of the hands and the expression of the face tell the story. Or the screen curtain which plays the part of decorative background, sounding board and surface for light effects may part to disclose the time and mood of the action. The cyclorama may be lighted with an autumnal grey crossed by the shadows of nearly leafless trees, or again the aperture may indicate a room lighted with myriads of flickering candles for the celebration of some great feast.

Aside from introducing the risk that doing away with scenery would cost Urban a substantial part of his income, the plan raises many questions. Perhaps Reinhardt could have made the theatre work, but one has to wonder whether other directors would have been able to master a performing space that appears to demand so much from both actor and spectator. In a study of modern theatres, Hannelore Schubert discusses the limits of those with stages similar to that of the Reinhardt, and notes that "now that the old make-believe stage-sets have vanished, we find the bareness of a scene in which the actor performs in an empty space, a positive disadvantage."[6] Schubert goes on to describe the actor standing on the stage apron as performing "in a vacuum."[7] Urban's design was stunning and innovative, but it may have posed too many difficulties for directors less gifted than Reinhardt to overcome without scenery.

The Reinhardt Theatre was never built, most likely because of the stock market crash of 1929. Urban's plans for a new Metropolitan Opera House were also never realized, despite all the effort and time Urban lavished on an endeavor so important to him. It was the second greatest disappointment of his career, following the aftermath of the *Festzug* in Vienna.

The Metropolitan Opera House, which stood on Broadway between Thirty-ninth and Fortieth streets, opened on October 22, 1883, but the familiar, elegant maroon-and-gold Edwardian auditorium dated from a 1903 renovation. While the auditorium was unquestionably lavish, there were no spacious foyers or salons. Rehearsal rooms, dressing rooms for chorus and orchestra, and stage facilities were all severely limited. Even the auditorium, however plush, was far from satisfactory, for only the very center seats offered an unobstructed view of the stage.

The building occupied a full, irregularly shaped block that did not allow any possible expansion. The only solution, therefore, was to build a new opera house, and in the late 1920s a flurry of activity almost did produce a new theatre. Before discussing Urban's plans for this project, it is necessary to recount briefly the history of the Metropolitan, since its origins in part explain why the new house was not then built.

The Academy of Music on Irving Place became New York's opera house upon its completion in 1854, and its boxes soon were the proud possessions of the city's most socially prominent and wealthy families. After the Civil War the possessors of great new fortunes wished to mark their arrival into society by also having boxes at the opera. When the directors of the Academy declined to provide more boxes in the auditorium to accommodate the *nouveaux riches*, those thus excluded from the privileged ranks of boxholders announced that they would build their own opera house. Goelets, Goulds, Morgans, Vanderbilts, and Whitneys, among others, then formed a corporation, built an opera house, and made sure there were boxes enough for all shareholders.

Originally the new opera company permitted a general manager to produce the operas and share the profits, but in 1908 a different organizational structure was created. Henceforth the Metropolitan Opera and Real Estate Company, which consisted of the shareholders/boxholders, would own the building and the land beneath it, while the Metropolitan Opera Company, with its own board of directors, would be responsible for the performances. There would be a salaried general manager, and any profits were to be used for new productions.

At the time under consideration here, Otto Kahn was the chairman of the board of directors of the Metropolitan Opera Company, and the general manager, Giulio Gatti-Casazza, reported directly to him. Kahn knew all too well the limitations of the house, and despite his own great wealth and position genuinely believed that the Met should attract as wide an audience as possible. However, Kahn's democratic spirit inevitably conflicted with the aristocratic tendencies of boxholders jealously guarding privileged positions both in the opera house and in society itself. They were described in the November 25, 1925, issue of *Time*, which featured a cover story on Otto Kahn: "As feudal barons clung to their castles and patents of nobility, so the elect of Manhattan's social register cling to their boxes at the Metropolitan."[8]

Gatti-Casazza shared with Kahn the dream of someday building a new home for the company, and in 1924 he wrote Kahn a letter reminding him

The stage, proscenium, and auditorium of the proposed new Metropolitan Opera House. Urban compared the flaring stage opening to "an open mouth." The sides of the opening were part of the auditorium, and the aprons in front of the side walls could be used for action and processions. New York City. 1927.
Columbia University.

of their frequent discussions. He concluded with his feeling that "perhaps the right moment has arrived to take a decision." [9]

A piece of real estate became available on West Fifty-seventh Street between Eighth and Ninth avenues that Kahn thought would be an ideal site for the new opera house. The plot was two hundred feet deep and ran through to Fifty-sixth Street. Unable to arrange a quick meeting with the board of the Real Estate Company, and fearing that the property would either sell or become too expensive, Kahn bought it at his own risk and expense for $2,930,000. He was willing to sell this location to the Real Estate Company at cost if they were to build on it.

R. Fulton Cutting, the new president of the board of the Real Estate Company, who replaced a man known for his antipathy toward a new building, heard of Kahn's purchase and asked about his plans. Kahn gave four main reasons for building a new house, the first of which shows his concern for the general public and his conception of the Met's role in the cultural life of New York:

> The accommodations for those patrons of the opera who cannot afford to buy the more expensive seats, i.e. the masses of the music-loving public, is inadequate as to quantity and wholly unsatisfactory as to quality. Indeed, a considerable number of the seats are so bad that it is really an act of unfairness to take money for such seats—especially from people of small

222

means. It seems to me a particularly compelling obligation for an institution like the Metropolitan Opera, standing as it does morally in a kind of trust relationship to the opera-loving public of New York, to provide amply and generously for those of its patrons who are of small or modest means and in whose case the price of a ticket means close economy and the denial of other things.[10]

Kahn's other reasons concerned the inadequate and antiquated backstage facilities, the insoluble traffic problems before and after performances, and the fact that the existing house did not produce additional revenue to meet the ever-increasing costs of opera. This last point implied that a new building would include office or residential space.

Kahn developed his ideas about the project in some detail in his initial communication with Cutting; it was obvious that a great deal of thought already had been invested in the project. Seating capacity would be increased from thirty-five hundred to not less than four thousand. There would be only one tier of boxes, those on the parterre level, and their number would be reduced from thirty-five to twenty-eight. Ownership of the boxes, Kahn wrote, had proved to be "inconvenient, troublesome and expensive to the owners."[11] He proposed, therefore, that boxes in the new house would be leased for each of the five weekly subscription series.

Kahn also had formed clear ideas about the building:

> It is not contemplated that the new Metropolitan need be a monumental and ornamental building, rivalling European Opera Houses in appearance. Our conception is that it should be plain, simple, dignified, seeking its distinction rather in being perfectly adapted to its purpose, both on the stage and in the accommodation to the public, than in outward appearance.[12]

The press and the public reacted favorably to such a project, and by February 1927 the idea was unanimously approved by the board of the Real Estate Company. Although the land had been purchased late in 1925, little progress seems to have been made until 1926 when Benjamin W. Morris, who had designed the Cunard Building on lower Broadway and the annex to the Morgan Library, was named architect. According to the *New York Times*, Morris was chosen for his ability to combine beauty with modern steel construction.[13] Boston critic H. T. Parker described Morris as a man "who has signed no plans for a theatre, but who has fulfilled various commissions for men of wealth."[14]

Joseph Urban was named associate architect, but to operagoers he was less well known as an architect than as a scenic designer. The general assumption was that Morris would be in charge of the overall design while Urban would chiefly concern himself with the stage and the technical requirements of opera production. Urban was clearly Kahn's first choice, and the two men had discussed the project in great detail before Kahn's intentions were made public. Early in 1926 Urban was able to submit a proposal to Kahn that was to be the first of six done before he and Morris were officially appointed architects.

The relationship between Morris and Urban was specified in an exchange of letters between Morris and Kahn in February 1927. Morris wrote that he understood his commission to be as follows:

> I am to prepare, in consultation with Mr. Joseph Urban all matters relating to Operatic Production, Stage Arrangements, etc., Preliminary

Drawings, adequate in study, Scale, and Presentation to give the Board a complete understanding of the Design and arrangements of the Building, both internally and externally. I am to pay Mr. Urban's fee in connection with his services following the Preliminary Studies. . . . Mr. Urban is to be cordially welcomed as a Consultant with me to the extent desired by you, on the basis that his subsequent fee will be paid by me, and that it will not exceed one sixth of the fee to be paid to me.[15]

In his reply Kahn specified that Urban was to receive 20 percent of Morris's fee in payment for his services and concluded his letter as follows: "The Board understands that you are prepared to collaborate and consult in every way with Mr. Urban, and to accord him full and public recognition in his capacity as Associate Architect." [16]

Discussions began in March 1927 about such basic matters as seating capacity and engineering. By the first of April, Morris had prepared a working schedule for the building: demolition of structures currently on site was to start on December 1, 1927; the house would be completed and ready for rehearsal by September 15, 1929; and the first performance would take place on November 1, 1929. At this early stage, however, there was no agreement about the actual design of the building, and a set of plans had yet to be approved by all concerned parties.

It was understood that when Otto Kahn returned from Europe in June 1927, plans were to be submitted for his approval. The two architects accordingly visited his home in Cold Spring Harbor on June 25 and 26, at which time two very different approaches were offered. Urban made an elaborate presentation with what Morris described as a "very handsome set of drawings, of plan sections and elevation, and exceedingly artistic photographs of a model which he had prepared taken from various points of view." [17] Since Morris had not earlier seen these plans for a three-tiered, fan-shaped auditorium with thirty-five boxes, he did not feel prepared to comment on it. His own plan was in the traditional horseshoe style, but it would not be ready until July 18.

Resentment between the two architects was already starting to build, for obviously both were working alone on separate plans instead of collaborating.

This drawing shows the grand foyer of the proposed new Met that corresponded to the orchestra level of the auditorium. The second level (surrounding the well) was reserved for the boxholders. 1927.
Columbia University.

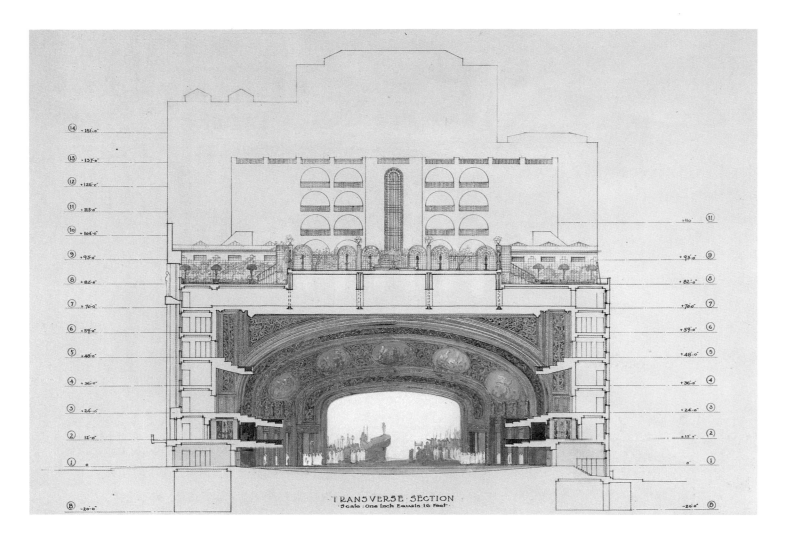

TRANSVERSE SECTION
Scale: One Inch Equals 16 Feet

That summer both architects went to Europe with their respective plans, visited various opera houses and theatres, and consulted with technical experts, architects, and producers. Before he departed, Urban had completed his designs for new productions of *La Rondine*, *Norma*, *Hänsel und Gretel*, and *Violanta*, which would be presented during the Met's 1927–1928 season.

As might have been expected, each man returned with testimonials for his own design and criticisms of the other's. Urban had collected evidence that since Wagner opened Bayreuth in 1876 more fan-shaped theatres had been built in Germany than the horseshoe-shaped variety. Morris came back claiming that everyone he contacted expressed preference for his plan and criticized the inferior sight lines and acoustics in the Urban plan. Based on comments gathered abroad, Morris wrote Kahn that he supported his own "Scheme C" and would not care to assume any responsibility for Urban's "Scheme IX." [18] Urban was by then furious and explained in a letter to Morris the theory behind his "scheme" as though he were talking to an architectural novice:

> The object of the plan is to have as few as possible, or preferably no seats, loges, boxes or balconies right and left of the stage, the concentration of all seats being in the form of an amphitheatre with the idea that every one in the audience has almost the same view of the stage and that the loges are in back of the amphitheatre or at their starting point on the sides as far removed from the proscenium as conditions will permit. [19]

View of the proscenium and stage for the proposed Metropolitan Opera. 1927. Columbia University.

225

Against the really unsupportable claim that sight lines in his proposal were bad, Urban stated: "I can make no defense to this except to say that a study of the plans will reveal that the sight lines of Scheme IX are as near perfection as it is possible to make sight lines and are far superior to those of Scheme C."[20] Urban noted that Morris's antagonism to ideas that he "considered entirely sound and most vital" had naturally led to a condition of competition.[21] Claiming that he had cooperated fully with Morris's staff, Urban clearly stated that further collaboration was impossible:

> My main thought was to get the best possible opera house for New York, but it seemed to me that you apparently laid greater stress upon who was the architect. This policy of complete cooperation I maintained for almost half a year until what is now a fact became apparent—that is, that we are entirely in disagreement. . . . [S]ince I have strong faith in Scheme IX I feel that I should fight for it to the extreme even at the cost . . . of cooperation.[22]

Critic and composer Deems Taylor (whose operas *The King's Henchman* and *Peter Ibbetson* were given productions at the Met with Urban settings) saw Urban's plans for the new Met in his studio and asked permission to publish them. He did so in the October 8, 1927, issue of *Musical America*, including his own favorable comments on the project. Until then the Urban-Morris conflict had been kept from the general public.

Taylor stated clearly in his article that the plans shown had not officially been approved by the Met and that the reproductions were not of Urban's actual drawings but of his own sketches based on the architect's work. However, one striking drawing by Urban of the interior of the auditorium did appear on the first page. The New York press picked up the story, some papers giving the distinct impression that the new Met would follow Urban's plans.

Otto Kahn issued a statement reaffirming that Morris was the architect, Urban the associate architect, and that they had been retained as collaborators, not competitors. The plans that appeared in the journal, Kahn continued, had not been authorized by Morris, the Metropolitan Opera Company, or the Real Estate Company. The statement concluded with Kahn's pledge that when the plans were approved they would be made public in a duly authenticated and official manner.[23] Although Kahn did not mention it in his statement,

Floor plan of the new Met's box level, which was isolated from the other public areas of the opera house. Urban offered the boxholders their own separate entrance, elevator, lounges, salons, and smoking rooms in hopes they could be persuaded to back the building of his proposed version of the theatre. 1927. *Theatres.*

Opposite top. Elevation of the proposed Met, with the stage loft and workshops to the left and the studio apartment tower to the right. 1927. *Theatres.*
Bottom. Cutaway view of the opera house showing the seating levels of the auditorium. Urban's broad fan-shaped design was intended to provide every seat with a full view of the stage. 1927. Columbia University.

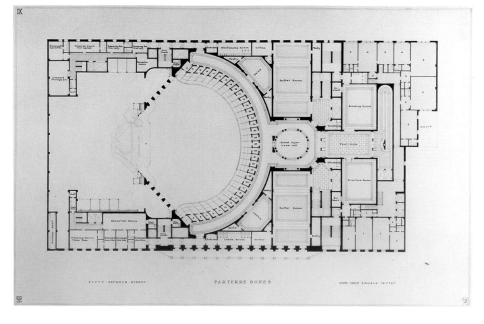

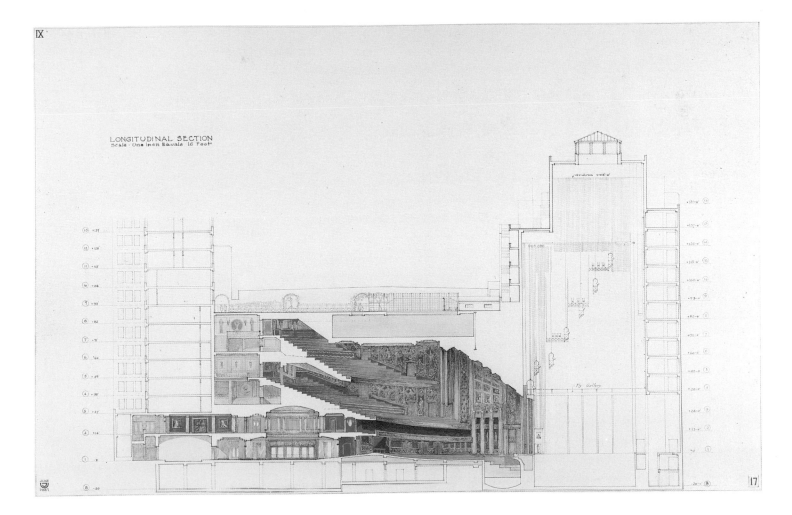

LONGITUDINAL SECTION
Scale - One Inch Equals 16 Feet

the chief reason the plans had not been submitted to either board, even though the "schemes" of both architects had been ready for about three months, was that so many of the board members, most importantly J. P. Morgan, were in Europe for the summer.

The issue of a more "democratic" house, so important to both Kahn and Urban, was raised in Taylor's article: "The new Metropolitan is a democratic opera house. Whether the directors consider it or not, they have made it one by demanding an auditorium to accommodate 5000 people." [24] (Actually it was Kahn who insisted on seating a larger audience.) The magazine added more fuel to the fire in its October 18 issue with a front-page headline: "Publication of Urban Plans for Metropolitan Crystallizes Situation in Which Conflict Between Democratic and Conservative Elements Point to Delay in Construction of Home for New York Music Drama." [25] If the publication of the plans did not divide the boxholders into rival factions, this headline surely did, and it also killed the project.

Objections to the site were raised by boxholders, and a committee of five, among them R. Fulton Cutting and J. P. Morgan, was appointed by the board of the Real Estate Company to look for other suitable locations. To show how absurd the situation had become, one alternate site the committee said it was considering, while Kahn was left holding the property acquired at his own expense, was Fifth Avenue and 110th Street!

Meanwhile, Urban became increasingly upset by his treatment at the hands of both Morris and his staff. In a memo apparently written in advance of a conversation with Kahn, Urban noted that Morris would see him for only a few minutes at a time, leaving him to talk with his employees, "young boys who did not know anything about a theatre." [26] He was also concerned about his reputation as an architect after learning of unpleasant remarks made against him. The *New Yorker* conducted an interview with Morris during which Kenneth Murchison, an architect-financier who wrote a column in *Architecture*, was said to have said: "Don't worry, Urban won't touch a pencil or brush to this opera house; we will see that he is kept well behind the footlights." [27] And in front of a group of architects Murchison had said, "Morris will wipe out [the] scene painter." [28]

On January 26, 1928, Cutting wrote Kahn that "regrettably and decisively" the plans for the new opera house were not acceptable to the committee that studied them and could not be recommended to the stockholders/boxholders.[29] Kahn's dream had failed to materialize because he lost the support of those who would ultimately have to approve the project. The objections of the boxholders to the plans, the site, and the financing, however legitimate some of them might have been, were really of secondary importance. The primary concern of the boxholders was for what they felt was a threat to their social position; they really had nothing to gain in a new house. They cared little about backstage facilities or how well others could see or hear. One wonders what might have resulted had Kahn, and Urban as well, proceeded more diplomatically.

Urban and his staff spent an incredible amount of time and effort on the nine separate "schemes" he prepared. The archives at Columbia preserve piles of finished drawings for elevations, seating arrangements, and floor plans. In *Theatres* Urban expressed some of the ideas that influenced his thinking and designs:

The purpose back of the building of a new opera house today must be to find an architectural form so free that it can in turn set free every modern impulse which would tend to heighten and develop the form of grand opera, to make it not grandiose, but grand, majestic, as large in spirit as in scale. . . . The growth of the modern opera orchestra, the pageantry required for modern production of operas, like *Aïda*, the wishes of Wagner in decoration, still unfulfilled, demand a more elastic stage, a larger orchestra pit, a more flexible arrangement.

The auditorium, too, must change. What was originally a large house holding two thousand people must today be enlarged to hold five thousand, all of whom must hear and see well. In such a house with the stage enormously widened, probably to cover the whole width of the auditorium, there will be no room for the present diamond horseshoe. The loges will at least have to retire to the back of the house, and the seats will be arranged in the forms of as many, or rather, as few, amphitheatres as necessary.

The drawings published in *Theatres* are taken from Urban's "Scheme IX" and represent plans specifically for the Fifty-seventh Street location. The facilities the architect incorporated into his plans are indeed most impressive: a fan-shaped auditorium seating 5,378, lounges, promenades, restaurants, the latest in backstage equipment, an enormous stage, and a revenue-producing apartment tower. There were even separate dressing rooms for white and colored supernumeraries.

Urban was most generous in providing for the comfort of the boxholders, who had their own private entrance with a private staircase and two private elevators. There was a vestibule and foyer reserved for their exclusive use in addition to two smoking rooms, a directors' room, and restrooms. The entire box level was isolated from the rest of the house, and all boxes enjoyed a full view of the stage, which neither Met at Broadway nor Lincoln Center could claim.

The Fifty-seventh Street façade reflected the three separate but related units that catered to three distinct constituencies. Viewed from left to right there was first the stage house and workshops for the opera staff, the auditorium in the middle for the spectators, and on the right the apartment units. Urban's exterior was handsome, certainly very much in the style of the time, and could not have jarred too seriously the sensitivities of the most conservative patron of the diamond horseshoe.

Urban's auditorium is grand and massive with a stage that projects well out beyond the proscenium and continues along the sides of the orchestra level. Seating over five thousand, the theatre might have had trouble presenting more intimate works, but for spectacles it would have offered ample resources. As with the Reinhardt Theatre, one has to wonder how many directors and designers could have used the facilities effectively and not be either defeated or intimidated by them.

Had the new house been built in the late 1920s as Kahn and Urban wished, ironically it could well have spelled the end of the Metropolitan Opera Company. The move to Lincoln Center showed that economies expected from a new plant are not always realized and that there are more likely to be unanticipated expenses. It also showed that while a larger house might produce more receipts at the box office, increased operating costs could easily offset the additional revenue. These factors seriously upset the financial stability of the Met when it moved uptown; had the opera company been

MUSIC CENTRE. THE MASS OF THE GREEK THEA-
TRE CLOSED AT THE SIDES BY THE ELEVATOR
AND FIRE TOWERS. ON THE TOP IS AN ENCLOSED
RESTAURANT WITH OPEN DINING TERRACES
ABOVE, WHICH WOULD COMMAND A BROAD PROS-
PECT AROUND THE THEATRE. LOWER, THE
PROMENADE SURROUNDING THE THEATRE

In these drawings for a proposed music center, Urban presented his conception of an ideal theatre and opera house. Mid-1920s. *Theatres.*

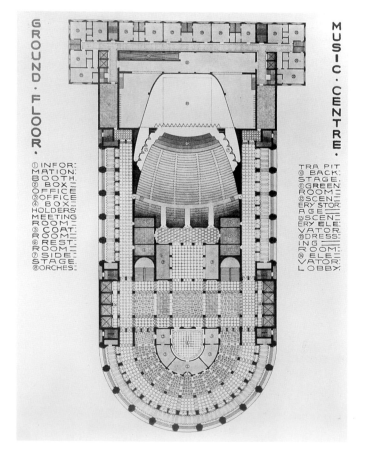

GROUND · FLOOR ·

MUSIC · CENTRE ·

① INFOR-
MATION-
BOOTH.
② BOX-
OFFICE-
③ OFFICE-
④ BOX-
HOLDERS'
MEETING-
ROOM-
⑤ COAT-
ROOM-
⑥ REST-
ROOM-
⑦ SIDE-
STAGE-
⑧ ORCHES-

TRA PIT-
⑨ BACK-
STAGE.
⑩ GREEN-
ROOM-
⑪ SCEN-
ERY STOR-
AGE-
⑫ SCEN-
ERY ELE-
VATOR-
⑬ DRESS-
ING-
ROOM-
⑭ ELE-
VATOR-
LOBBY-

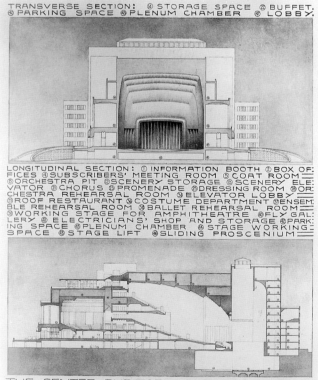

TRANSVERSE SECTION: ④ STORAGE SPACE ㉒ BUFFET.
④ PARKING SPACE ㉒ PLENUM CHAMBER ⑧ LOBBY.

LONGITUDINAL SECTION: ① INFORMATION BOOTH ② BOX OF-
FICES ④ SUBSCRIBERS' MEETING ROOM ⑤ COAT ROOM-
⑧ ORCHESTRA PIT ⑪ SCENERY STORAGE ⑫ SCENERY ELE-
VATOR ㉒ CHORUS ㉒ PROMENADE ⑬ DRESSING ROOM ⑨ OR-
CHESTRA REHEARSAL ROOM ⑭ ELEVATOR LOBBY ㉒
⑳ ROOF RESTAURANT ㉒ COSTUME DEPARTMENT ㉒ ENSEM-
BLE REHEARSAL ROOM ㉒ BALLET REHEARSAL ROOM-
㉒ WORKING STAGE FOR AMPHITHEATRE ㉔ FLY GAL-
LERY ㉒ ELECTRICIANS' SHOP AND STORAGE ㉒ PARK-
ING SPACE ㉒ PLENUM CHAMBER ㉒ STAGE WORKING
SPACE ㉒ STAGE LIFT ㉒ SLIDING PROSCENIUM-

THE CENTRE AUDITORIUM IS A FURTHER DE-
VELOPMENT OF THE MEGAPHONE FORM. THE
SURFACE IS ARRANGED FOR DELICATE VARI-
ATION FROM DARKNESS TO DAZZLING LIGHT,
ONE MOOD EVOKED BY STAGE AND AUDITORIUM.

230

forced to cope with similar problems during the depths of the Depression, one questions the possible outcome. As it was, the Met barely survived, thanks largely to Mrs. August Belmont and the creation of the Metropolitan Opera Guild.

Frustrated in his desire to build a new home for the Met, Urban presented his designs for an ideal opera house in *Theatres*: a music center not subject to limitations imposed by site, budget, or the social sensitivities of a board of directors. What he designed was a free-standing building very similar to such performing arts complexes of today as Lincoln Center or Kennedy Center. Urban's years of experience in the theatre and his knowledge of theatre history were applied to this plan.

The music center was intended for a parkland setting that would provide ready access to patrons arriving by automobile. The auditorium was, in Urban's words, "a strongly unified space within which the audience sits and the performers play. No definitely marked proscenium emphasizes the line of demarcation between actor and audience. Stage and auditorium are included in one vast dome-like form."

The main auditorium could provide traditional staging for grand opera on a proscenium stage, or with a screen lowered to close off the stage, the hall could become "one vast room wherein the actor plays." Side stages, as in the plans for the Met, were also available to bring the action closer to the audience. Curtains could also be used to reduce the auditorium space by thirds for chamber music or orchestral concerts. Many of the new theatres in post–World War II Europe, such as the *Neues Festspielhaus* in Salzburg, were designed for such varied programs.

Lighting was central to Urban's conception of the ideal opera house:

> The auditorium itself lives or disappears through lights. Like the theatres of the Greeks, where plays began in the starlight before dawn and continued into the blaze of noonday, this auditorium can enfold the beginnings of a drama in obscurity, and gradually disclose it to the audience. A blaze of light can mask the movement of actors behind it and effect a gradual change of scene. . . . The decoration of this room is plastic, dependent entirely upon light to reveal it. At the time of performance it is unlighted, vanished. At the intermission it can again become apparent to divert the unoccupied gaze. Changing lights can give it movement, and colored light, mood. It can even be brought into the production and made to contribute the whole auditorium to the effect.

Of course the stage was to be superbly fitted out with lighting equipment and machinery: "The stage equipment is mainly electric lighting. The change of practicable scenery is effected by lowering the stage; while one act is being struck, another, already set, is rolled out and raised to stage level."

Directly behind the center's curved front façade was a small Greek theatre in arena style that was both a lobby for the main auditorium and a theatre in its own right. A rendering of this room is the only color plate in *Theatres*. Among other events Urban foresaw for such a space were "certain civic functions such as the presentation of awards by the City for distinction in civic services, [and] ceremonies attending the visit of foreign musicians and people of note."

Many ideas Urban worked out for his music center and for the new Met were actually incorporated into Radio City Music Hall, including side stages, an elaborate lighting system in the auditorium, and stage lifts.

Top. Urban incorporated a small arena theatre into the music center. This Greek theatre could be used to present plays, to serve as a lobby for the music center itself, and to accommodate municipal functions and ceremonies. Mid-1920s. *Theatres.*

Bottom. This drawing of the Greek theatre was the only color plate Urban included in his book, *Theatres.* Mid-1920s. *Theatres.*

THE GREEK THEATRE IN THE CENTRE USED AS A LOBBY IN CONNECTION WITH THE OPERA. THE AMPHITHEATRE IS TRANSFORMED TO A PLACE LIKE A GARDEN WHERE ONE MAY MEET FRIENDS AND SIT TO TALK AND SMOKE AND WATCH THE COLORFUL MOTION OF THE CROWD.

232

With the Ziegfeld Theatre, Urban shifts the scene from the ideal to the very practical world of a Broadway theatre designed to present musicals on a seven-shows-a-week basis. Of the projects described in *Theatres*, only this one and the Paramount in Palm Beach were actually realized.

There had been no *Ziegfeld Follies* in 1925 due to the impresario's prolonged legal battle with Abe Erlanger, owner of the New Amsterdam, the theatre to which the *Follies* had moved in 1913. Ziegfeld was galled that Erlanger benefited so handsomely from his successes while sharing none of the risk. Flo's relations with other producers, fueled by envy and by his devious business practices, were likewise hostile. Friction between Flo and the Shubert brothers dated back to 1906, when Flo refused to return a $1,000 advance on a production of *The Parisian Model* for Anna Held. By the twenties the Shuberts controlled most of the theatres in New York, as well as on the road, and they had long memories; no Ziegfeld production ever played in a Shubert house. For Ziegfeld, the answer obviously was a theatre of his own. Fortunately, he was able to find someone to finance his dream.

William Randolph Hearst owned a good deal of property on upper Sixth Avenue, which in the mid-1920s was undergoing a period of development. Hearst had just finished constructing the Warwick Hotel on the corner of Sixth Avenue and Fifty-fourth Street when he heard of Ziegfeld's plan. A handsome new theatre opposite the Warwick could hardly fail to increase property values, so Hearst volunteered to finance the entire project. Both he and Ziegfeld agreed that Joseph Urban was the man to build the Ziegfeld Theatre, and the architect was delighted by the prospect.

"The whole idea back of the Ziegfeld Theatre," Urban wrote in *Theatres*, "is the creation of an architectural design which shall express in every detail the fact that here is a modern playhouse for modern musical shows." The Ziegfeld could not have been mistaken for anything other than a theatre; its façade clearly and boldly reflected the building's purpose:

> The swelling proscenium-like facade clearly expresses the curves of the auditorium back of it. The elevation—the strong decorative elements of this part of the facade—have nothing to do with architectonic proportions. They are meant as a poster for the theatre. At night this poster is brilliantly illuminated by floodlights.

The auditorium, however, was the most innovative feature—elliptical, perfectly smooth, no corners or moldings, encompassing the audience in its egg-shaped ambience. The stage, framed by a simple gold arch, projected into the audience, creating a high degree of intimacy between players and spectators and forming an apron that could be used for solo numbers during scene changes.

The auditorium was softly illuminated from a central source, and the carpeting and seats were in gold tones that flowed up the walls into a soaring mural. Amid leaves and blossoms blurred in detail by waves of color, there appeared fleeting, fanciful medieval figures. Of this mural Urban wrote:

> The aim in the decoration . . . was to create a covering that would be a warm texture surrounding the audience during the performance. In the intermission this design serves to maintain an atmosphere of colourful gaiety and furnish the diversion of following the incidents of an unobtrusive pattern. . . . During the performance the pattern should be felt rather than seen.

Left. Hugh Ferriss's rendering of the billowing façade of the Ziegfeld Theatre in New York City. Thomas W. Lamb was Associate Architect. 1927. Columbia University.
Right. Photo of the Ziegfeld's smooth, egg-shaped auditorium with its decorative mural. 1927. Columbia University.

In the dome of the theatre was a hidden space from which Ziegfeld and friends could watch the action onstage. A handsome suite of offices was provided, and Ziegfeld himself designed a chamber like a baronial dining hall that was large enough to accommodate one hundred guests and display his ever-growing collection of elephants in silver, gold, porcelain, and jade. Facilities backstage were also impeccable—rehearsal and storage spaces, proper dressing rooms with showers, and even a dining area. Among performers it was agreed that Urban was the only designer who took as good care of the actors as he did of the audience.

The person responsible for the mural with its 850 figures was the talented young artist Lillian Gaertner, who had studied with Josef Hoffmann in Vienna and would work with Urban in Palm Beach and also design costumes for the Metropolitan Opera. The mural, which took eighteen months to paint, became quite an attraction in the Yonkers studio for Gretl and her friends, who would drop in from time to time to apply a few daubs of paint.

Everyone was eager to see how the mural would look when finally installed in the theatre. To preserve the delicate colors, the required fireproofing spray was not applied until after the oil paint dried completely. The sections were then trucked to New York and installed in two days of painstaking work. Karl Koeck, head of the studio, who was in charge of hanging the mural, called Gretl and asked her to be in the theatre next morning before eleven o'clock. He wanted her to see the results before the fire inspector arrived:

Even with the ordinary lights we were spellbound by the stupendous effect of the mural. We were embracing and congratulating each other in triumph when the fire inspector arrived with several attendants and an air of gloomy importance.

Before we realized what he was doing, he had out a huge . . . acetylene torch and put it right up against a corner of the mural. Within minutes he had burned about a foot-square hole in it.

I told him, "You can't do that!"

He said, "It's my job. The murals have to come down."

I was speechless, but Karl jumped in and showed him it was evident that the murals would not burn except on the spot where a red-hot flame was applied. The fire inspector was unperturbed and told us if there was a fire the murals would start coming down, burst into flame, and cause the deaths of hundreds of people, an unheard-of catastrophe. Therefore he could never give his approval.

Bernie McDonald, who was working on the stage, heard the commotion and came to join us. He greeted the fire inspector as an old friend and after a few amenities led him and his cohorts out. Lillian had retired to a corner ready to weep, while Karl and I stood rooted to the spot in helpless despair.

After a bit, Bernie came back and told us not to worry, that this was just a brazen demand for political graft: "The fire chief said to tell you he would okay the murals if you fireproofed them once again."

We groaned and told him that an additional coat of fireproofing would dim the brilliance of the colors. He winked and said, "Spray them with water. That won't hurt, will it?"

"What about the fire chief?" I asked.

Bernie answered, "Two firemen will come to watch the spraying tomorrow, so be sure you are at it. The rest I will take care of."

I had always heard that Bernie was quite a political figure in New York, but this was the first time I had seen him in action. He told me he would get in touch with the Hearst people who handled such matters; they had the real political clout and money. Then he added that we would have to give a banquet for about two dozen important people in the fire department, at which time presents from Mr. Hearst would be given. With Father working in Florida, I would have to be the hostess unless I could persuade him to come here for the occasion. I *couldn't*. All Buschi said when I told him on the phone was that he could not get away and I was not to get excited. Small comfort that was.

The banquet, for which Bernie made all the arrangements, was in a private room (maybe at Luchow's, I'm not sure). It was an experience I will never forget, but even when it was over I would not have missed it for the world.

Sue [Goldklang, Urban's devoted secretary], Bernie, and I arrived early, as did Karl, who had to be there as manager of the studio. The table was festively decorated with a mountain of silver. I remember a huge soup tureen, meat and vegetable platters, and what have you.

Karl said, "It looks like a goddamned wedding!"

In his pocket Bernie had the pièce de résistance, an envelope with a card of thanks for all the help from the fire department, signed by William Randolph Hearst, Florenz Ziegfeld, and Joseph Urban. Bernie added that folded into this were a few nice big bills.

I marveled at how Bernie had managed it all so smoothly, particularly as we had received the permit from the fire department even before the presentation. The fire chief and fire marshal, lord knows what their titles were, arrived with lesser luminaries, all in their Sunday best, as were Sue and I at opposite ends of the table.

Overleaf. The mural in the Ziegfeld auditorium at various stages of design and completion. Urban wrote that in the mural "heroes of old romances form the detail in flowering masses of color interspersed with gold." 1927. Columbia University and author's collection.

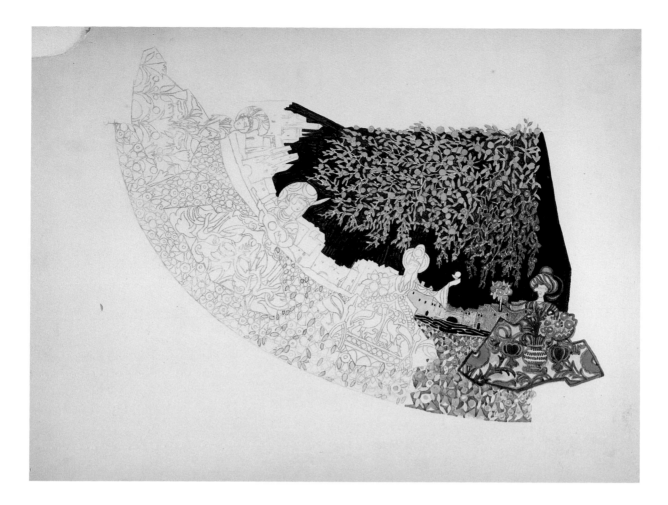

Liquor flowed freely; there were many long speeches, all in praise of the fire department; and finally Bernie ended the affair with his presentation of a speech of thanks. While waving his hands over the silver riches on the table, he handed the envelope to the head man. Bernie was superb. The head man made a speech of thanks, everybody loved and congratulated everyone else, the silver was to be delivered to the fire department headquarters, and it was over.

One morning near opening night of the theatre, Gretl came to see how Bernie McDonald was getting along with hanging the *Rio Rita* settings, scenery that she actually had designed while her father was occupied with architectural projects in Palm Beach. Gretl found the usually taciturn stage manager positively ecstatic. Never had he walked on such a magnificently planned stage! All of her father's ideas worked flawlessly. The cyclorama fit neatly, and the head electrician had told him that the light board, now that he was used to its many innovations, worked like a charm. Above everything else, even the bigger sets could be changed quickly and noiselessly unless some "damned fool" dropped a prop. With everyone out to lunch, Gretl found herself alone on the stage:

I was fussing with some artificial flowers that were out of line when Flo made an unexpected appearance. He came up on the stage, and we both looked out into the auditorium. Even in the faint working light we were aware of its beguiling beauty. Flo put his arm around me and said, "Your father sure hit the jackpot this time."

In a sudden feeling of elation, we hugged each other and kissed warmly. Within a moment, there was Bernie telling me I was needed backstage. Flo asked for more light so he could see better, gave me a quick peck on the cheek, and returned to the auditorium.

Plan and longitudinal section of the Ziegfeld Theatre, the first truly modern theatre in the United States specially designed and equipped for musicals. 1927.
Theatres.

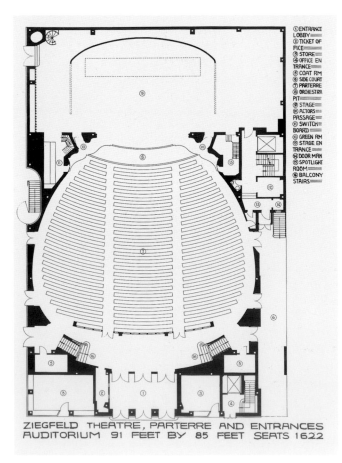

ZIEGFELD THEATRE, PARTERRE AND ENTRANCES
AUDITORIUM 91 FEET BY 85 FEET SEATS 1622

① ENTRANCE LOBBY ② TICKET OFFICE ③ STORE ④ OFFICE ENTRANCE ⑤ COAT RM ⑥ SIDE COURT ⑦ PARTERRE ⑧ ORCHESTRA PIT ⑨ STAGE ⑩ ACTORS PASSAGE ⑪ SWITCH BOARD ⑫ GREEN RM ⑬ STAGE ENTRANCE ⑭ DOOR MAN ⑮ SPOTLIGHT ROOM ⑯ BALCONY STAIRS

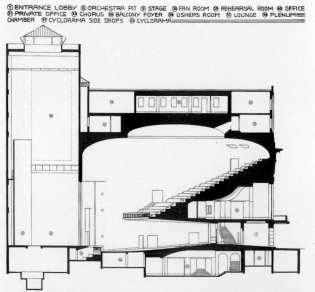

① ENTRANCE LOBBY ② ORCHESTRA PIT ③ STAGE ④ FAN ROOM ⑤ REHEARSAL ROOM ⑥ OFFICE ⑦ PRIVATE OFFICE ⑧ CHORUS ⑨ BALCONY FOYER ⑩ USHERS ROOM ⑪ LOUNGE ⑫ PLENUM CHAMBER ⑬ CYCLORAMA SIDE DROPS ⑭ CYCLORAMA

ZIEGFELD THEATRE: THE SECTION SHOWS THE CLEAR CORRESPONDENCE BETWEEN INTERIOR OF AUDITORIUM AND FACADE. THE MAIN PROMENADE ON THE SECOND FLOOR IS EXPRESSED OUTSIDE BY THE MARQUISE AT THE FLOOR LEVEL AND THREE TALL WINDOWS. AS SHOWN IN THE SECOND FLOOR PLAN THE OVAL OF THE AUDITORIUM PROJECTS ON THE FACADE IN A BAY. A BOLD CORNICE MARKS THE TOP OF THE GALLERY ON THE EXTERIOR. ABOVE IT A CHANGE IN SCALE IN THE FACADE EXPRESSES TWO FLOORS OF OFFICES. SIMPLICITY OF THE AUDITORIUM FORM, SUPPRESSION OF THE PROSCENIUM AND USE OF ACTORS DOORS ON THE APRON HELP, BY PLACING PERFORMER AND AUDIENCE IN THE SAME ROOM TO ESTABLISH GOOD THEATRICAL CONTACT.

Curtain and setting for *Rio Rita*, the first production staged in the Ziegfeld Theatre. Since Urban was commuting between New York and his architectural work in Palm Beach, Gretl was primarily responsible for the designs of *Rio Rita* and *Show Boat*. 1927. Columbia University.

I said, "Now Bernie, you don't really think Flo was trying to seduce me!" Bernie looked sheepish and assured me that he did not know, but he had promised Father to keep an eye on me when Flo was around. I told him he was a dear but that maybe it would be better not to tell Father.

"Christ, no!" said Bernie.

When I came back on stage, there was Flo with his legs straddled over the seat in the front of him, looking around with a beatific smile on his face. That's the way I like to remember him—sitting in his very own theatre built by Joe Urban.

On February 27, 1927, searchlights were played on the billowing façade of the Ziegfeld Theatre as *Rio Rita*, with tickets selling for the then astronomical price of $27.50, opened to sensational notices. Not only was the show the season's biggest musical hit, but that evening the first truly modern theatre specifically created to present musicals was publicly unveiled. In his review of the theatre itself, Brooks Atkinson of the *New York Times* observed:

> For the wall and ceiling decorations of this elliptical playhouse Mr. Urban has unfolded one of the most extravagant and bizarre cycloramas of imaginative designing to be found this side of fairyland. It is not only splendid but appropriate. According to Socrates . . . beauty is perfection in usefulness. By the terms of that Athenian definition, the Ziegfeld Theatre is the divination of beauty in playhouses, for it fits the type of entertainment Mr. Ziegfeld proposes to foster there like the proverbial glove. Indeed, it sets a standard. Mr. Ziegfeld must take care lest his productions on stage prove inferior to the sweep of carnival beauty on the walls of his theatre.[30]

The evening was a triumph for Urban. During the intermission, however, those who flocked to congratulate him were puzzled as to why, on this joyous occasion, he appeared so reserved. He stood rigidly fixed against one wall, closely flanked by Gretl and Mary. The reason was quite simple. Hans had brought to Urban's Plaza suite a pair of dress trousers that no longer fit. There was no time to make the trip back to Yonkers before the opening, and Mary had been forced to piece together a gusset with pins and elastic. Urban's

239

movements were consequently considerably restricted until Hans eventually returned from Yonkers with a suitable pair of pants. At the parties and celebrations after the performance, Urban was his old ebullient self.

Architect Ely Jacques Kahn reviewed the theatre for *Architectural Record*. His only real criticism was of the presence of stores on either side of the theatre's front: "When they become filled with the average shop merchandise, flaunt their own signs and illumination, they are likely to be extremely discordant notes." [31] About the auditorium he was more enthusiastic:

> The interior, apparently, interests Mr. Urban more than his exterior, for here he has emphasized his break with the classic tradition by hurling to one side the entire category of architectural forms and has expressed his own version of what a theatre might be. The basis of his plan is the ellipse, as contrasted with the normal use of the fan-shaped auditorium. By projecting part of the stage into the body of the house—the Shakespearean plan, incidentally—the audience is brought into more intimate touch with the actors. The forestage permits minor action to take place while the curtain is drawn, permitting flexibility that is different in the customary stage set apart and sharply cut from the audience.[32]

In 1926 while the theatre was nearing completion, Gene Buck brought Oscar Hammerstein and Jerome Kern up to Yonkers to talk with Urban about their new musical based on Edna Ferber's novel *Show Boat* and to play the score. Urban and Kern had, of course, worked together in the *Follies*, and in 1925 Urban had designed Hammerstein's *Song of the Flame*, which was produced by Oscar's uncle, Arthur Hammerstein, who had turned down *Show Boat*. Ziegfeld, who already had been approached about the show, liked the music but was less than enthusiastic about the book. Gretl tells what happened in Yonkers: "When Oscar and Jerry came that Sunday afternoon, Jerry sat down almost immediately and played the unforgettable score while Oscar told the story in dialogue and lyrics. Father said that Ziegfeld must produce

While *Rio Rita* looked back to the operettas of the past, *Show Boat* was a milestone in the development of the American musical theatre. Based on Edna Ferber's novel, with book and lyrics by Oscar Hammerstein II and a brilliant score by Jerome Kern, it was Ziegfeld's greatest artistic and most enduring achievement. The bayou scene reflects the influence of Urban's trip with Hearst to New Orleans and Mexico. 1927. Columbia University.

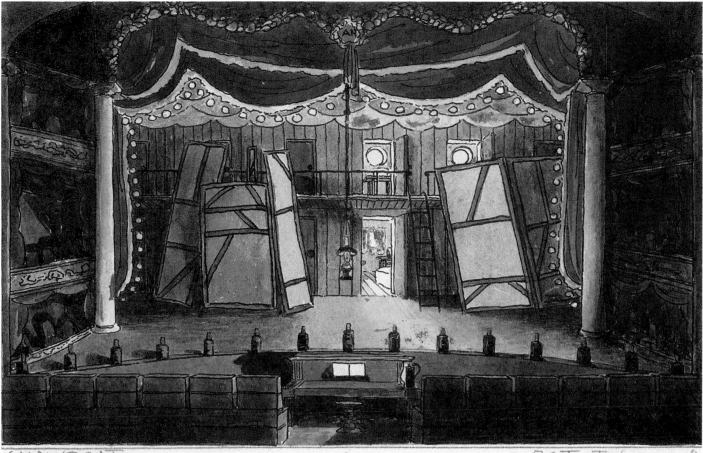

SHOWBOAT. — ACT·I·Scene·4·

SHOW·BOAT. ACT·I·Scene·7,

Show Boat right after *Rio Rita* and told Oscar that he was as fine a poet as Hugo von Hofmannsthal."

Flo was not so easy to convince, but Urban assured him that a dazzling finale could be devised. Knowing that Flo considered Arthur Hammerstein a rival, he pointed out that Arthur had turned down his own nephew's work and that Flo might take this opportunity to show Arthur what a *really* great producer could do with the material.

Oscar Hammerstein made the changes in the book that Ziegfeld requested, and Ziegfeld added a spectacular scene that was set at the 1893 Chicago World's Fair—which Urban recreated onstage. As with *Rio Rita*, most of the scenery was actually designed by Gretl Urban, with finishing touches applied by her father.

Showboat opened at the Ziegfeld Theatre on December 27, 1927, a critical and financial success as well as a major landmark in the development of the American musical—not to mention the great songs by Jerome Kern: "Ol' Man River," "Make Believe," "Why Do I Love You?" "You Are Love," "Bill," and Helen Morgan's big number, "Can't Help Lovin' Dat Man." *Showboat* was the first musical in which the disparate elements of song, dance, comedy, and production numbers all emerged naturally, even inevitably, from the play's book. It was light-years beyond the "naughty" musicals Ziegfeld had produced for Anna Held.

While working on *Showboat*, the producer was preparing two other musicals: *Rosalie*, starring Marilyn Miller, which opened at the New Amsterdam two weeks after *Showboat*, and *The Three Musketeers*, which appeared two months later. Both were successes. *Rosalie* combined the many talents of Guy Bolton, P. G. Wodehouse, George and Ira Gershwin, and Sigmund Romberg. *The Three Musketeers* featured lavish Urban settings and a score by Rudolph Friml that turned out to be the composer's last successful effort.

By the end of the 1926–1927 season, Ziegfeld had three smash hits running on Broadway. He had his own theatre and a lavish suite of offices, but he produced just one more smash hit, *Whoopee*, which opened on December 4, 1928, at the New Amsterdam. The cast included Eddie Cantor, Ruth Etting, and Ethel Shutta. The score was written by Walter Donaldson and contained such standards as "Makin' Whoopee" and Ruth Etting's "Love Me or Leave Me." The show with its Wild West setting was given a lavish production complete with live horses and Urban's version of the Grand Canyon. Ziegfeld's career had truly reached its zenith.

So confident was Ziegfeld about his future that he announced a major new undertaking. A clipping in Urban's crumbling scrapbooks at Columbia, from an unidentified newspaper dated January 22, 1929, tells of the producer's plan to build a theatre in Chicago. Because of trouble finding suitable houses for his shows on tour, Ziegfeld felt that his own theatre was once again the best solution. Although the article said that work was to begin in sixty days on the site at Eighth and Michigan, nothing ever materialized.

Flo's optimism and apparent financial security lasted only until the fall of 1929. He, like so many others, was wiped out in the stock market crash of October 29. To recoup his losses, Ziegfeld turned to what he could do best: produce musical comedies. By February of 1930 he had raised money enough to present Rodgers and Hart's *Simple Simon*, starring Ed Wynn. In it Ruth Etting introduced the other song with which she is identified: "Ten Cents a Dance." The show lasted only 135 performances. Ziegfeld's next venture, *Smiles*, starred Fred and Adele Astaire and Marilyn Miller and had music by

Vincent Youmans. It opened on November 18, 1930, and lasted a mere 63 performances.

No *Follies* had appeared on Broadway since 1927. Its final edition opened on July 21, 1931, at the Ziegfeld, the only *Follies* that played in the producer's own theatre. One last time Urban provided beautiful settings, but the show ran for only 165 performances. Gerald Bordman, author of the definitive compilation of the American musical theatre, explains why the revue failed:

> . . . the depression was not solely responsible for the relatively short run. Elaborate annuals had begun to seem dated even in the affluent heyday of the twenties. A faster pace of life, as reflected in other entertainments, and an undeniable, if not general, rising of intellectual standards in musicals foredoomed them.[33]

Ziegfeld's last original musical was *Hot-Cha*, starring Bert Lahr and Lupe Velez. The show, financed in part by the gangsters Waxie Gordon and Dutch Schultz, opened at the Ziegfeld on March 8, 1932. Unfortunately, the ailing producer's hopes that he would have another hit like *Rio Rita* were not realized. *Hot-Cha* proved to be just one more in a string of flops.

Urban provided one final setting with elephants for the 1931 *Follies*, the last that Ziegfeld himself produced. Columbia University.

In spite of these disasters, Ziegfeld did pass from Broadway in a final blaze of glory. He revived *Showboat* with the original sets and costumes and with Paul Robeson as Joe. Even better than the original production, this revival received great reviews. Nevertheless, when the hot summer months of 1932 arrived, attendance dropped. Ziegfeld was by then unable to carry on his business affairs, and they were turned over to his ever-reliable secretary, Goldie Clough. Funds provided by the tycoon husband of former Ziegfeld Girl Peggy Fears kept the show running as long as possible.

Ziegfeld, under doctor's orders and to escape his creditors (he owed Urban fifty thousand), decided that California's climate would help combat his pleurisy. On the arduous train trip west with Billie, the exhausted Flo was incoherent most of the time. He rallied a bit at Billie's bungalow in Santa Monica, started sending his famous lengthy telegrams and making long-distance phone calls, but when the pleurisy flared again he was moved to the Cedars of Lebanon Hospital.

On the afternoon of July 22, 1932, while Billie was shooting a screen test with Walter Pidgeon for *A Bill of Divorcement*, she was summoned to the hospital. Shortly before she arrived, Flo died, at 3:45 P.M. There was a quiet funeral. A column Will Rogers wrote after Ziegfeld's death could serve as his eulogy:

> He picked us from all walks of life and led us into what little fame we achieved.... He brought beauty into the entertainment world. To have been the master amusement provider of your generation, surely a life's work has been accomplished.... He left something that hundreds of us will treasure till our final curtains fall, and that is a "badge," a badge of which we are proud and I want to read the lettering: "I worked for Ziegfeld." [34]

Burial was in Hollywood's Forest Lawn, so very far from Broadway.

At the opening of Ziegfeld's beautiful theatre, Will Rogers is reported to have said to the impresario, "I hope you never have to put in a movie screen." [35] Sadly, in 1933, six years after it opened, the Ziegfeld became a Loew's movie house. In 1944 showman Billy Rose bought the building for $630,000 (it had cost $2.5 million to build) and restored it as a legitimate theatre, where several more hits appeared, among them *Brigadoon*, 1947, *Gentlemen Prefer Blondes*, 1949, and *Kismet*, 1953.

In 1955 the National Broadcasting Company leased the Ziegfeld for seven years for use as a television studio. Although Rose threatened to tear the theatre down when the lease expired, he ultimately decided to save it. Otto Teegan, who inherited Urban's architectural business, was called in to restore the theatre, once again, as a legitimate house. One of its last shows was *Foxy*, a 1964 musical adaptation of the classic *Volpone*. The star of *Foxy*, Bert Lahr, had appeared on the Ziegfeld stage thirty-two years earlier in the ill-fated *Hot-Cha*; he made what proved to be his last appearance on Broadway on this same stage.

Built during one period of development on Sixth Avenue, the Ziegfeld Theatre was torn down during another, as Rockefeller Center expanded west of the avenue. After Billy Rose died in February 1966, his estate sold the property he had assembled along Sixth Avenue to developers. Attempts to save the theatre proved futile, and demolition started in September 1966.

The last word on the Ziegfeld Theatre belongs to the current architectural critic of the *New York Times*, Paul Goldberger:

Here, classicism was given a shot of adrenalin, and the result was something voluptuous and lush; the building, which was demolished in 1966 to make way for the banal Burlington House skyscraper, brought the simmering energy of the Baroque to monumental classicism. The Ziegfeld was one of those buildings that went just a few years too soon—had it been able to hold on just a bit longer, a later age would surely have seen its value and refused to sanction its destruction.[36]

THE LAST YEAR

The final months of Joseph Urban's life were characterized by remarkable achievement, as well as vindication. His extraordinary career in America was rounded out in a fitting form of symmetry, for it both opened and closed with a world's fair, and he died at the very height of his creative powers and success. The scale of his last four major projects ranged from an apartment for a famous novelist to the color scheme and lighting for a world's fair that attracted almost fifty million visitors.

The earliest of Urban's final projects was his setting for the Metropolitan Opera's premiere of Richard Strauss's one-act opera *Elektra*. His penultimate set design for the Met, Urban's *Elektra* has been acknowledged as his masterpiece. The designer had discussed his ideas with the composer much earlier and refined them in talks with his longtime friend Artur Bodanzky, who was to conduct the performances. By June 1932, after his usual historical research into the period of the opera, Urban had developed a design and color scheme that he was ready to submit to stage director Alexander Sanine. In a letter on June 10 he described his conception of the setting in terms that encompassed the three key elements in all of his work: color, light, and simplicity:

> I will keep the whole scene in a deep brown-red which is only broken up by a small stubborn piece of sky, of which both Strauss and Bodanzky talked. This piece can change color from the red of a sunset to the blackness of the night. I will of course change in the execution some of the forms expressed. I think it is still a little restless—maybe not simple enough, which I think I will get by more careful and closer study of the composition.[1]

Urban explained his concept to Edward Ziegler in another letter: "That the whole scenery will be in mysterious deep color, light and shadow effect, is a matter of course which can be really only achieved on the stage."[2] He went on to tell Ziegler that the stage director had suggested the use of columns

Top. A photograph of the model of the setting for Richard Strauss's *Elektra* that is all but indistinguishable from the Met's actual set. 1932. Columbia University. *Bottom.* A drawing for *Elektra.* Urban based his designs on recent archaeological discoveries as well as conversations with Strauss and conductor Artur Bodanzky. 1932. Columbia University.

similar to those found in the recently excavated Palace of Knossos, which of course was unknown when the opera was first performed in 1909. Urban then described the architecture of the palace to Ziegler:

> The Palace of Knossos which is connected with the legendary figure of Minos was built 2000 B.C. and has unusually strange beauty. In connection with the cyclopean stone walls of the Palace were heavy *wood* beams *highly colored.* The staircases and ceilings of verandahs and galleries were carried by columns which are strange to all other Greek architecture.[3]

These columns were not of the classic orders, but more simple and from a much earlier period than the opera. Urban nevertheless incorporated the stage director's idea into a second design that Sanine accepted. He also submitted a third plan that conveyed his own preferences: "After studying No. 2 I think the use of the Knossos columns robbed the architecture of its sinister character.... I studied the situation again, kept the *ground plan exactly as Sanine accepted it* and made Number 3 which I think is *by far the best* of these three studies.[4]

Urban's own opinion notwithstanding, Ziegler wrote the designer on October 18 that "Mr. Gatti has chosen #2, and you said you would begin painting on same at once." [5]

The action of the opera was set in the rear of Agamemnon's dwelling in a yard strewn with abandoned building stones. The palace itself emphasized long, horizontal lines and had deep, brooding shadows emanating from the dark recesses of the porch. The color and lighting scheme Urban described above further heightened the atmosphere of menace and evil.

Elektra had been given only one previous New York performance, the Hammerstein opera company's version in 1910. The Met's premiere took place at the Saturday matinee of December 3, 1932. Olin Downes wrote the *New York Times* review under the headline "Strauss's 'Elektra' Creates a Furor." Although he failed to mention Urban or the setting specifically, his enthusiasm for the production might, by inference, be extended to include Urban's role in the general triumph:

> Events which stirred an immense audience to its depths took place yesterday afternoon in the Metropolitan Opera House.... The performance, as a whole, was the most eloquent interpretation that the writer remembers in eight years of listening to opera in this city. In the same period no such demonstration of enthusiasm has been seen after a Metropolitan performance, or perhaps any performance of a serious musical work given here. The moment that the last chord crashed from the orchestra was the moment for an outbreak of applause which had hardly less resonance. For precisely fifteen minutes by the watch the audience, in slowly diminishing numbers, cheered and called the principal artists back to the stage.[6]

Over the years the New York Architectural League's annual shows had degenerated into poorly organized displays that were architectural only in the broadest definition, ranging from landscaping to statuary to stage design. In 1931, when some of the younger architects who espoused the principles of the new International Style had their entries rejected for the League's fiftieth anniversary show, they presented their own exhibit organized by Philip Johnson. In 1933 the League called on Urban to mount the annual show, which was to run from February 18 to March 12, and it turned out to be one of Urban's greatest personal triumphs. However, once again, during the run of the "orthodox" League exhibition, "less conservative" architects dedicated to the International Style were holding a separate show of their own. Among the participants were Mies van der Rohe and Le Corbusier. The irony is that their exhibition was held in a building designed by Urban, the New School, and that he himself was a participant while also exhibiting in the Architectural League show.

Photographs reveal that Urban planned and arranged the League show much as he did those for the Hagenbund in Vienna over a quarter century earlier. Rather than fall back on the usual floor-to-ceiling temporary panels

for dividing the rooms and displaying the works of art, he provided a low,
counterlike display stand that created more exhibit area but allowed the
gallery to be open and uncluttered. As usual with Urban's work, photographs
let us see the simplicity of the design but not the transforming effects of the
other two major components of his talent: color and light. Fortunately, an
article in *Architecture* has left us the following description: "The color scheme
is of white and red for the walls, the carpet being in yellow, orange and green.
The ceiling of the high galleries was lowered by stretching muslin over a
grille of wires diffusing through this the lighting from above." [7]

Other commentaries about the League's 1933 presentation make it plain
that what was so special was not the works on display but the manner in
which they were displayed. Lewis Mumford, writing in the *New Yorker*,
contrasts this show with previous ones:

> In the days when buildings were syphoned up into the skies scarcely
> five minutes after a charcoal sketch had been rendered by Hugh Ferriss
> [the leading architectural illustrator of the day], the annual show of the
> Architectural League of New York resembled the city outside: it was a jungle.
> There was too much to see and too little reason for seeing it. . . . The
> exhibition arranged at the Fine Arts Building by Mr. Joseph Urban is such
> a superb piece of showmanship that one readily forgets how few of the
> buildings or works of art have any real significance. The choice of materials,
> the scheme of presentation (namely lowering the ceiling and utilizing
> adroitly the space between the floor and the usual first line of drawings and
> photographs), the emphasis and concentration on the whole show are
> admirable.[8]

The League awarded Urban the President's Medal for the "architectural treatment of the galleries and the effective installation of the exhibits." [9] Of even more significance to Urban, however, was the League's award of a gold medal for native and industrial art for a now-lost stage setting for a religious pageant and play. The award was for "excellent craftsmanship and design used in keeping with its grand purpose." [10] This recognition of his work as an architect by his peers came only four short months before his death, but the League's Medal meant as much to this man of sixty as the Emperor's Prize had meant to the youth of twenty-five. It was for all too brief a time his most cherished possession, as it was for his daughter over the following half century.

To understand what this honor meant to Urban, it is helpful to recapitulate the course of his career as an architect. As a youth in Vienna, he had gone against his family's wishes to pursue a career in architecture, only later to abandon this in the aftermath of the 1908 *Festzug*. He was then employed as a scenic designer until 1925, when he was able to use his earnings from working for Hearst in films to open his own architectural firm. As an architect Urban was undeniably successful and prosperous, creating at least two masterpieces: the Ziegfeld Theatre and the New School for Social Research. Still, critics and other architects were most likely to categorize Urban as a scene painter, and such a slight must have deeply hurt a man of his sensitivity, no matter how self-confident, self-possessed, and jovial he seemed to those around him. In a way his position was similar to that of the novelist whose books rise to the top of the best-seller list but who receives only condescending reviews from the literary establishment. There also had to be some resentment that Urban did so many things well and with such seeming ease and lack of effort.

During the 1930s, while many architects had no work at all, Urban was able to keep his staff busy with commissions for decorating hotel lounges, ballrooms, and dining rooms. While interior decoration was less ephemeral than stage settings, it was not so permanent as architecture, and Urban was

Top. The gold medal that the Architectural League awarded Urban in 1933 was a meaningful and tangible recognition of his success as a practitioner of the art he so dearly loved. The medal was all too briefly his prized possession.
Gretl Urban collection.
Bottom. Joseph and Mary Urban in Egypt early in 1933.
Gretl Urban collection.

251

desperately eager to be remembered as an architect—grateful to receive any lasting recognition from his peers for work in that field.

In March of 1933 Urban and his wife had returned to the scene of one of his earliest architectural projects: Egypt. Since 1929, at her father's bidding, Gretl had been spending the summer months in Paris to develop her painting skills, and that spring she was given an exhibit of her work at the Galerie Zaks. Although Urban was unable to reach Paris for the vernissage, he and Mary did join Gretl in early April before the show closed. Those of her works that impressed Urban most were not in the show but left in her studio, decorative paintings that were just what the architect needed as themes for murals in his interior design commissions. Gretl was to stay in Paris until her exhibit was over and then a final few months to learn as much as possible about mural painting from her teacher, Lilli Steiner.

Urban visited his mother every summer in Austria and had planned to come back to Europe in late July or early August to spend a week with her. He and Mary would then meet Gretl on the Lido for a week and all return to New York together. The farewells, as Gretl recollects them, "were carefree and gay. When he left he said, 'Be a good girl, Gretsie, work hard, and be happy. I'll see you on the Lido in August.' " That was the last time Gretl saw her father.

Starting with late reviews of the Architectural League exhibition, commentaries on Urban's work became mixed with obituary tributes, as is the case with the following remarks from *Theatre Arts Monthly*:

> To those who worked with him it was a splendid gesture of farewell, one that showed in action all the qualities that made "the myth of Urban," the free experimental mind and hand and eye, the giant energy, the never ending kindness, the rich humanity which made him as proud of another man's good work as though it were his own. It was a last hail, too, to a host of younger artists, many of whom had never exhibited before, some of whom had never—through union limitations—had the coveted opportunity to work in the professional theatre, and who will remember Joseph Urban for his graciousness to them and his effort to present their designs to the best possible advantage beside the works of men already famous.[11]

The last project Urban completed was a New York City apartment for the novelist Katharine Brush. He was at his elegant best in working on this small-scale project for a client for whom money was no object. Once again the surviving black-and-white photographs show the splendor of the Art Deco rooms but give no indication of the ravishing color schemes; fortunately, Mary Fanton Roberts captured all of this in a tribute to Urban in a 1936 issue of *Arts and Decoration*:

> This unique apartment was the swan-song of the great designer. It is hard to describe such a place, but Joseph Urban had a feeling about color that was like a sixth sense. I could never picture him actually trying to harmonize curtains and carpets, using mirrors to separate distances. He did all these things, but he seemed to design a room as a man painted a picture or composed music or carved a shaft of marble.[12]

The key area of the apartment was its two-story living room, where two circular mirrors, each ten feet in diameter, were placed opposite each other to create an effect of great space. One of the mirrors was hung on a white wall over the fireplace, where on its white marble mantel there was a Dagobert Peche silver piece from the Wiener Werkstätte. Flanking the fireplace were

Opposite top. Two views of the two-story living room in the Katharine Brush apartment in New York City, Urban's last completed project. The color scheme was black, red, and white. Columbia University. *Bottom.* Katharine Brush's circular writing studio is a final example of Urban's use of lavish materials in a simple, uncluttered design. Quilted green leather panels on the walls went from the floor to the level of a single row of books. Polished redwood continued to the dull-silver ceiling. 1933. Columbia University.

two deep niches into which white leather seats had been built, each adorned with a white velvet cushion striped in red. Against the wall opposite the fireplace Urban placed a sofa covered in geranium-red velvet, and in corresponding niches finished in white and lined with red lacquer were books and a silver bust by Josef Hoffmann.

The north side of the room was painted blue-black. Between the windows, framed by geranium-red drapes, was a handsome picture of an elephant. To compensate for the cold north light, the southeast corner of the room was fashioned into a kind of solarium where, as described by the *New York Sun*, "orange and yellow chiffon curtains bring the sunlight streaking into the room in glowing warmth."[13]

The major piece of furniture in the room was a large white sofa in two sections placed at right angles to each other. Urban liked to display books in an unusual manner, and here he made the backs of the sofas serve as bookcases. Zebra-striped cushions were used to accent the white couch, which itself rested on a black carpet inlaid with red and zinnia tones.

The writer's workroom was an Art Deco masterpiece. The soundproofed chamber was perfectly circular, as were the desk and light fixtures. The bottom third of the encircling wall was covered in quilted green-leather panels behind which were concealed bookcases. Between the dado and the polished redwood panels that extended to the ceiling was space for a single row of books. The ceiling itself was of tarnished silver set off from the walls by a black molding that had a circular motif. This elegant and carefully ordered room was hardly the tiny, cramped, book-littered den one usually pictures as a writer's quarters. It was more an executive's office as fabricated by a scenic designer for a 1930s Hollywood musical.

The Louisiana Purchase Exposition of 1904 in St. Louis was Urban's first work in America; almost thirty years later the Century of Progress International Exposition of 1933 in Chicago was his last. The board of trustees of the Chicago fair had organized an architectural committee to serve as advisors, and those selected for it in turn nominated Joseph Urban early in 1932 "to serve as an advisor on coloring."[14] This assignment was a tremendous undertaking, not only in terms of the sheer size of the fair and the number of buildings involved but also in terms of the use of new materals and lighting techniques. As early as 1927 Urban had predicted the use of more color in buildings, but he was then thinking mainly in terms of terra-cotta decorative elements and night lighting: "When we look at the city at night . . . we see lights of many tones. Some are dazzling white; others are soft and warm. A building can have the same distinctiveness of tone in the daytime. Its color may express its personality."[15]

The earlier Chicago fair of 1893 offered little to which the architect could refer for guidance or inspiration, for, with the exception of Louis Sullivan's Transportation Building, the buildings were all of the same classical style, all colored white, and all made of the same material, stucco. A manuscript in the Urban archives details the difficulties confronting him:

> The problem presented to him was to coordinate and give life and vitality to a huge group of buildings of widely varying use and design—to bring together in a unifying whole buildings designed by many different architects, each of whom had a particular problem of his own to solve. The Fair buildings were planned fundamentally for exhibition purposes, so that they differ from ordinary office architecture or factories or classical temples in many ways. There are large unbroken spaces. Many have no windows.

They are built of many materials, for here is the opportunity to try out these new materials turned out by the machines of the great factories of today.[16]

Urban's solution was color. What he had used so successfully on a relatively small scale at the New School he was now going to use on a vastly larger canvas:

> 1. Color to be used in an entirely new way.
> 2. Color used to co-ordinate and bring together all these vastly different buildings.
> 3. Color to unify and give vitality.
> 4. Color to give brightness and life to material not beautiful in itself.
> 5. Color to give the spirit of carnival and gayety, to supply all atmosphere lacking in our daily life.
> 6. Color that should transport you from your everyday life when you enter the fair grounds.[17]

Urban called for new kinds of paint and in brighter colors than had been used before, for they had to withstand Lake Michigan's fierce weather conditions. As had been the case forty years earlier, when the new incandescent bulb was a major feature of the 1893 fair, the latest in lighting techniques were brought into play. Neon, or "rare gas," tubes were presented in their first major application at the 1933 fair.

The experience of Vienna's 1908 *Festzug* served Urban well in Chicago, for there was to be an imposing grand avenue of flags with flower-bedecked light poles, colorful kiosks, and other such amenities, all coordinated with each other and with the pavilions.

The man charged with coloring the fair made just one visit to the site, at a time when only four buildings had been completed, two of which were three miles apart. Nevertheless, Otto Teegen remained on-site and oversaw the work to completion when Urban was unable to return. Architect Raymond Hood, himself just out of the hospital, gave this report to Urban in late May of 1933: "Your color was just being begun at the agricultural end. It was marvelous—swipes of pure color 40 feet high and 400 feet long. They messed up the plan with a small exhibit building—but your color will bring back the form. It is going to save the show." [18]

A guidebook to the fair describes some of the major buildings and records Urban's treatment of them:

> The many colors, all tints of the rainbow, made the Fair a wonderland of color. Across the lagoon stand [*sic*] the Architectural Building with its long red streak of light extending all the way across its top.
> ... the Federal Building with its bright lights making the building stand out magnificently.
> ... the blacks and yellows of the German-American Building.
> ... the vividness of the Sears, Roebuck Building, brought out by bright white lights.
> ... the vivid blues and greens of the Administration Building; the orange and reds blended into the lighting for the Czechoslovakian structure.
> ... the outstanding yellow hue of the Swedish Pavilion.
> ... the North Court of the Hall of Science. The lighting of this court is arranged as to bring out to its best advantage the color of the building itself. The blue background of the court is wonderfully contrasted with the white statue of a man struggling with a serpent in the background.
> ... The Social Science Hall is a beautiful contrast of blues and greens,

Soon after he had returned from Europe, Urban found himself unaccountably tired, as well as suffering pain in his lower back. He kept working, nevertheless, with Otto Teegen and his staff on the Chicago fair. Finally, when he was examined by his physician, a fellow Viennese named Dr. Max Wolf, it was discovered that a tumor had appeared since the patient's rather recent physical exam. Hospitalized at Doctors Hospital, Urban had a large room for himself and an adjoining room for Mary. Surgeons found an inoperable, rapidly spreading malignancy.

Gretl became alarmed about her father's health after receiving a vaguely worded note from his secretary, Sue Goldklang. Immediately Gretl telephoned Mary, who broke down in tears and told her that her beloved father had only a few weeks to live. Nevertheless, Mary forbade Gretl from returning home because Urban would then realize he was dying. Ida Gaertner, one of Urban's closest friends, telephoned Gretl that Mary had become frantic and would allow only her and Sue by Urban's bedside, afraid that anyone else might tell him of his real condition. Sue also advised Gretl that her return would cause Mary great distress and in turn adversely affect her father.

Sue and Ida telephoned Gretl frequently, while she sought in her painting distraction and comfort. Even after more than fifty-five years, Gretl recalls those terrible days of waiting and how she felt about her stepmother: "I believe I truly hated Mary." However, when Gretl did return to New York, she quickly forgave Mary once she saw her:

> Mary, to make it up to me, did have an exhibit for me at [a gallery on] Fifty-seventh Street when I returned. And when I saw how she had shrunk to nothing from a rather plump, young-looking woman to an old shriveled-up one, my heart went out to her, and I forgave her because I knew how much she had suffered. I had lost a father I loved more than anyone else, but she had lost her god. There is no question about that.

Urban, of course, knew that he was dying but found it easier for himself and Mary to maintain the pretense that he would recover. He told Sue that he was resigned to dying and that his only concerns were for Mary, Gretl, and his "children" at the studio. (His younger daughter, Elly, had died previously, also from cancer.) Assured that Mary and Gretl were provided for, Urban told Sue that despite the Depression he had already contracted for, and made sketches for, enough work to keep the three Viennese painters in Yonkers busy for at least a year. Then he made Sue promise over and over again that she would not let go any of the architects in his Manhattan office until they found suitable work elsewhere.

Since his days working with Heinrich Lefler in Vienna, money had meant little to Urban beyond something to spend. He was fortunate both in earning enough for his extravagant lifestyle and great generosity and in having someone as faithful and competent as Sue to look after his financial affairs. With the assistance of her brother-in-law, an accountant, Sue had managed to put money aside, and she did keep the promise made so many times to Urban on his deathbed. None of the architects had to be dismissed.

The news Gretl so long dreaded arrived on July 10, 1933. Sue quietly informed her over the transatlantic phone that her father had died peacefully at seven-thirty in the morning. When Gretl told Tony Biddle, he could not believe that the man he had seen so happy at his sixty-first birthday party on May 26, at the Atlantic Beach Club, was really gone. Gretl sent a telegram to the Bodanzkys in Vienna, and the conductor responded with these words of consolation: "A bright light has gone out for many, many of us because he was greatly admired and much loved, and we shall weep."

At Urban's death, Mary collapsed and everything fell upon the shoulders of Sue Goldklang. Although Mary wanted a private funeral, there was such a public clamor for a chance to pay last respects to so famous and well-liked a man as Joseph Urban that arrangements were made at Campbell's funeral home. No flowers were on the closed mahogany casket until Mary placed there a single spike of delphinium she had marked "From Gretl" and a single red rose from her, both grown in the Yonkers garden. Sue put two blue cornflowers, such as Urban used to wear as a boutonniere, in one of his favorite vases and placed it at the foot of the casket. Blue was, of course, Urban's favorite color, and over the years he had found the delphinium and cornflower acceptable substitutes for his beloved Austrian bluebell.

A service was held in the chapel of the Sleepy Hollow Cemetery in Tarrytown, New York. Among the mourners were fellow architects Raymond Hood and Ely Jacques Kahn and composer and critic Deems Taylor. On his tombstone was inscribed the final couplet of "Der schönste Mann":

> Da liegt der Urban Pepprl d'rin,
> Er war der schönste Mann von Wien.

> ([On my tombstone will be written,
> So that all the world can see,]
> The Urban Pepperl lies herein,
> The most beautiful man from Vienna.)

Urban had earlier dictated a letter to Sue intended for Gretl, and Ida Gaertner delivered it to her in Paris shortly after the funeral. These were the last words Gretl received from her father:

> Don't grieve for me, Gretl, after I am gone. I've had great happiness in my life, most of which you have shared, Gretsie. You know that I always said I did not want to live if I could not work, and so I am getting my wish, and I am satisfied as long as I know that you are a good girl, work hard, don't weep and have an occasional dry martini on me. I don't want to hurt Mary, but remember I loved you better than anyone else and always have.

A year after his death, *Architecture* published a memorial edition devoted to Urban. Otto Teegen wrote that with the Chicago Century of Progress Exhibition, which had been visited by almost fifty million people, Urban's life mission had been fulfilled:

> In embarking on this radical color scheme he expected it to shock— perhaps offend—but he had learned from past experience that with every advance there is opposition. He deliberately set out to make people consider—if possible to feel—the stimulating quality of color. That some were made to realize this for the first time in their lives, and that some were at first sight actually frightened there is no doubt, but to every one who objected, a hundred acclaimed, and, it is to be hoped, returned to their own colorless homes with new courage to do something about making them brighter and happier. And so, in the last analysis, Urban's last work fulfilled what he had made his life's purpose—to bring happiness through the creation of beauty.[20]

NOTES

Chapter 1 (pages 9–43)

1. Deems Taylor, "The Scenic Art of Joseph Urban," *Architecture*, May 1934, pp. 286–89. This memorial issue devoted to Urban has long been the chief source of information about the artist.

2. Quoted in David Ewen, *Wine, Women and Waltz* (New York: Sears Publishing Company, 1933), p. 29.

3. Quoted in Peter Vergo, *Art in Vienna 1899–1918* (London: Phaidon Press, 1975), p. 90.

4. Josef Roth, "The Bust of the Emperor," in *Hotel Savoy* (Woodstock, N.Y.: Overlook Press, 1986), pp. 158–59.

5. Stefan Zweig, *The World of Yesterday* (Lincoln, Nebr.: University of Nebraska Press, 1964), pp. 1–2.

6. After her father's death in 1933, Gretl Urban went to Vienna to interview as many people as she could find who knew him. These transcripts are in the Joseph Urban Collection, Rare Books and Manuscript Library, Columbia University, New York, and subsequent quotes from these interviews will not be cited again.

7. Otto Teegen, "Joseph Urban's Philosophy of Color," *Architecture*, May 1934, p. 257.

8. Vergo, *Art in Vienna*, p. 90.

9. Ibid., p. 91.

10. Untitled manuscript, Joseph Urban Collection, Rare Books and Manuscript Library, Columbia University, New York (hereafter cited as Urban Collection).

11. Robert Musil, *The Man Without Qualities* (New York: Capricorn Press, 1965), p. 13.

12. Otto Freidlander, *Letzter Glanz der Marchenstadt* (Vienna: Ring-Verlag, 1948), p. 319.

13. Bruno Walter, *Theme and Variations* (New York: Alfred A. Knopf, 1946), p. 135.

14. Gretl Urban, unpublished manuscript in authors' collection.

15. *Kunst und Kunsthandwerk*, 1899, p. 116.

16. Ibid., p. 121.

17. Ibid., 1900, p. 475.

18. Charles Holme, ed., "The Art Revival in Austria," *The Studio*, Summer 1906, see captions to plates C57–62.

19. *Kunst und Kunsthandwerk*, 1908, pp. 393–94.

20. Arthur Schnitzler, *The Road to the Open* (New York: Alfred A. Knopf, 1923), p. 28.

Chapter 2 (pages 45–69)

1. Henry T. Parker, "The New Stagecraft," *Evening Transcript*, September 7, 1912.

2. John Corbin, " 'The Riviera Girl' Charms Musically," *New York Times*, September 25, 1917.

3. John Corbin, "The Urban Scenery and Some Other Matters," *New York Times*, September 30, 1917.

4. Ibid.

5. Quaintance Eaton, *The Boston Opera Company* (New York: Appleton-Century, 1965), p. 25

6. Henry Russell, *The Passing Show* (London: Thornton Butterworth, 1926), p. 104.

7. Ibid., p. 25.

8. Ibid., p. 149.

9. Ibid., p. 151.

10. Eaton, *Boston Opera*, p. 6.

11. Ibid, p. 14.

12. Lawrence Gilman, "Boston as an Operatic Centre," *Harper's Weekly*, November 20, 1909, p. 13.

13. Eaton, *Boston Opera*, p. 41.

14. Ibid., pp. 42–43.

15. Ibid., p. 43.

16. Mme. Leblanc was, in fact, not really Mme. Maeterlinck as the world, including Russell, discovered when the poet married a very young actress who had appeared in his play *The Bluebird*.

17. Russell, *Passing Show*, p. 160.

18. Ibid., pp. 160–61.

19. H. T. Parker, Editorial, *Evening Transcript*, January 11, 1912.

20. Ibid.

21. Philip Hale, Review, *Boston Herald*, January 11, 1912.

22. Eaton, *Boston Opera*, p. 209.

23. "Plans for Great Opera Season," *Boston Herald*, March 15, 1912.

24. "68 Soloists in Boston Opera," *Boston Herald*, October 18, 1912.

25. Adalbert Albrecht, "The Opera's Factory of Illusions," *Evening Transcript*, September 25, 1912.

26. Ibid.

27. Ibid.

28. Ibid.

29. Ibid.

30. Ibid.

31. Ibid.

32. H. T. Parker "At the Opera House," *Evening Transcript*, October 19, 1912.

33. Joseph Urban, manuscript, Urban Collection, production box 32.

34. Ibid.

35. H. T. Parker, "The Opera Outdoes Itself . . . ," *Evening Transcript*, November 26, 1912.

36. Ibid.

37. Philip Hale, Review, *Boston Herald*, December 19, 1912.

38. *Evening Transcript*, January 11, 1913.

39. Philip Hale, Review, *Boston Herald*, January 18, 1913.

40. H. T. Parker, Review, *Evening Transcript*, February 25, 1913.

41. Ibid.

42. H. T. Parker, *Evening Transcript*, March 17, 1913.

43. Ibid.

44. Eaton, *Boston Opera*, p. 255.

45. "Opera Stars Hurt in Crush," *New York Times*, March 30, 1914.

46. Eaton, *Boston Opera*, p. 260.

47. Ibid.

48. Ibid.

49. Ibid.

50. George C. Tyler, *Whatever Goes Up* (Indianapolis: Bobbs-Merrill Company, 1934), p. 257.

Chapter 3 (pages 71–97)

1. "New Sheldon Play Lavishly Staged," *New York Times*, November 30, 1914.

2. Louis Defoe, "A New Experiment with the Fairy Play," *Greenbook Magazine*, February 1915, pp. 270, 277.

3. "Mr. Ziegfeld and His Follies," *New York Times*, June 18, 1916. Ziegfeld was probably wrong about the month of his first meeting with Urban. The play opened at the end of November and only ran for about ten performances; December seems a more likely time.

4. "Anna Held and Others," *New York Times*, September 22, 1896.

5. Edward A. Dithmer, "The Theatre," *New York Times*, September 27, 1896.

6. Eddie Cantor, *Ziegfeld the Great Glorifier* (New York: A. King, 1934), p. 41.

7. Robert Baral, *Revue* (New York: Fleet Publishing Company, 1962), p. 5.

8. "Sculpture and Painting in a Theatrical Environment," *New York Times*, November 11, 1903.

9. "Urbanity of the 'Follies,' " *Arts and Decoration*, October 1919, p. 302.

10. Billie Burke, *With a Feather on My Nose* (New York: Appleton Century Crofts, 1949), p. 118.

11. Ibid., p. 120.

12. Ibid.

13. Ibid., p. 131.

14. Lady Duff Gordon, *Discretions & Indiscretions* (London: Jarolds Publishers, 1932), p. 124.

15. "A High Priestess of Clothes," *Vogue*, April 15, 1910, pp. 27, 80.

16. Duff Gordon, *Discretions*, p. 134. Lady Duff Gordon quotes what she says was the reaction of the American press to her arrival.

17. Lady Duff Gordon, Letter to the editor, *Harper's Bazaar*, December 1914, p. 34.

18. "High Priestess," *Vogue*, April 15, 1910, p. 27.

19. Duff Gordon, *Discretions*, p. 218.

20. Review, *New York Evening World*, June 13, 1917.

21. Baral, *Revue*, p. 268.

22. For Ziegfeld's sentiments see *Theatre Magazine*, December 1923, p. 66. For Urban's see the interview he did with Oliver Saylor in 1923 for *Shadowland*. All references used are taken from Transcripts, Urban Collection.

23. "Ziegfeld," *New York Times*, June 18, 1916.

24. Oliver Saylor, Interview with Urban, *Shadowland*, 1923, unpaginated.

25. Ibid.

26. Ibid.

27. "Ziegfeld Follies Here Resplendent," *New York Times*, June 22, 1915.

28. This account of the preparation of the *Follies* is mainly taken from "Urban the Ambidexterous," *New York Times*, June 17, 1917, and Gretl Urban's recollections.

29. Ibid., *New York Times*, June 17, 1917.

30. " 'Follies of 1917' Is a Fine Spectacle," *New York Times*, June 13, 1917.

31. Louis Sherwin, Review, *New York Globe and Advertiser*, June 20, 1918.

32. Review, *New York Telegraph*, June 13, 1917.

33. "When Joseph Urban Forgot His American Citizenship Papers," *Musical America*, June 27, 1918, p. 12.

34. P. G. Wodehouse and Guy Bolton, *Bring on the Girls!* (New York: Limelight Editions, 1984), p. 50.

35. Ibid., p. 51.

36. Ibid., p. 52.

37. " 'Midnight Frolic' Is Launched," *New York Times*, October 4, 1916.

38. "Ziegfeld's 'Midnight Frolic,' " *New York Telegram*, April 26, 1917.

39. Review, *New York Telegram*, December 11, 1918.

40. Ibid.

41. Saylor, Interview, unpaginated.

42. Ibid.

Chapter 4 (pages 99–113)

1. Renold Wolf, "Around the Map," *New York Morning Telegraph*, November 2, 1915.

2. Joseph Urban, "Caliban . . . 1916," Urban Collection, production box 4.

Chapter 5 (pages 115–43)

1. Saylor, Interview, unpaginated.

2. Giulio Gatti-Casazza, *Memoires of the Opera House* (New York: Vienna House, 1973), p. 20.

3. Ibid.

4. "A New Era at the Metropolitan," *Vogue*, January 1918, p. 218.

5. Ibid.

6. Quaintance Eaton, *The Miracle of the Met* (New York: Meredith Press, 1967), p. 245.

7. Ibid., p. 201.

8. Urban to Edward Ziegler, December 7, 1925, Metropolitan Opera Archives, New York (hereafter cited as MOA).

9. Mary Urban to Edward Ziegler, March 28, 1922, MOA.

10. Edward Ziegler to Mary Urban, March 30, 1922, MOA.

11. Kenneth MacGowan, "The Myth of Urban," *Theatre Arts Magazine*, May 1917, pp. 105–6.

12. Deems Taylor, Review, *New York World*, November 26, 1922.

13. Ibid.

14. "Viennese Art Wrought on the Shore of Boston," *New York Times*, November 7, 1915.

15. Ibid.

16. Olin Downes, " 'Turandot' Opens, Scores a Triumph," *New York Times*, November 17, 1926.

17. Lawrence Gilman, "Music," *New York Herald Tribune*, November 17, 1926.

18. Cable from Otto Kahn to Giulio Gatti-Casazza, March 31, 1927, MOA.

19. Giulio Gatti-Casazza to Otto Kahn, April 20, 1927, MOA.

20. Irving Weil, " 'Jonny Spielt Auf'—New York," *Musical America*, January 26, 1929, p. 5.

21. Urban to Edward Ziegler, October 19, 1929, MOA.

22. Helen Noble, *Life with the Met* (New York: G. P. Putnam and Sons, 1954), p. 29.

23. Urban to Edward Ziegler, October 30, 1929, MOA.

24. Urban to Giulio Gatti-Casazza, February 14, 1930, MOA.

25. Urban to Edward Ziegler, February 14, 1930, MOA.

Chapter 6 (pages 145–67)

1. "Film People Explain," *New York Times*, December 14, 1918.

2. Quoted in W. A. Swanberg, *Citizen Hearst* (New York: Collier Books, 1986), p. 402.

3. Marion Davies, *The Times We Had* (New York: Bobbs-Merrill Company, 1975), p. 265.

4. Ibid.

5. Ibid., unpaginated introduction by Orson Welles.

6. Contract, Urban Collection, production box 1.

7. Joseph Urban, manuscript, Urban Collection, production box 1.

8. Ibid., pp. 1–2.

9. *The Sunday Journal*, October 3, 1920.

10. Quoted in Swanberg, *Hearst*, p. 402.

11. Quoted in Fred Laurence Guiles, *Marion Davies* (New York: McGraw-Hill, 1972), p. 382.

12. *Chicago Herald Examiner*, October 6, 1922.

13. "The Screen," *New York Times*, September 15, 1922.

14. Louella Q. Parsons, *The Gay Illiterate* (Garden City, N.Y.: Doubleday, Doran and Co., 1944), p. 68.

15. Ibid., p. 69.

16. Davies, *Times*, p. 28.

17. "The Newest New York Picture-Play House," *Arts and Decoration*, October 1923, p. 40.

18. "The Screen," *New York Times*, August 2, 1923.

19. Guiles, *Davies*, p. 125.

20. *Los Angeles Examiner*, August 27, 1924.

21. *Newark Star Eagle*, October 29, 1924.

22. "Thomas H. Ince Dies," *New York Times*, November 20, 1924.

23. "Ince's Death Natural," *New York Times*, December 11, 1924.

24. Swanberg, *Hearst*, p. 376.

25. Guiles, *Davies*, p. 149.

26. *Evening Journal*, April 22, 1925. City of newspaper unknown. Clipping is in Marion Davies's scrapbooks at the Lincoln Center Library, New York.

Chapter 7 (pages 169–213)

1. Frank Cady, "Joseph Urban Excels Because He Doesn't Specialize," *Brooklyn Eagle Magazine*, March 30, 1930.

2. *Buffalo Times*, March 26, 1927.

3. "Cocoanut Ball at Palm Beach Brilliant Event," *New York American*, March 5, 1927.

4. "Persian Ball at Palm Beach Thursday Night," *New York Evening Post*, March 5, 1927.

5. "Annual St. Patrick's Day Dance . . . ," *New York Evening Post*, March 12, 1927.

6. "Mr. & Mrs. Hearst Give Ball in a Palm Beach Setting," *New York Herald Tribune*, April 29, 1927.

7. Helen Worden, "About Society: Hutton Debut," *New York American*, December 23, 1930.

8. Joseph Urban, *Theatres* (New York: Theatre Arts Press, 1929), unpaginated.

9. *New York Times*, November 11, 1926.

10. T. Square, "The Skyline," *New Yorker*, March 24, 1928, p. 75.

11. Joseph Urban, "World's Greatest Magazine Center at Columbus Circle," *New York American*, April 15, 1928.

12. Arthur North, "A Modern Store Alteration," *Architectural Forum*, June 1929, p. 957.

13. "The Bedell Company's Store," *Architecture and Building*, July 1929, p. 200.

14. Theodor Muller, "Store Elevators and Escalators," *Architectural Forum*, June 1929, p. 944.

15. Quoted in Lewis Mumford, "Notes on Architecture," *The New Republic*, March 18, 1931.

16. "Bedell," *Architecture and Building*, July 1929, p. 200.

17. "Central Park Casino," *Architectural Record*, August 1929, p. 97.

18. "Biddle Defends Walker Palace in Park Bower," *New York Herald Tribune*, November 30, 1928.

19. "Opening Rehearsal at the Park Casino," *New York Times*, June 4, 1929.

20. Ibid.

21. Ibid.

22. Ibid.

23. Ibid.

24. Robert A. Caro, *The Power Broker* (New York: Alfred A. Knopf, 1974), p. 339.

25. Ibid.

26. This account is based on Caro's definitive study of Robert Moses.

27. Walter K. Kilham, Jr., *Raymond Hood, Architect* (New York: Architectural Book Publishers Co.), pp. 79–80.

28. For a complete account of the school's origins and guiding philosophy, see Peter M. Rutkoff and William B. Scott, *New School* (New York: Free Press, 1986).

29. Alvin Johnson, *Pioneer's Progress* (New York: Viking Press, 1952), p. 318.

30. Brendan Gill, *Many Masks: A Life of Frank Lloyd Wright* (New York: Ballantine Books, 1987), pp. 299–300.

31. A. Johnson, *Progress*, p. 320.

32. Ibid., p. 321.

33. Philip Johnson, "The Architecture of the New School," *Arts*, March 1931, p. 393.

34. Rita Susswein, "The New School for Social Research," *Parnassus*, January 1931, p. 11.

35. Shepard Vogelgesang, "The New School for Social Research," *Architectural Record*, February 1931, p. 143.

36. Ibid.

37. Edmund Wilson, *The American Jitters* (New York: Charles Scribner's and Sons, 1931).

38. Ibid., p. 29.

39. A. Johnson, *Progress*, p. 321.

40. Ibid., p. 323.

41. Eugene R. Clute, "Lighting Made a Part of Architecture in the New School for Social Research," *American Architect*, May 1931, p. 40.

42. Wilson, *Jitters*, p. 28.

43. A. Johnson, *Progress*, p. 323.

44. For more on Urban's influence on Rockefeller Center and the Music Hall see Carol Herselle Krinsky, *Rockefeller Center* (New York: Oxford University Press, 1978).

45. Roberta Smith, "New School Unveils Its Restored Orozco Murals," *New York Times*, October 11, 1988.

46. Ibid.

47. P. Johnson, "New School," p. 393.

48. Ibid., p. 395.

49. Ibid., p. 397.

50. Ibid., p. 398.

51. Ed Sullivan, "Ed Sullivan Sees Broadway," *New York Evening Graphic*, November 4, 1931.

52. Alvin Scott, "A Motion Picture Theater for a Suburban Town in New York," *Architectural Record*, August 1931, p. 111.

53. "A Small Suburban House," *Architectural Record*, November 1931, p. 361.

Chapter 8 (pages 215–45)

1. Statement prepared for the *New York Times* for the opening of the Architectural League's 1933 exhibit, Urban Collection, production box 42.

2. Urban, *Theatres*, unpaginated.

3. Joseph Urban, "The Stage," *Theatre Arts*, April 1919, p. 125.

4. Urban, *Theatres*, unpaginated. Because of the brevity of this text, future references will not be listed in these notes.

5. Joseph Urban, "Wedding Theatre Beauty to Ballyhoo," *New York Times Magazine*, August 19, 1928, p. 10.

6. Hannelore Schubert, *The Modern Theatre* (New York: Praeger, 1971), p. 13.

7. Ibid.

8. "The Boxholders," *Time*, November 2, 1926, p. 24.

9. Giulio Gatti-Casazza to Otto Kahn, November 19, 1924, MOA.

10. Otto Kahn to R. Fulton Cutting, December 26, 1925, MOA.

11. Ibid.

12. Ibid.

13. "Pick Men to Design New Opera House," *New York Times*, February 27, 1927.

14. H. T. Parker, "Urban Opera Plan Raises Chorus of Praise," *Musical America*, October 22, 1927, p. 1.

15. Benjamin Morris to Otto Kahn, February 21, 1927, MOA.

16. Otto Kahn to Benjamin Morris, February 25, 1927, MOA.

17. Memo by Benjamin Morris, June 25, 1927, MOA.

18. Benjamin Morris to Otto Kahn, no date, but presumably late September or early October 1927, MOA.

19. Urban to Benjamin Morris, October 5, 1927, MOA.

20. Ibid.

21. Ibid.

22. Ibid.

23. Otto Kahn to Edward Ziegler with press release, October 10, 1927, MOA.

24. Deems Taylor, "An Impressive New Home for the Metropolitan Opera Company," *Musical America*, October 8, 1927.

25. Ibid.

26. Memo by Urban, October 17, 1927, MOA.

27. Ibid.

28. This is a quote from Urban's memo, not a direct quote of Kenneth Murchinson's.

29. R. Fulton Cutting to Otto Kahn, January 26, 1928, MOA.

30. Brooks Atkinson, "The Play," *New York Times*, February 4, 1927.

31. Ely Jacques Kahn, "The Ziegfeld Theatre," *Architectural Record*, May 1927, p. 396.

32. Ibid.

33. Gerald Bordman, *American Musical Theatre* (New York: Oxford University Press, 1986), p. 469.

34. Will Rogers, *The Autobiography of Will Rogers* (Boston: Houghton Mifflin Company, 1949), p. 26.

35. "News of Realty," *New York Times*, September 22, 1966.

36. Paul Goldberger, "At the Cooper-Hewitt, Designs of Joseph Urban," *New York Times*, December 20, 1987.

Chapter 9 (pages 247–59)

1. Urban to Alexander Sanine, January 10, 1932, MOA.

2. Urban to Edward Ziegler, August 29, 1932, MOA.

3. Ibid.

4. Urban to Edward Ziegler, October 13, 1932, MOA.

5. Edward Ziegler to Urban, October 18, 1932, MOA.

6. Olin Downes, "Strauss's 'Electra' Creates a Furor," *New York Times*, December 4, 1932.

7. "The Architectural League's Annual Exhibition," *Architecture*, April 1933, p. 212.

8. Lewis Mumford, "The Architects Show Their Wares," *New Yorker*, March 4, 1933, p. 57.

9. "Annual Exhibition of the Architectural League of New York," *Pencil Points*, March 1933, p. 140.

10. Ibid., p. 141.

11. "The Myth of Urban," *Theatre Arts Monthly*, September 1933, p. 668.

12. Mary Fanton Roberts, "Remembering Joseph Urban—Timeless Modernism," *Arts and Decoration*, August 1936, p. 11.

13. Elizabeth Boykin, "Where Katharine Brush Lives and Plays," *New York Sun*, January 3, 1933.

14. Rufus C. Dawes, *Report of the President of a Century of Progress to the Board of Trustees* (Chicago: Century of Progress, 1936), p. 37.

15. "Colorful Buildings," *New York Times*, May 29, 1927.

16. "Chicago Fair," manuscript, Urban Collection, production box 47.

17. Ibid.

18. Raymond Hood to Urban, no date, but postmarked May 23, 1933, Urban Collection, production box 47.

19. Robert Alexander, *A Century of Progress* (Chicago: Millar Publishing Company, 1933), pp. 20–21.

20. Otto Teegen, "Joseph Urban's Philosophy of Color," *Architecture*, May 1934, p. 271.

A GUIDE TO SOURCES

The major source for information on Joseph Urban and his work has long been the memorial edition of *Architecture* that appeared in May 1934, a year after his death. Subsequently, his name virtually dropped from sight—until the much later revival of interest in fin-de-siècle Vienna and in Art Deco.

Thieme Becker, the German-language artists' lexicon, through its bibliography, was an invaluable tool in locating references to Urban's work in Vienna. The entry on Heinrich Lefler was also very helpful, as was the mention of Gretl Urban.

Quaintance Eaton's thorough and meticulously researched *The Boston Opera Company* (Appleton-Century, New York, 1965) will long remain the standard work on this important part of American operatic life. Extensive coverage devoted to the opera company by Boston's *Herald* and *Evening Transcript* provided very complete contemporary descriptions of, and reactions to, the new stagecraft that Urban introduced to America.

For our coverage of the life and work of Florenz Ziegfeld, we relied on two major biographies by Randolph Carter (*The World of Flo Ziegfeld*, Praeger, New York, 1974) and Charles Higham (*Ziegfeld*, Regnery, Chicago, 1972).

Robert Baral's *Revue* (Fleet, New York, 1962) and Stanley Green's *The World of Musical Comedy* (Ziff-Davis, New York, 1960) were useful in the checking of dates and casts of the various editions of the *Follies* and other shows that Urban designed. Gerald Borman's comprehensive work *American Musical Theatre* (Oxford University Press, New York, 1986) is indispensable to anyone delving into the early days of this uniquely American art form.

It is most fortunate that so many newspapers were published during the span of Urban's career in New York, but it would have been exceedingly difficult now to identify, let alone locate and read, all of them. Nevertheless, Urban's very diligent clipping service has preserved for us a tremendous number of articles about him, often from papers and magazines now long forgotten. These clippings are to be found crumbling away in scrapbooks deposited in the Urban archives at Columbia University.

The Metropolitan Opera has preserved notices of its activities, including numerous references to settings by Urban, in huge volumes that recently were microfilmed. Urban's correspondence with the company's management can be found in the Met's archives.

The third set of clippings that offered the authors more extensive material than they could otherwise have gathered is found in the Marion Davies scrapbooks now at the library and research center in New York's Lincoln Center. These rapidly deteriorating pages should be microfilmed for posterity.

Miss Davies has also left us her autobiography *The Times We Had* (Bobbs-Merrill, New York, 1975), where we found extensive information on her relationship with William Randolph Hearst and her films that Urban designed. There is a comprehensive list of Miss Davies's films with plot summaries and production data in Fred Guiles's *Marion Davies* (McGraw-Hill, New York, 1972).

Urban's architectural career was quite extensively covered in major media journals of the day such as *Architectural Record* and *Architectural Forum*, which, along with other publications, have been cited in the text of this study. For the Four Theatres chapter, most of the material in Urban's own words came from his book *Theatres* (Theatre Arts Press, New York, 1929), which was issued in a strictly limited edition and is now a very rare collector's item.

ACKNOWLEDGMENTS

After Joseph Urban's death in 1933, Aldous Huxley, Deems Taylor, and Somerset Maugham, all friends of Urban, wanted to write his biography. All three, however, were dissuaded by Urban's widow, Mary, who two decades later commissioned a German writer to produce the biography. She was bringing it back with her from Europe in the summer of 1956 when her ship, the *Andrea Doria*, sank. Mary was rescued, but not the manuscript. Never to fully recover from the accident, Mary did not attempt to recreate the book.

Urban was all but forgotten by the mid-1950s. However, one person who could not forget was Urban's daughter, Gretl, who wanted to see her father's remarkable life and career duly acknowledged through a biography published in her lifetime. She is now in her mid-nineties. We hope that we have fulfilled her dream by creating a book worthy of Urban the man and artist.

Gretl worked closely with her father in his Yonkers studio. Her memories of him and the now almost legendary people he knew were recorded on a series of tapes she very generously prepared for us. These transcribed recollections form an integral and invaluable part of the text. Without them, we could only have presented Urban's artistic legacy. Thanks to Gretl, we have been able to offer a more complete picture of the man and the times in which he lived.

To Gretl we owe many thanks for all that she has done for *Joseph Urban*. In addition to her recollections, she made available to us her own collection of her father's and uncle's work as well as family photographs. Over the many years it took to realize this project, her encouragement and support were steadfast and greatly appreciated.

It must be noted that while we referred to Gretl for clarifications of details about her father's life and work, the opinions and analyses we express are entirely our own, as are any errors of fact or interpretation.

We thank Kenneth A. Lohf, librarian for Rare Books and Manuscripts at Columbia University, where the Urban archives are located, for his part in this study. He made the entire collection readily available to us, and without his consideration and generosity this book could not have been so comprehensively illustrated.

Jane Rodgers helped us locate photographs and drawings in the Urban archives that we would not otherwise have found. Yvonne Cunningham, library assistant for reprographics, oversaw the efficient reproduction of the many items we withdrew from the collection, and photographer Martin Messik somehow made old, faded photographs look like new ones.

Joseph Urban owes its existence to the commitment and dedication of

Walton Rawls, senior editor of Abbeville Press. It was he who suggested how to present the many diverse and ongoing activities of Urban in a logical order, who upon seeing firsthand the quality and magnitude of Urban's work allowed us to include many more illustrations than originally planned, and who is responsible for a book that turned out to be far better than either of us could ever have expected.

Thanks to the efforts of our agent, Christine Bernard, the manuscript reached Abbeville.

The National Foundation of the Arts awarded Mr. Carter a much appreciated grant for this biography.

INDEX